The Black Pacific

THEORY FOR A GLOBAL AGE

Series Editors: Gurminder K. Bhambra and Robin Cohen

Globalization is widely viewed as a current condition of the world, but there
is little engagement with how this changes the way we understand it. The
Theory for a Global Age series addresses the impact of globalization on the
social sciences and humanities. Each title will focus on a particular theoretical
issue or topic of empirical controversy and debate, addressing theory in a more
global and interconnected manner. With contributions from scholars across
the globe, the series will explore different perspectives to examine globalization
from a global viewpoint. True to its global character, the Theory for a Global
Age series will be available for online access worldwide via Creative Commons
licensing, aiming to stimulate wide debate within academia and beyond.

Also in the series:

Connected Sociologies
Gurminder K. Bhambra

*Eurafrica: The Untold History of
European Integration and Colonialism*
Peo Hansen and Stefan Jonsson

*On Sovereignty and Other
Political Delusions*
Joan Cocks

*Postcolonial Piracy: Media
Distribution and Cultural Production
in the Global South*
Edited by Lars Eckstein
and Anja Schwarz

Forthcoming titles:

Cosmopolitanism and Antisemitism
Robert Fine and Philip Spencer

*Debating Civilizations: Interrogating
Civilizational Analysis in a Global Age*
Jeremy Smith

*John Dewey: The Global
Public and its Problems*
John Narayan

*Stark Utopia: Debt as a Technology of
Power*
Richard Robbins and Tim Di Muzio

The Black Pacific

Anti-Colonial Struggles and Oceanic Connections

Robbie Shilliam

Bloomsbury Academic
An imprint of Bloomsbury Publishing Plc

B L O O M S B U R Y
LONDON • NEW DELHI • NEW YORK • SYDNEY

Bloomsbury Academic

An imprint of Bloomsbury Publishing Plc

50 Bedford Square	1385 Broadway
London	New York
WC1B 3DP	NY 10018
UK	USA

www.bloomsbury.com

BLOOMSBURY and the Diana logo are trademarks of Bloomsbury Publishing Plc

First published 2015

© Robbie Shilliam, 2015

☺①⑤⊜

No responsibility for loss caused to any individual or organization acting on or refraining from action as a result of the material in this publication can be accepted by Bloomsbury or the author.

British Library Cataloguing-in-Publication Data

A catalogue record for this book is available from the British Library.

ISBN: HB:	978-1-4725-1923-8
PB:	978-1-4725-3554-2
ePDF:	978-1-4725-1925-2
ePub:	978-1-4725-1924-5

Library of Congress Cataloging-in-Publication Data

A catalog record for this book is available from the Library of Congress.

Series: Theory for a Global Age

Typeset by Fakenham Prepress Solutions, Fakenham, Norfolk NR21 8NN
Printed and bound in Great Britain

Contents

Series Foreword

The Theory for a Global Age series investigates what theory would look like if we started from places and peoples other than those with which 'Theory' usually begins. The series examines how our understandings of the global might alter if we began with processes, connections, entanglements and peoples other than the standard accounts of globalization as endogenous to the West and diffused out from it. Robbie Shilliam, in his book, *The Black Pacific: Anti-Colonial Struggles and Oceanic Connections*, provides us with an exemplary account of both concerns. In this remarkable book, he forcefully demonstrates both the possibility and the very necessity of a different kind of theory for a global age.

The Black Pacific, Shilliam argues, is both a provocation and a problem. It addresses the populations and narratives of Oceania and locates them in their, usually forgotten, relations to other parts and peoples of the world. In doing so, Shilliam recovers the deep relations between (but not only) formerly colonized subjects in order to redeem the possibilities generated by and generative of anti-colonial solidarities. He does this in the terms and concepts of 'colonial science' as well as in the terms and concepts of 'decolonial science', which is, as he suggests, another kind of science. In navigating with skill and expertise between and through colonial and decolonial science, Shilliam offers us possibilities of seeing the world again and anew.

This is not an easy book to read for those of us schooled only in the language of colonial science. Even those of us committed to other ways of knowing the world and other visions of the world might be challenged by the journeys Shilliam prompts us to take alongside him. That challenge is itself part of the journey and the reward of this provocative, powerful theorization of the politics of the world we inhabit and the effort needed to cultivate the worlds we wish. From the prosaic and mundane, the political and social, Shilliam takes us also to the spiritual and poetic and the redemptive powers and prophecies that animate decolonial science in service of our deep relations. *The Black Pacific* not only presents a history, politics and sociology of self-determination in other places, but contributes to the very determining of self that is constitutive of all projects of liberation.

Gurminder K. Bhambra

Acknowledgements

I acknowledge the support and expertise of my colleagues at Victoria University of Wellington. Maria Bargh, Teresia Teaiwa, April Henderson, Cherie Chu, Elizabeth Mcleay, Kate Mcmillan and Richard Hill were especially instrumental in the development of my ideas. I acknowledge Te Herenga Waka marae at Victoria University for its warm hosting of events. I acknowledge Tangi Te Keo, the backbone of Wellington, as well as Porirua, Ōtara, and Otatara Pā – places that I regularly visited. The Te Reo courses that my wife and I took through Te Wānanga o Aotearoa helped to open the door. I am indebted to Tiopira McDowell, Erina Okeroa and Tony Fala for reading and critically commenting upon a draft of this book. Your support, knowledge and principled guardianship is humbling. I thank Gurminder Bhambra for exemplary editorship of this book series, and for the people at Bloomsbury Academic for so ably supporting her vision. Thanks as well to Maureen Roberts at London Metropolitan Archives for facilitating a Keskidee link-up. One love to BE.BOP Black Europe Body Politics curator Alanna Lockward and advisor Walter Mignolo for journeys into decolonial aesthesis. Raspect to the Centre of Caribbean Thought and the Rastafari Studies Unit at the University of West Indies for inspirations and clues. Special shout-out to Tahu Wilson, Erina Okeroa and Sun Ku, perfect graduate students who took part in this research in various ways. Big ups to all the Welly and P-Town poets and artists: 'as well the singers as the players on instruments shall be there'. Peace and love to my wife Cynthia, my family and my friends.

I dedicate the book to all those in Aotearoa NZ who share similar stories to my friend, who found the strength to survive homelessness in the music of the crown prince Dennis Brown. Finally, and most importantly, I acknowledge all the persons who I have been honoured to build relationships with in the course of writing this book. Your presence, knowledge systems, stories and ancestors constitute its spirit.

Some of you have since passed on to become even more powerful agents for reparation of the breaches to humanity caused by Cook and Columbus. This book is in your service. *Mā pango mā whero ka oti te mahi.*

Introduction

In May 1979 a Black theatre troupe called Keskidee along with a RasTafari band called Ras Messengers left the UK to undertake a tour of predominantly Māori and Pasifika communities in Aotearoa New Zealand. Upon arrival in Auckland, the organizers of the tour drove the troupe almost immediately to the very tip of the North Island. There, at a small hamlet called Te Hāpua, Keskidee and Ras Messengers gathered outside a *marae* (traditional meeting place) of Ngāti Kuri, the local *tangata whenua* (people of the land). A *karanga* (call) was given, acknowledging the dead and welcoming the *manuhiri* (guests) onto the land. A *kaumātua* (elder) of Ngāti Kuri then proceeded to introduce his guests to the significance of the place where they now stood. He asked them to consider that, although they had the Queen of England living among them in London, Ngāti Kuri lived at 'the spiritual departure place throughout the world'. The *kaumātua* concluded with the traditional greeting of *tātou tātou* – 'everyone being one people'. Then Rufus Collins, director of Keskidee, responded on behalf of the visitors:

> You talked of your ancestors, how they had taken part in our meeting, and I do agree with you because if it was not for them you would not be here. You talked of our ancestors, taking part and making a meeting some place and somewhere; the ancestors are meeting because we have met. I do agree with you.

But Collins also recalled the association made by the *kaumātua* between themselves and the Queen and politely refuted the association: 'we are here *despite* the Queen'.[1]

There are three aspects of this meeting that are noteworthy. First is the modality of the greeting. The Māori *kaumātua* does not treat these visitors as aliens or 'others' but as peoples who already share a relation that must be creatively retrieved because it is not just individuals who are meeting but their ancestors too. Second is the response to the greeting. Collins accepts the modality of relating provided by the *tangata whenua* (people of the land) and confirms, indeed, that the ancestors are meeting and that the Māori are no more 'others' to them as they are to Māori. Nevertheless, third, Collins also finds within this indigenous modality the resources with which to critically cultivate the relationship. Māori have often appealed to their partner, the Crown, to compel British settlers to honour in good faith Te Tiriti o Waitangi (the Treaty of Waitangi) that many of the *rangatira* (chiefs) had signed in 1840. The *kaumātua* therefore recognized the auspicious provenance of the visitors – in terms of their proximity to the Queen – yet also sought to inform them of the different but equally significant provenance of the land on which they now stood. For Cape Rēinga was close by, which in many Māori cosmologies is the departing point for spirits to journey back to the homeland of Hawaiki. Nevertheless, the Queen had been no partner to the Black actors and musicians visiting from London; she was, rather, a symbol of (post)colonial oppression that had to be replaced. Following Collins' comments, the Ras Messengers began the chant that rerouted the provenance of the troupe from the halls of Buckingham Palace to the highlands of Ethiopia: 'Rastaman come from Mount Zion …'[2]

Despite the separations of oceans (Pacific, Atlantic), of geo-political position (peripheral Aotearoa NZ, metropolitan Britain), of race (brown, black), and of sociological hue (the indigenous, the descendants of enslaved), a deep relationship binds these groups, one that seems to belie a separated reality. This incommensurability between rich relationality and poor material connectivity provokes a set of questions. What cosmologies underpin this greeting at Te Hāpua? What techniques of relating enable it? What stories buttress it? What projects of self-determination accompany it, and how do they inform a sensibility of global injustice over colonial rule? My book seeks to provide insights that might help answer these questions so that the greeting at Te Hāpua does not appear as a peculiar and arcane episode but rather becomes intelligible as part of a deep, global infrastructure of anti-colonial connectivity. I also hope that the book will help to cultivate the spiritual, ethical, intellectual and political sensibilities required to critically support, renew and extend this infrastructure. To my mind, this is the most urgent and challenging task of cultivating theory for a global age.

But in order to start the journey a prior question must first be addressed: why are engagements with meetings such as that which took place at Te Hāpua so rarely engaged with in academic inquiry? To answer, it will be instructive for us to consider a modality of relating that is quite different to that utilized at Te Hāpua.

In July 1886 the *Graphic* magazine published a map of the world that accompanied an article by John Charles Ready Colomb on the status of British imperialism.[3] The map, commissioned by the Imperial Federation League, has since become one of the most iconic cartographic representations of empire.[4] Ready's article reflected the anxieties felt by British commentators at the time over the need to maintain the integrity of their empire in the face of increased imperial competition.[5] For this purpose the map brings together the peoples who populate colonial territories – both settlers and non-settlers – and depicts them in cartoon relief around the peripheral areas of the map. They are all captured by the gaze of Britannica, the figure that is centrefold on the Greenwich meridian. In this depiction the peripheral figures, especially the colonized among them, can only understand themselves in mute relation to the imperial centre.[6] And there is certainly no possibility of the colonized relating to each other across the global spaces, as in the greeting at Te Hāpua, and cultivating knowledge 'sideways' so as to possibly inform a decolonial project.

The pretensions of this cartographic gaze have been thoroughly protested in the Western academy by many intellectuals in their critical investigations of the key tropes of Western social theory: 'self/other',

'master/slave(servant)'. Indeed, the turn towards theorizing repre-
sentation, discourse and culture across the social sciences has been
dependent upon and in a sense has breathed new life into these tropes.
Before this turn, however, Jean-Paul Sartre had dared to do something
different. As a French intellectual, Sartre engaged with the problem of
colonialism by displacing himself from the centre of the world so as
to witness a relationship between other selves. In his preface to Frantz
Fanon's *Wretched of the Earth*, written in 1961, Sartre bid his fellow
Europeans to enter the book with these words:

> After a few steps in the night, you will see strangers gathered round a
> fire, draw closer, listen: they are discussing the fate they have in store
> for your trading posts, for the mercenaries who defend them. They
> will see you perhaps, but they will continue to talk among themselves
> without even lowering their voices. Their indifference strikes at our
> hearts …[7]

Sartre's attempt to displace the cartographic gaze rather than to
dwell solely upon its operation was part of a political commitment to
anti-colonial struggle for which Fanon, of course, had made the quintessential statement. But even though promoted by a white metropolitan
intellectual, Sartre's standpoint quickly disappeared from subsequent
conversations of social theorists in the Western academy. The cartographic master tropes of the *Graphic* were quickly re-inhabited and,
through them, these theorists returned to primarily intra-European
controversies.[8]

Sartre's provocation did, however, find a resonance in a group of
largely Indian intellectuals who, in the early 1980s, sought to break the
cartographic gaze of the *Graphic*'s imperial world map by proposing
that those colonized peripheral figures – the subalterns – had lucid
minds behind their fixed stare. Truth be told, the intellectuals of
Subaltern Studies were influenced not by Sartre but mostly by E. P.
Thompson's approach to 'history from below' and its Gramscian sensi-
tivities to culture and meaning as key sites of social struggle. Above
all, though, Subaltern Studies was an intellectual response to the

popular-democratic movements that gained prominence for a period of time after the ousting of Indira Gandhi and her rule by state of emergency.[9] Subaltern Studies sought to create a cognate space of democratization within the historiography of India, a practice of story-telling that had heretofore been dominated by the 'Cambridge School' and Marxism, both of which had produced elitist accounts wherein the peasantry were rendered an unreasoning or pre-political mass.[10]

Ranajit Guha's ground-breaking work on peasant rebellions argued that colonial elites might have dominated the hinterlands of India, but had not achieved hegemony over them.[11] Instead, the peasantry had engaged with colonial rule through their own forms of political consciousness, the seedbed of which lay in spiritual lore. In this sense, the consciousness of the peasantry could not be categorized as pre-political but rather as political in ways other-wise to the idealized version of secular European reason pronounced by colonial (and indeed native) elites.[12] Guha implored historians to listen to these 'small voices' of the past and, in their presence, to consider 'what kind of history would be written?'[13] This historiographical intervention had contemporary political import. For if the peasantry had now become citizens then the register of political rationality also required democ-ratization. In this movement the elitist profane logic of state and social interest would have to be disturbed and displaced by the 'small voices'.[14]

The Subaltern Studies project soon ran into a series of problems laid out most famously by Gayatri Spivak via an engagement with the figure of the subaltern woman.[15] Spivak's work posed a set of questions. Was it possible to recover the political consciousness of the subalterns as knowledge untainted by the exercise of power? To what extent was the notion of a 'resisting subject' itself a category born of European fantasies of their own mastery? And, in this respect, was the very attempt to represent the subaltern not also an act of epistemic domination akin to those undertaken by other elitist historians? In sum, did sympathetic ventriloquism induce the same affect as elitist silencing? Addressing these questions, Spivak carefully argued that Subaltern Studies was a politically necessary but necessarily irresolvable intellectual project.[16]

Yet she went further than this. Because the subaltern could not appear 'without the thought of the elite', Spivak also proclaimed that the subaltern provided 'the model for a general theory of consciousness'. Specifically, she argued that 'the historical predicament of the colonial subaltern' could be considered the 'allegory of the predicament of *all* thought, *all* deliberative consciousness'.[17] Philosophically, then, Spivak bade the subaltern to travel from the periphery to the centre, but only to become there the 'recalcitrant difference' that structured elite discourse.[18] As the project was taken up in Western intellectual spaces, enabled by what I would call an opportunistic utilization of Spivak's sympathetic critique, Subaltern Studies was made to proffer less an opportunity to decolonize knowledge regimes and more another faculty through which to deconstruct knowledge of the Western self. As such, Subaltern Studies could interface with – even be collapsed into – the post-structuralist project (broadly conceived), a project that was also decidedly post-Sartre in its singular obsession with the modern (read colonizing European) subject.[19]

With these movements the peripheral figures on the *Graphic's* imperial world map, now encoded as subalterns, were once more emptied of epistemic authority so as to become the cipher through which to interpret the proclivities of Britannica – the self and master. Perhaps these incorporations were reflective of the general trajectories of the Western academy after the defeat of the Third World project and the apparent re-incorporation of troublesome populations back into neo-imperial orbits through neo-liberal governance. No doubt, the end of the Second World project (i.e. global communism) did nothing to arrest this movement; nor did the subsequent internationalization of the staff and student constituencies of Western universities through the globalization of elites rather than through the global democratization of life chances and the attendant decolonization of knowledge.

Nevertheless, the originating democratic impulse has remained seminal to Subaltern Studies. Dipesh Chakrabarty still hopes for a 'subaltern historiography that actually tries to learn from the subaltern',[20] although in his own work he marks the subaltern as only an epistemic limit to historical knowledge.[21] Spivak, meanwhile, has always read Subaltern Studies as a political intervention, that is, as 'a strategic use of positivist essentialism in a scrupulously visible interest'.[22] More recently, however, Spivak has focused on pedagogy, a move honed through her practitioner work with marginalized communities. She has given up her 'apologetic formula' for Subaltern Studies as the strategic use of essentialism, and has found instead, 'a different one emerging from my own subaltern study: learning to learn from below'. 'This one', Spivak suggests (and here I would recall the fate of Sartre's intervention in the Western academy), 'will have had few takers'.[23]

I want to dwell on these (somewhat slim) openings in Subaltern Studies because to my mind the transmogrification of Subaltern Studies from an engaged democratic project into postcolonial critique has (unintentionally) serviced the colonial 'fatal impact' thesis.[24] This thesis rests on the assumption that indigenous cultures could not withstand or compete with the sophistication of European civilization: they would have to die or transform into substitute versions of the conquering culture. At the epistemic level I would argue that the category of the subaltern is part of this erasure. In his own way, even Gramsci, the immediate source of the category of the subaltern, is complicit in this erasure. He states that some social strata – especially the peasantry – seem to be incapable of developing their own intellectuals because in the very moment of their formation as intellectuals they cease to be 'organic' to that stratum.[25]

But what if, in the pursuit of 'epistemic justice',[26] the democratic impulse of Subaltern Studies were to be separated from the very term 'subaltern'? The seedbed of such a decolonial project would not, then, be found in academic discourse but in the living knowledge traditions of colonized peoples.[27] Maligned, ridiculed, attacked and disavowed by colonial forces, these traditions have nevertheless retained a tenacious thread of vitality that provides for the possibility of a retrieval of thought and action that addresses global injustices in ways otherwise to the colonial science of the gaze. Crucially, these projects have refused – and more often than not ignored – the injunctions of the fatal impact thesis. Their ethos of living other-wise is expressed by Bob Marley in the following verse: 'we refuse to be what you wanted us to be, we are what we are, that's the way it's going to be'.[28]

In light of these decolonial projects, the category of the subaltern becomes singularly unhelpful, if not meaningless. For the colonized figures on the periphery of the *Graphic*'s world map have always named and re-named themselves as, for example, 'sufferers',[29] Black Israelites, Ethiopians, RasTafari, Tūhoe, Ngāti Kuri, Māori, Ham and Shem. And, heretically, these peoples have often determined the meaning of Britannica on her behalf as they cultivate useful understandings of their relationships to power. This is precisely what Reitu Harris, president of the predominantly Māori Black Power gang, does when he states that 'to me the word "Pākehā" no longer stands for "European" ... it stands for a type of person who ... when it rains, will rush for shelter themselves and not care about others getting wet'.[30]

In this respect it is not possible to speak of a 'decolonial project' in the abstract, that is, as an academic enterprise separated from living knowledge traditions. For instance, Kaupapa Māori is a knowledge framework that, while utilized academically in Māori Studies, has a constituency, purview and knowledge base that encompasses the wider Māori world (*Te Ao Māori*). Kaupapa Māori is a critical project of self-determination at the level of knowledge cultivation, and frames intellectual priorities and working practices through *mātauranga* Māori (Māori knowledge systems).[31] Kaupapa Māori and other grounded decolonial projects of epistemic justice undermine the fatal impact thesis in so far as they refuse the colonial conceit that European knowledge traditions hold supreme interpretative authority over the varied cosmologies and cultures of humanity.

The disciples of anthropology and sociology have long claimed that Western academia institutionally embodies modern self-reflexivity, that is, a superior ability to critically examine oneself as well as – and in relation to – others. Social scientific interpretations of reality, because critical, are assumed to be more mobile and hence more universalizable than particular context-specific 'lay' interpretations. Poststructural/

postcolonial justifications for fixating upon the gaze of Britannica implicitly reproduce the assumption that a qualitative difference exists between interpreters: the lay/subaltern/colonized practitioner is unknowable to herself but, thank God, at least the academic/expert/ modern subject is knowable to himself at the limit of his experience.[32] However, if we mark the fatal impact thesis as a fantasy, then we must at least consider that self-reflexivity (personal and institutional) is in no way a unique product of modernity but is rather, in the basic sense of the word, traditional. And if self-reflexivity is institutionally traditional, then even the interpretative superiority of Western academia must be radically questioned. In this decolonial apprehension, there can exist in principle only a *quantitative* difference between the representations made by academics and those made by practitioners – a difference predicated upon the infrastructural power to disseminate knowledge of others.

So by this reasoning I remind myself that entering academia is not a fatal impact, a transmogrification of my being into a modern reflexive self, but rather, a problematic mapping of the legacies of collective struggles and their living knowledge traditions onto an institution of privilege. It is my decision as to whether I wish to cash in that privilege wisely by contributing to a decolonization of knowledge regimes with a liberatory intent, instead of passively deferring to the valorization of Britannica. I choose, then, to return us to Te Hāpua and a greeting, not between subaltern A and subaltern B, but between Keskidee, Ras Messengers and Ngāti Kuri (the people of that land). I cannot speak for Sartre or his people, but I notice that he follows me back to the campfires. There I ask to fold myself into this greeting at Te Hāpua, on the terms given by the greeters, terms that in at least some way I am already invested in. Through these terms I critically contribute to the support, renewal and extension of a global infrastructure of anti-colonial connectivity. Hence the title of this book, *The Black Pacific*, which is both a provocation and a problem.

The term 'Black Pacific' has, in the main, been used to refer to the variable and shifting nature of African-American and North-Pacific

Asian ties of kinship, politics and ideology against the backdrop of US imperial ambitions in the region.[33] 'Black Pacific', of course, is a comparative remix of 'Black Atlantic',[34] a term popularized by Paul Gilroy in his endeavour to recast Western modernity by reference to the double consciousness of Diaspora Africans living in North American society.[35] And yet in some ways Gilroy's seminal work reproduces the cartographic imagination of the *Graphic*'s imperial world map: continental Africa is hardly treated as agental within modernity; it sits mostly silent besides the vocal Americas where its progeny have taken on life as 'moderns'.[36] Likewise, the dominant cartographic imaginary of the Black Pacific tends to focus on its Rim and less so on the 'sea of islands' composed of a dazzling array of related peoples, languages, cultures and polities.[37] Here the question arises as to whether the indigenous peoples of this vast Oceanic region are to be muted in the analysis of global interconnections. (I will now follow Epeli Hau`ofa in preferring the term Oceania rather than Pacific.[38])

With these challenges in mind, Teresia Teaiwa's warnings on analogical reasoning are extremely valuable.[39] Teaiwa notes that while, in the early twentieth century, Oceania was a region of intense interest for ethnographic and anthropological inquiry it subsequently lost much of its value for Western academia. More recently, scholars of the region have tried to reinject value through analogy, i.e. the 'Caribbeanization' or 'Africanization' of the Pacific. The title of this book was enthusiastically suggested to me by my publishing company no doubt for such purposes of valorization. Nevertheless, I agreed to this title because it has a purchase beyond the market and besides analogy. The peoples and projects that we will walk with in this book have in various ways identified Black and its inferences to Africa – both continental and diasporic – as a key site of struggle for indigenous self-determination in Aotearoa NZ and, to some extent, Oceania at large. Less an analogy, these engagements reference Black (and African) as part of a global infrastructure of anti-colonial connectivity. I follow these sensibilities and join this book with cognate intellectual enterprises.[40]

The fundamental aim of this book is to redeem the possibilities of anti-colonial solidarity between colonized and (post)colonized peoples on terms other than those laid out by colonial science. This will entail a wilful movement across various academic fields of study guided not by abstract concerns for interdisciplinarity but by the analytical imperatives of this redemption. And for the same reason, this aim will necessitate a plural register of argumentation spanning the social scientific, narrational, poetic and personal.

The most important purpose of this book is to retrieve the relationship between African and Māori anti-colonial struggles as a space that supports spiritual, intellectual and political commitments to *mana motuhake*, a central term for the following investigations, which in Te Reo (the Māori language) can be glossed as 'self-determination'. Such retrieval is especially important for a society – Aotearoa NZ – which tries to bury its living colonial frontier under a worldly 'multiculturalism', thereby stifling the spirit of Te Tiriti o Waitangi (the Treaty), signed in 1840 between many *rangatira* (chiefs) and Queen Victoria, and additionally, whitewashing imperial legacies in Oceania. A second purpose is to strengthen the confidence of peoples of African heritage as to the global (and never marginal) importance of our anti-colonial struggles and ongoing decolonial projects. A third purpose is to underline the fact that European colonization has depended upon an interlocking super-exploitation of labour and super-dispossession of land organized along lines of race.[41] Hence, the exorcism of racial inequality requires the cultivation of spiritual, philosophical and political standpoints that reach across these lines to rebind the various descendant communities who have and continue to suffer from such exploitation and dispossession. A fourth purpose is to build a political commitment among intellectuals to what I would call 'deep relation', that is, a commitment to leave behind current academic endorsements of privileged narcissism.

In the next chapter I shall elucidate a decolonial science adequate to the task of cultivating knowledge of deep relation between peoples who, like Keskidee, Ras Messengers and Ngāti Kuri, appear on the imperial world map to be irrevocably distant and disconnected subalterns. A science of deep relation allows us to reason and walk some way with Black Power and young Māori warriors, with Panthers of the Polynesian type, with Black liberation theologians as they encounter indigenous struggles and spirituality, with Black thespians and RasTafari musicians as they attempt to catalyse the soul powers of Oceania, with the RasTafari of the House of Shem, with prophetic movements that chant down Babylon but that are indigenous to Oceania, and with all the peoples and projects who seek to heal the wounds suffered at the hands of Cook and Columbus.

Deep Relation

Introduction

In this chapter I build a decolonial science of 'deep relation'. The depth that I am retrieving can be found in a relationality that exists underneath the wounds of coloniality,[1] a cutting logic that seeks to – but on the whole never quite manages to – segregate peoples from their lands, their pasts, their ancestors and spirits. Decolonial science seeks to repair colonial wounds, binding back together peoples, lands, pasts, ancestors and spirits. Its greatest challenge is to bind back together the manifest and spiritual domains. For in the latter domain there exist hinterlands that were never colonized by Cook and Columbus, and therein lie the supports of a global infrastructure of anti-colonial connectivity. Decolonial science affirms Rufus Collins' reply to the *kaumātua* (elder) at Te Hāpua that 'the ancestors are meeting because we have met'. This science will become our compass and energy store.

The knowledge traditions of Māori and Pasifika peoples utilize sophisticated practices of relating – and valuing relations – that are firmly embedded in particular locales and peoples yet at the same time proffer general principles of engagement without laying claim to abstracted universals.[2] These practices, in part, depend on a participatory criterion which renders the categorical segregation of the 'researcher' from the 'researched' impossible.[3] For this reason the chapter is organized along partially autobiographical lines. The living and growing knowledge traditions of Oceania – especially *mātauranga* Māori – were an edifying gift that enabled me to dispense with the colonizing methodology of social science that I had previously been trying to work through/against. I learnt aspects of these traditions sometimes through university engagements but much more commonly through the intellectuals outside of academia who I worked with and for whom philosophy, ethics and application are not distinct pursuits.[4] This work impelled me to recover, work in and work with the living knowledge traditions that were most urgent for the collective repair of the colonial wounds that had directly affected me. And ever since, I have been embedding myself back in the 'continent of Black consciousness'[5] that I claim personal historical allegiance to via the Indian Ocean human trafficking of Africans.

The flow of the chapter reflects this journey. As a clearing exercise I decolonize Hermes, the European agent that interprets relations. I then bring forth respective agents of Oceania – Tāne/Māui – and Africa – Legba – who cultivate knowledge through deep relation. As they meet, Tāne/Māui and Legba find existing commonalities between their relating skills, skills that are encompassed by the term 'grounding', and that enable them to know themselves better by knowing each other.

Hermes, Tāne/Māui and Legba

Hermes is the ancient Greek agent of communication and provides for the term hermeneutics, which in the Western academy stands for interpretative method.[6] In the Homeric Hymn, Hermes must mature from a cunning child thief of cattle, representing the primitive pastoral tribes, to an adult who, via a binding oath to his elder brother Apollo, becomes a subordinate messenger to Olympus, the agent of commerce and city-state diplomacy.[7] Hermes is therefore colonized by Homer and forced into urban civilization. I want to decolonize this personality. The St Lucian poet Derek Walcott compares the islands of the Caribbean with the Aegean and suggests that if the ancient Greeks were resurrected today they would be considered Puerto Ricans – brown, gaudy, sensual etc.[8] So, following Walcott, let us cast aside a certain 'progressive' narrative of Greek development that mirrors the fatal impact thesis of moderns – from myth and magic to reason, philosophy and history. Let us instead acknowledge that the magic of Hermes possesses its own rationalities.[9]

Before and besides the Homeric Hymn, Hermes appears as part of nature – a force in life, death and regeneration.[10] And rather than city-states, Hermes' provenance is the pastoral province of Arcadia.[11] There, he is the agent of the crossroads, of pathways that intersect, of thresholds and boundary stones.[12] As spiritual agent of the traveller, Hermes possesses the magic of translation that must be utilized when crossing from one domain to another. This magic, or 'skill at the oath', is not quite deceit or wilful misdirection and neither is it a use of trickery.[13] In fact, the Greek word for trick can also be glossed as 'technical skill';[14] and magic more accurately infers the act of binding together.[15] Hermes' prime skill, therefore, is to bind together different domains – geographical, social, spiritual. In this respect, Hermes is the quintessential craftsman and sometimes appears in Attic dramas as the 'heavenly counterpart of the menial labourer'.[16] Hence, despite his propensity for trickery, Hermes is considered the giver of good things to those in need. His regenerative force might even be intentionally wielded to address issues of redistribution and restitution.

I choose, therefore, to dispense with Homeric Hermes, the colonized messenger, and resurrect the Arcadian Hermes who is concerned with creatively cultivating knowledge of deep relations for the restitution of colonial wrongs. Why 'deep'? Because the domains that are being bound back together reach to the seedbed of creation; we are not concerned here only with the cause-and-effect laws of the manifest domain. Moreover, unlike Homeric Hermes, Arcadian Hermes is not the supreme and singular messenger of the gods; he is a mundane agent rather than an exceptional world-historical figure masquerading as the colonizing European modern. Thus, the science and skill of deep relation that Hermes holds can be found everywhen and everywhere. So let us meet some of Hermes' contemporaries.

Māori cosmologies speak of an entity known as Tāne (occasionally Tiki) who is the progenitor of humankind and of forest life. Tāne forcibly separates his parents Papatūānuku (earth mother) and Ranginui (sky father) from their loving embrace thereby creating the space within which humans live.[17] Yet Tāne also races against his evil brother Te-ika-a-whiro to ascend to the realm of Io-mata-ngaro (the begotten, i.e. the hidden face) in order to bring back to the manifest domain of human beings the three baskets of knowledge.[18] Tāne, similarly to Hermes, is a generative force of human life and also a 'messenger of the gods' to the extent that he translates their sublime knowledge so that humans might live well in the manifest world. In short, Tāne creates meaningful human life by redeeming deep relation between the manifest and spiritual domains that he himself had rent asunder. In this respect, Tāne embodies a fundamental predicament but also ethos of humanity: to *relate*, that is (to follow the Latin etymology of the word), bring back – re-bind – that which has been rent asunder.

However, the skill of binding together different domains is practised most acutely in Māori cosmologies by Māui. Māui is well known throughout Oceania, although he is always integrated in particular ways into particular cultural constellations.[19] Here I follow the key contours of North Island Māori narratives. Māui is neither good nor absolutely bad, but he is a great voyager and, like Hermes, well practised in trickery, especially in changing shape. Māui utilizes these skills in order to shape the environment of the manifest world such that it is better suited for human habitation.[20] For example, Māui tricks Mahukia into giving to humanity the technology of fire; and Māui ensnares the sun, and forces it to travel more slowly so that the day might be longer in which humans can perform useful activity.[21] In this respect, one of Māui's key characteristics is the will power he exercises in order to meet his objective. This wilfulness is partly related to Māui's low-born status. He is, in fact, a miscarried foetus, and survives initially in the sea before being found and cared for by a surrogate family.[22] So in his endeavours Māui often seeks to overcome his lowly status.[23] And for this, he regularly breaks *tapu* (a state of sacredness).

chaotic
good/nuera.

Here we might note that the ethos of humanity – to relate – is closely linked to the pursuit of restitutive justice.

Māui's fate is eventually sealed when he attempts to break the ultimate *tapu* and climb back into his ancestress Hine-nui-te-po, who crushes him by closing her thighs.[24] Cognizant of this warning, I want to assert that the restitutive ethos of humanity is not an imperial process of convergence that seeks to homogenize all the diverse experiences of humanity and dimensions of existence. Rather, the act of binding implicates diverse but relatable matters, and hence this ethos of humanity should be conceived of as a wilful relating. Indeed, this wilfulness is suggested by Māui's very name. *Mā* can be glossed as to be freed of the restrictions of *tapu* (a state of sacredness); and *ui* can be glossed as to ask or inquire. So Māui embodies the skill of open inquiry in order to creatively make a path.[25] This creativity borders on the irreverent; however, it does not seek to destroy but rather to manipulate arrangements, perhaps even for the purpose of addressing injustices. Thus I submit that the Tāne/Māui complex embodies a decolonial science of deep relation, that is, the binding back together of different domains in order to cultivate useful knowledge through which to provide restitution for a disadvantaged social position.

A cognate personality to Tāne/Māui exists in many cosmologies of the African Diaspora, that is, those persons and their descendants trafficked to work enslaved on the plantations of the Americas (as well as South-East Asia and elsewhere). Legba, a key personality in West African Fon cosmology, is one such agent who dwells at the thresholds of temples and houses.[26] Legba is also present at the threshold of communications between humans.[27] As the interpreter of fate Legba enjoys a close relationship to Fa, who rules over divination and expresses the destiny of the cosmos.[28] Fa resides on the top of her tree, and every night Legba climbs up to open the eyes of his sister to survey the manifest world.[29] In this respect, Legba, similar to Tāne, moves between the manifest and spiritual domains, especially by revealing to human beings their fates but also, similarly to Māui, by providing them with the ability to 'trick' fate, i.e, to utilize certain binding skills to their advantage.[30]

Similar to Arcadian Hermes, Legba is a trickster who cannot be relied upon, yet is nonetheless a guardian of human beings.[31] There is, moreover, a restitutive aspect to Legba's relationship with humanity, an aspect that can also be gleaned in Tāne/Māui. As time goes by, human beings remember Fa (destiny) yet forget Legba (malleable fate). In fact, wars break out because those who have been given kingdoms have forgotten the language of their parents. Legba must be remembered, even if only by certain pivotal people, so that fate can be 'tricked' and war cease.[32] In this respect, Legba embodies a certain irreverence to ordained fates, as does Māui. And this characteristic takes on especial importance in the African Diaspora with regards to reparation for the wounds of enslavement.

In this book we will walk at different times with both the continental and diasporic children of Legba. However, while diverse articulations of Legba exist in West African cultures, in this chapter I will focus more on the diasporic children's conceptions. For the enslaved that are forced to make the middle passage, Legba's prime aspect becomes that of the gatekeeper,[33] his key purpose: to provide redemption from the fate of slavery.[34] In Haitian Vodou, Legba stands at the crossroads between the manifest world of humans and the spiritual realms of *loa* (spiritual agencies), domains that map respectively onto the Americas – the place of plantations, enslavement and suffering – and the domain of the island below the sea, populated by the ancestral and spiritual agencies of Guinea (Africa).[35] Legba helps the diasporic sufferers in the manifest domain to repair the breach with the spiritual domain that has rendered them dehumanized. He does so by facilitating useful communication between manifest beings and their ancestors/spirits. For those who dare, Legba might be mobilized for even grander schemes of redemption, that is, repatriation out of the living death of the American plantations to African homelands. By these means, the colonial destiny (Fa) of enslavement might be reduced to a malleable fate (Legba) to be decided through liberation struggles.

In sum, Tāne/Māui and Legba (as well as Arcadian Hermes) are personalities that embody the creative cultivation of deep relation.

Their magic, i.e. their decolonial science, binds different domains together – individual, social, geographical and spiritual – in the pursuit of restitutive justice. The problem of binding back together is germane to the human condition. It is not a colonial creation. Colonial science was never that innovative. We will, nevertheless, dwell in the particular dispensation of this problem caused by the European colonial science of segregation, which stands opposed to the decolonial science of cultivating deep relation.[36] A brief excursus into anthropology can help us to clarify this difference.

Categorical segregation versus deep relation

Let us recall the image of the *Graphic's* imperial world map that I discussed in the last chapter. In the first part of the twentieth century, anthropologists made claim to the method of ethnography, that is, the examination of other cultures from a position of intimacy usually achieved through extended fieldwork in a native community. The term ethnography has a Greek provenance, referring to the study of foreign places in order to construct the difference and distance between there and home.[37] In this sense, the expectations of ethnographic writing diverge from the cultivation of deep relation. Indeed, ethnography, as a tool of colonial administration, sought to mark, justify and police precisely the categorical difference between native and modern. And it is this ethnographic gaze that is behind the *Graphic's* imperial world map, fixing the subaltern in its subordination to Britannica. Caught in this ethnographic gaze, Tāne/Māui and Legba could never relate to each other (or with an Arcadian Hermes) because, as non-moderns, they do not possess the competency to interrelate; they are merely 'unreflexive' agents, practising the old mystic arts of magic and trickery. To become competent, therefore, Tāne/Māui and Legba would have to look to a third force – a modernizing force of self-reflexivity – that could render the meaning of their actions on their behalf.

With independence from colonial rule, many traditional ethno-graphic sites became less easily accessible to Western anthropologists as the peripheral characters began to take back their own voices on the world stage. In this new era the supposedly higher sciences of trans-lation and interpretation practised by the white ethnographer were at least partially revealed to be simply political instruments of colonial rule.[38] We should be careful to suppose that anthropological inquiry is incapable of breaking out of colonial science.[39] Nevertheless it is still rare to find studies that engage with the relationship of (post)colonized to *each other* 'sideways' without having to call upon Britannica to interpret and provide the meaning of these relationships.[40]

How might deep relation be a different practice of knowledge cultivation to that of categorical segregation? We must start by acknowledging that the manifest world is a broadly (post)colonial one, structured through imperial hierarchies that encourage the one-way transmission of political authority, social relations and knowledge from the centres outwards. But Tāne/Māui and Legba use their skills to bind this manifest domain to the hinterlands of the spiritual domains wherein colonial logic and lore is certainly an intrusion, although only an intrusion, and not a foundation. This is why I term this particular aspect of the spiritual domain as 'hinterland', that is, a space that has not been colonized yet faces the colonial frontier. Most importantly, the spiritual hinterlands provide the expanded agency to redress colonial fates in the manifest domain by providing the compass and energy store for anti-colonial self-determination.[41]

With these points in mind let us return to Tāne and his retrieval of the three baskets of knowledge from the begotten domain of Io-mata-kore, as detailed by the scholar Māori Marsden. In one basket lies knowledge of Te Ao Tua-ātea – the world beyond space-time. This is the ultimate sublime reality – of the spirit, of potential, and of the first cause (*Io-taketake*). It is also the condition from which and towards which the cosmos as a whole is tending.[42] In another basket is knowledge of Tua-uri, dark worlds (*te pō*) that are nevertheless the 'seedbed of creation' wherein space-time is gestated, evolves and refined, ultimately, into the various and specialized manifestations of the natural world. In these sublime worlds, *hau-ora* [the breath of life] begets shapes, shape begets form, form begets space, space begets time and time begets Rangi and Papa.[43] Ranginui the sky father and Papatūānuku the earth mother embrace each other in this world of becoming until Tāne forces their separation and births Te Ao Mārama – the manifest world of light. This, then, leads us to the final basket of knowledge of Te Aro-nui, the natural world of being that can be apprehended through our senses in terms of events, sequences, cycles, regularities and, in general, relations of cause and effect.[44]

In recounting this genealogy of creation, Māori Marsden is at pains to point out that different domains have different competencies, traits and purposes. This point resonates with the caution that I took from Māui's ultimate fate. In short, the binding skills of Tāne/Māui do not seek to collapse domains but, rather, to make their agents relatable and their energies traversable. We might also remember that Tāne, after causing a breach that creates the manifest world, seeks knowledge through which to repair the breach. I have suggested that this could be considered an ethos of humanity, one that requires a science. And in this science of deep relation, the material must be apprehended as material-and-spiritual, whereas in colonial science the spiritual must be profaned, that is, it must be transmogrified into a material cause (or ideology or symbol) so as to be captured by imperial logic.

We must now examine how these binding skills open temporal and spatial pathways that subvert the colonial segregations that structure the manifest domain. Let us first examine the temporalities that allow colonized history to be displaced by decolonial pasts.[45]

Contrary to a developmentalist understanding of time, which is focused upon the creation of a pristine future, both Tāne/Māui and Legba practise deep relation as, principally, the reparation of ancestral ties.[46] In Te Reo (the Māori language), *mua* functions both as a locative indicating in front and also the past, while *muri* indicates behind and also the future. Therefore, the future is behind us, because it is unknown and yet to be inhabited. The past, however, are the days which lie in front (*ngā rā o mua*).[47] This temporal orientation can also be identified in cosmologies associated with Legba. One Akan symbol that has gained popularity among enslaved Africans and their descendants is Sankofa – a bird that looks back to take an egg off its back. The imperative of Sankofa, meaning to 'go back and take', is to retrieve valuable heritage for the present day.[48] Likewise, Haitian Vodou ceremonies will often begin by halting profane time; the *hougan* (priest) will emerge out of a sacred chamber in a backward motion orientating the congregation forward to the first human and ultimately to the godhead, the source of all cosmic agency and relation.[49] The RasTafari faith provides a short-hand for this temporality: the 'i-ncient [ancient] future'.[50]

Legba facilitates a reparative process by way of this temporal sensibility. He stands at the crossroads, a site of orientation.[51] The cosmogram of the crossroads is composed of a vertical pole that denotes the centre of the world while the horizontal pole denotes the boundary of water called *nzadi* – the great river – that separates the mountains of the manifest (alive) and the spiritual (alive other-wise) that are nevertheless connected at their bases under the water.[52] The greater the distance between these two mountains the more that equilibrium is required by means of communication between the entities of the two domains.[53] In many faith systems in the African Diaspora, that great river is the Atlantic and great polarity had been created by the human traffic crossing it. Thus, even greater skill would be required for the enslaved if they were to repair the breach, escape the lands of death (Americas) and return to the lands of the living (Guinea).[54]

These temporal orientations provide a means to heal the colonial wound of segregation in so far as they bind post(colonized) peoples back to their ancestors and other spiritual agents that are not subaltern but still-living entities with their own integrity. Colonized presents cannot be sutured by uninhabited futures but by meaningful, already inhabited pasts. Moreover, the temporal (re-)orientation of decolonial science enables and requires the cultivation of different spatialities and relationalities that are also categorically ruled out by colonial science.

In the manifest domain of colonial governance, entities are racially segregated into enslaved, indentured, native, free poor and masters. None can relate sideways to each other. They are fixated by the gaze of Britannica, the master. However, Legba allows for these segregations to be re-rendered as meaningful relations by binding together the manifest and spiritual domains, and the colonial present back to decolonial pasts. Ultimately such binding is made possible because the spiritual hinterlands are arranged not according to colonial logics of segregation but to those of relation. For instance, in the Caribbean island of St Vincent, the Converted, an African Baptist faith, practise spiritual journeying through which they will receive guidance for problems that plague their everyday life. In this journeying they freely visit Africa, India and China – originating regions of the various labourers brought to the islands by British colonialism. They might also visit Ethiopians, 'a tribe of very small, eerie dark people in Africa'; however, in order to meet them the 'tone has to be deep in the Spirit' of the sojourner.[55] Samoan writer Sia Figiel poetically expresses a similar science of deep relating for those who journey with Tāne/Māui:

> alofa [love] for the dead
> that live inside us
> nurturing our imaginations of ancestors across continents
> across time and space.[56]

Therefore, instead of fatalism in the face of manifest colonial domination, Tāne/Māui and Legba turn cause and effect to run forward in order to redeem the past. And when the past is redeemed as a living site of anti-colonial agency, the spiritual hinterlands can redeem relationships between peoples segregated by the manifest forms of colonial rule. What is more, if Tāne/Māui and Legba are walking together in the spiritual hinterlands, their children might be moved to do the same in the manifest domain. Thus, beyond the imperial gaze, subalterns cease to be as they relate to each other as other persons of integrity; the ancestors are meeting because we have met. We can mark this material-and-spiritual relationality with the Māori term *tātou tātou,* that is, 'all of us and all of us', meaning, everyone must be recognized as relatable entities rather than as categorically segregated objects.

In this section I have not made statements of belief. Neither have I been trying to convince you to believe with me. Rather, my statements are avowedly substantive – ontological, even. The material is material-and-spiritual. Temporalities that bind back together the material and spiritual also bind (post)colonial presents back to decolonial pasts as well as persons and collectives spatially segregated by colonial logics. Knowledge is cultivated as part of this political pursuit, and that is decolonial science. This science is not waiting to be profaned in order to become a higher-order science of modern self-reflexivity for that would be, first and foremost, an imperial move rather than an epistemic revolution.[57] As Māori Marsden confirms, it is certainly true that profane matter has its own competencies. Nevertheless, these competencies manifest quite late in the day in cosmological terms and do not constitute the deep structures of existence.

We have arrived, then, at the prospect of a radical expansion of agency made possible in the practice of binding together the manifest and sublime domains so as to redeem and refigure the past in an expanded and interconnected global arena. My concerns in this book are to apprehend this expansion of agency and energy as part of a pursuit of global justice in colonial conditions that practically and epistemically outlaw such pursuits, relationships and solidarities. I now elaborate on the particular skill of relating practised by Tāne/Māui and Legba known as 'grounding'.

Grounding

To my mind, decolonial science *cultivates* knowledge, it does not *produce* knowledge. Using the Latin roots of these words, we could say that to produce knowledge is to lengthen, prolong or extend, whereas to cultivate knowledge is to till, to turn matter around and fold back on itself so as to rebind and encourage growth. Knowledge production is less a creative endeavour and more a process of accumulation and imperial extension so that (post)colonized peoples could only consume or extend someone else's knowledge (of themselves).[58] In short, a colonial science produces knowledge of and for subalterns. Alternatively, knowledge cultivation is a necessarily creative pursuit as it requires the practitioner to turn over and oxygenate the past. Most importantly, cultivation also infers habitation, which means that knowledge is creatively released as the practitioner enfolds her/himself in the communal matter of her/his inquiry. What is more, this constant oxygenation process – a circulatory one – necessarily interacts with a wider biotope, enfolding matter from other habitations. To cultivate knowledge of deep relation can therefore be understood as 'grounding'.

In Māori cosmology, the manifest world is created when Tāne separates Ranginui from Papatūānuku. Specifically, Papatūānuku refers to the sublime aspect of *whenua* – the manifest earth.[59] *Whenua* (land) is therefore never just a material object, because it connects the manifest world back to the seedbed of creation. Inhabitation is an enaction of creation; hence the term *tūrangawaewae* – glossed as 'stomping ground' but more accurately rendered as 'to stand is to be'.[60] This is why the land is an ancestor to human beings.[61] With regards to these considerations the term *whakapapa* takes on great importance. In a quotidian sense *whakapapa* can be glossed as 'genealogy'; for example, 'who do you *whakapapa* to?' means 'what are your tribal affiliations?' More accurately, however, *whaka* means to make or cause, and *papa* refers to ground or foundation. So *whakapapa* can be glossed as 'to make a ground/foundation';[62] and because of the constitutive relationship of land to being, the act of *whakapapa* is in many ways an enaction of creation.

As part of a decolonial science, *whakapapa* proposes that 'to understand phenomena we must understand relationship'.[63] And one of the key structuring principles of *whakapapa* is the relationship between junior (*tēina*) and senior (*tuākana*) relations. While this principle is heavily implicated in the web of family and tribal structures, it also operates on a broader cosmological scale: manifest entities hold a junior relation (*tēina*) to those senior entities (*tuākana*) that inhabit the spiritual domain. This being said, although *whakapapa* expresses hierarchical relations, these are always multiple and overlapping. Indeed, one of the most signal qualities of Te Ao Māori (the Māori world) is just how many diverse and sometimes conflicting stories peoples have of themselves and of their relationships.[64] Hence *whakapapa* are, to a certain extent, malleable. It is possible, for example, to identify more strongly with a junior descent line (*tēina*) than a senior (*tuākana*) or with one's matrilineal lines more than with patrilineal lines.[65]

The qualified malleability of *whakapapa* is amenable to the creative path making that is a signal quality of Māui's skills.[66] Indeed, the retrieval of particular lines and ancestors can be creatively mobilized to address present-day challenges. For example, if a child is taught the skill of weaving they might not only be taught about Hine-te-iwaiwa, the originator of the skill, but perhaps also about an ancestor who was noted for the skill.[67] Many of the people who I have cultivated relationships with in the course of writing this book similarly explain their present-day work, politics and direction by intentional reference to particular *tūpuna* (ancestors) and the living legacies that they now embody.

In this respect, *whakapapa* is not only a practice that concerns personal genealogy but can also be mobilized to relate through common experiences or the pursuit of common purpose.[68] For instance, in explaining how the Black Power gang should be more accurately considered an *iwi* (tribe), Eugene Ryder, Wellington spokesperson, mobilizes the concept of *whakapapa*. Iwi, like all collective groups, constitute themselves through their genealogy. But what binds Black Power members, argues Ryder, is not so much common personal lines of descent (although they can be these too), but, more so, common lines of purpose to which they are all committed, often inter-generationally so. Thus Ryder is a member of a number of *iwi*: Ngāti Kahu – his personal genealogical line – and Mangu Kaha (Black Power) – his line of purpose.[69]

In sum, *whakapapa* provides for the 'ultimate catalogue' of relations between people and all other entities in the manifest and spiritual domains – flora, fauna, land, ancestors, spiritual agencies etc.[70] Indeed, *mātauranga* Māori (Māori knowledge systems) are themselves organized through *whakapapa* and usually communicated by narrative, as is the case with Māori Marsden's cosmological recital that I rehearsed above.[71] All entities – tangible and intangible – are therefore related as part of creation. Less a passive rehearsal of genealogy, *whakapapa* is much more an intentional and creative (re-)cultivation of relations that constitute the cosmos, announced to the world in the form of storytelling (*whaikōrero*). *Whakapapa* demands persons to 'know their foundations and embrace a diverse humanity'.[72] To be and to know, absent of relating, is unthinkable. This is why the *tūpuna* (ancestors) teach that one must always '*whakapapa* to the world'.[73] In this way, knowledge cultivation through *whakapapa* epistemically and ethically demands the enfolding of diverse matters into the habitation of indigenous being. Perhaps, then, oceans (Pacific and Atlantic) and racial categorizations (black and brown) are only manifest barriers to peoples that can be bound back together at deeper levels. A ground can always be creatively prepared for relating.

Legba, keeper of the crossroads, is invoked in the 'invisible institutions' – the secret night-time congregations of enslaved peoples on plantations presided over by fellow enslaved preachers and prophets.[74] In the emergency conditions of the plantation, worship had to be physically and spiritually sheltered from the overseers and masters. In the 1930s and 1940s Caribbean, adherents of the RasTafari faith began the next iteration of this tradition.[75] Elder Bongo Spear notes that secluded meetings among RasTafari became synonymous with a theocratic assembly called the Nyahbinghi Order.[76] Referring back to a set of nineteenth-century religious and political movements in central Africa against European colonialism, Nyahbinghi came to denote a cardinal imperative of the RasTafari faith: (spiritual) death to all black and white oppressors.[77] The Nyahbinghi began to call their collective deliberations 'grounations'. Cognate to *whakapapa*, but adding an explicitly political impulse, grounation etymologically brings together ground, foundation and nation.[78] As such, grounation announces the binding together of manifest and spiritual domains guided by the collective pursuit of self-determination.

At grounation, reasoning, chants, prayers and meditation enable the faithful to be rejuvenated in order to focus on 'chanting down Babylon', quickening repatriation, and fulfilling the Nyahbinghi creed – the hungry be fed, the naked clothed, the sick nourished, the ancients protected, and the infants cared for.[79] Marijuana, the sacramental herb or 'wisdom weed', is consumed because it opens up the I-tes (the heights, the spiritual domain, the intellect). A 'fire key' is lit with the recitation of a set of Psalms that affirm salvation and refuge for the faithful and brimstone for the wicked.[80] Drums (or 'harps') are played for the duration of the congregation, their volume, style and speed varying according to the reasoning taking place and its affect upon the congregation. At grounation these various technologies facilitate the binding together of manifest and spiritual domains in order to bring Zion to earth in the pursuit of African liberation, as testified to in this popular rhyme:

> Natty dread shake him locks
> And a lightning clap
> And a weak heart drap! [drop][81]

It is true, though, that RasTafari do not expressly practise the same kind of ancestor veneration as many African Diasporic faiths.[82] This is an important observation in so far as it indicates that the RasTafari apprehension of spiritual intercession is also different from many indigenous practices. Nevertheless, I would argue that this difference is strategic and contextual rather than existential. Confronting the legacy of slavery as a living death, RasTafari disavow any notion of dying and hence pursue a more dramatic intercession for 'more life' via the powers of the Most High manifest in the human and living persona of the Ethiopian emperor, Haile Selassie I, alongside Empress Menen Asfaw. Direct intercession is, in fact, a component of much African ancestor veneration, although such a practice is only to be utilized in circumstances of extreme danger.[83] I submit that kidnapping, trafficking, enslavement and dehumanization can be considered as extremely dangerous circumstances. In this sense, the absence of direct ancestor veneration in RasTafari does not necessarily infer the absence of ancestors. Witness, for example, elder Bongo Ketu who explains that at grounation, 'when a skill man play 'pon de peta [repeater], de drums bring forth de spirits of all de Ancients ... de drum is de ancient Ethiopian form of communication'.[84]

While grounations are somewhat formal affairs, the practice of *grounding* is more often than not quotidian as is the case with the face-to-face practising of *whakapapa*.[85] And wherever RasTafari ground, they cultivate knowledge other-wise to the Babylonian institutions of knowledge production. Walter Rodney, the famous Guyanese academic and activist, returns to the University of West Indies (his *alma mater*) to teach in 1968. He relocates his classroom from the Mona campus to the shanties of downtown Kingston. There, Rodney and members of the RasTafari faith take part in informal grounding sessions, exchanging views on African history, politics and the liberation struggles.[86] Rodney comes with dead books but is 'amazed' at the living practices of knowledge cultivation pursued by RasTafari, the way in which they are able to traverse the segregations of colonial science, retrieve African personhood from 'thingification',[87] and recentre the peripheral and marginalized sufferers within a deep set of supportive and emancipatory relations.[88]

As is the case with *whakapapa*, RasTafari grounding tends to exceed its immediate habitation among the African Diaspora. The RasTafari pronoun 'I and I' is similar to *tātou tātou*, and specifically infers that my sanctified being must also be directly relatable to your sanctified being; the RasTafari pronoun for 'you' is, in fact, 'the I'. Additionally, RasTafari make use of 'spiritual anthropology', based on African fractal aesthetics, wherein research is 'insearch', i.e. what is inside is outside.[89] Sociological and/or racial segregational categorizations (native/negro, red, brown/black) cannot therefore frame grounding between I and I.

Rather, as is the case with African Baptists, RasTafari ground across these lines. For instance, RasTafari consider the Americas in general to be indigenous land and First Nation spiritual practices to be cognate to their own, especially in terms of the use of drums, fire and sacraments.[90] These considerations are manifested, whenever appropriate. Hence, the grounation that inaugurated the First International Gathering of RasTafari in May 1994 took place among the Miccosukee people of north-east Florida.

Grounding in Aotearoa NZ

Tāne/Māui and Legba have forged for us a decolonial science of deep relation that utilizes a key skill: the creative preparation of a ground for relating. Their decolonial science seeks restitution as a general ethos of humanity, but specifically as an anti-colonial pursuit, and will enable us to come to terms with a global infrastructure of anti-colonial connectivity that exists underneath and surreptitiously runs through the imperial hierarchy of Britannica. This decolonial science seeks to bind the manifest colonized world back to the uncolonized spiritual hinterlands, the colonized present back to decolonial pasts, (post) colonized peoples to other (post)colonized peoples, and the children of Legba to the children of Tāne/Māui. Perhaps even the children of Arcadian Hermes might have a part to play – or a relation to redeem – in this enterprise.

But the deep relation that we are retrieving in this book is of Africa in Oceania. And Oceania – specifically Aotearoa NZ – is not vacant nor a neutral space but one that is already inhabited. As a child of Legba I must address the fact that I am cultivating knowledge of the children of Tāne/Māui, on their own grounds. What, then, might be the ethical and methodological directives of this pursuit?

Here I follow the advice of Manuka Henare on the terms of engagement between *tauiwi* (non-Māori) and *mātauranga* Māori

(Māori knowledges). Henare affirms that there are particular stories whose guardians are particular groups – *whānau* (family), and *hapū* and *iwi* (larger social and political constellations). In these cases, the ethical and methodological imperative of knowledge cultivation addresses a primary question: 'who are the appropriate guardians'. Social science imperatives of '(how) can I extract the knowledge' must be subservient to the addressing of this primary question. After all, the principle of rightful guardianship (*kaitiaki*) is of foremost concern, especially when stories, as *whakapapa*, constitute being itself.

Yet Henare argues that there also exists a narrative that congenitally folds within itself numerous groups – Māori and *tauiwi* (non-Māori) – and is therefore, in principle, much more open to cultivation by all who feel compelled to claim an investment in it. This is the story of pan-Māori self-determination (*mana motuhake*) integrally connected to the arrival and building of relationships with Pākehā (European settlers).[91] I would respectfully add that the *tauiwi* (non-Māori) in this story are constituted by more multiple and diverse peoples than European settlers. Landmarks of this multicultural story include the Māori Declaration of Independence in 1835 (He Wakaputanga o te Rangatiratanga), the signing of Te Tiriti o Waitangi (The Treaty of Waitangi) in 1840, the emergence of the Kīngitanga (the Māori King Movement) in the 1850s as a response to breaches to Te Tiriti, and the renaissances of *mana motuhake* (self-determination) in the 1970s and 80s. I situate my engagement on these terms. That is, I retrieve the deep relation between the descendants of Africa and Oceania as part of the broader politics and narrative of the pan-Māori anti-colonial struggle for *mana motuhake*, a struggle that must involve *tātou tātou* – I and I.

Let me finish by rehearsing the cardinal skills of decolonial science that we have examined in this chapter. Grounding signals the cultivation of deep relation by variously binding different domains together. These domains are fundamentally the material and spiritual, domains that necessarily also enfold present and past, living and ancestors, and *tātou tātou* – persons and persons. For the purposes of this book, whenever an intentional attempt is being made by persons at some kind of binding along these lines (even in the absence of face-to-face relations) then grounding is taking place. *Whakapapa* is the particular expression and organization of these relations in the form of stories, or more accurately, as enactions of (a part of) creation, i.e. stories of creative constitution. Crucially, *whakapapa* do not simply describe mundane and material causal relations. Certainly, *whakapapa* cannot be composed out of fiction; however, their composition is an intentional, wilful rearrangement. In other words, there is a significant restitutive element to *whakapapa* – a creative redeeming of deep relation that material causality is in the service of rather than the master over. At various points in the book, I will recite *whakapapa* that will intentionally and creatively retrieve the depth of the grounding between the children of Tāne/Māui and Legba.

Many of the chapters in this book cluster around the time period of the 1970s and 1980s. However, the narrative of the book is not ordered chronologically; instead, its flow should be apprehended as an expression of a deepening relation with all its contentions. However, there are many crossroads along the way, delineated by the chapters of the book. As we proceed through the chapters, this contentious and staged deepening of relations between the children of Tāne/Māui and Legba will be signalled in the following movement: from comparison, to identification, to inhabitation and finally to enfolding.

The following chapters pursue the project of *mana motuhake* with this compass in hand. We begin in the late 1960s and 1970s when Māori activists start to compare their struggles and strategies with those of the Black Power movement of the USA. Here, the children of Tāne/Māui and Legba attempt to bind themselves together within the public sphere of the manifest domain, and they start to glean their deep relation through comparative exercises. But it is a contentious process. They then journey deeper into the relation and move from comparisons with Black Power to identifications with Blackness in public and personal arenas. We walk some way in this direction with the Polynesian Panthers, the struggles over sports and Apartheid, and the Black Women's Movement. Then we move from political

Blackness to spiritual and aesthetic Blackness, witnessing theological engagements with Black liberation and artistic projects that attempt to mobilize Black liberation for decolonial ends. At this point the children of Arcadian Hermes appear, seeking to appropriately support this deepening identification.

We then travel deeper still, from identification to mutual inhabitation in the arena of faith. We examine RasTafari as a faith of the children of Legba that the children of Tāne/Māui inhabit on their own grounds and terms. Subsequently we travel into the spiritual hinterlands using the Māori prophets of the nineteenth century as our vessel. There we find Tāne/Māui and Legba walking together in anti-colonial solidarity as the biblical Shem and Ham. We return to the present material-and-spiritual domain to witness how these traversable energies enfold RasTafari into the indigenous and endogenous prophetic traditions of Aotearoa NZ. Finally, we rehearse a general *whakapapa* of Africa in Oceania, and in so doing, make the greeting between ancestors at Te Hāpua intelligible as part of a deep, global infrastructure of anti-colonial connectivity.

Black Power and Mana Motuhake

Introduction

1950's

In the decade immediately following the Second World War, the percentage of Māori living in urban areas – as opposed to their mainly rural *tūrangawaewae* (places of belonging) – rose dramatically from approximately 35 per cent to over 60 per cent. The Hunn report of 1961, written for the Department of Māori Affairs, announced the official thinking on this development. The report recognized that the Māori population, long considered moribund, was now growing and urbanizing at a rate that was outstripping extant infrastructures. At the same time, however, the report actively promoted urbanization by encouraging Crown purchase of Māori land to facilitate development programmes, even while acknowledging that employment for Māori would be a future problem. The report proposed in a distinctly colonial-racial language that the 'integration' of Māori into predominantly Pākehā (settler European) urban areas had a modernizing effect on those who were 'complacently living a backward life in primitive conditions'.[1] Complicating but in many ways intensifying this confluence of urbanization, racism and assimilation was the migration of Tangata Pasifika (peoples of Oceania) over the same time period. Old colonial links with Western Samoa, Niue, Tokelau, Tonga and the Cook Islands were used to encourage unskilled and semi-skilled labourers into urban industry, especially around Auckland.[2]

By the late 1960s Pākehā media and politicians had framed these migrations in terms of a 'Polynesian problem'. To their minds, the problem was exemplified by a growing number of youth who seemed unable to integrate into the mainstream structures of urban life and preferred, instead, to hang out on the streets in groups.[3] Pākehā thought was occupied with the ways in which this phenomenon could be explained in terms of the pathologies of 'backward' Māori and Pasifika cultures. But Māori and Pasifika youth experienced their 'problem' in radically different ways: primarily through a sense of dislocation borne of living in urban areas run according to Pākehā rules and mores expressed through visceral and institutional racism. In this conjuncture a set of Māori and Pasifika activist movements arose that confronted the racist and colonial constitution of New Zealand society and state.

This chapter examines the ways in which predominantly young and urban Māori activists compared the radical politics of Black Power in the USA to the struggle for *mana motuhake* (self-determination), a struggle that they sought to radicalize. There now exists a rich literature on the diverse expressions and global determinants of Black Power.[4] In this and following chapters, I pick up the strands of Black Power that speak specifically to an oppositional aesthetic and ideology, to the practice of community self-sufficiency over dependency, to the redemption of Blackness as a positive mode of being expressed in Black love, and to a movement of spiritual liberation. In Aotearoa NZ the influence of Black Power upon Māori and Pasifika youth upset long-held mainstream assumptions that this particular settler society was exceptional in its enjoyment of racial harmony. However, for Māori youth Black Power also called into question the indigenous provenance of radical oppositional politics: were there no indigenous sources of Black Power? Engaging with these issues, we will witness the contentious ways in which the children of Tāne/Māui attempted to ground with the children of Legba in the public-political arena.

Black Power and New Zealand exceptionalism

By the late 1960s many Pākehā still held to the comforting myth that race relations in Aotearoa NZ, by comparison to the record of other settler colonies, were exceptionally good.[5] Only a minority of Pākehā who had invested themselves in the race question were critically examining its domestic coordinates. Most had imbibed the exceptionalist narrative and, following a well-established tradition, were looking abroad for a struggle to morally support, which they found principally in the anti-Apartheid movement. At worst, any claims of racial oppression suffered by Māori or Pasifika in Aotearoa NZ were treated at the time with derision. At best, discrimination was considered merely a temporary occurrence due to the arrival in cities of 'relatively unsophisticated immigrants'.[6]

It was in this climate that popular media started to make regular comparisons between the 'Polynesian problem' and the 'Negro problem' in the northern cities of the USA. Alarm bells rang over the assassination of Martin Luther King, the demise of the putatively accommodationist and peaceful civil rights movement that he represented, and its replacement by a putatively more violent and confrontational Black Power movement, exemplified in the popular imaginary by the Black Panthers.[7] Black Power presented itself as an unwelcome and threatening import when refracted through the lens of New Zealand 'exceptionalism'. And some started to worry that the disaffected and deracinated Polynesian youth might take a lesson from American Blacks and start burning Auckland and Wellington too. 'We have seen in the USA the kind of violence that can erupt when a depressed minority reaches the point of hopelessness and no return', noted a New Zealand Teachers Association report; '[w]e do not want to see such outbursts in our own … country'.[8]

Pākehā and Māori commentators alike tended to look for the flashpoint of Black Power radicalism among the unemployed and out-of-school youth who, congregating in groups, were apprehended

– in a somewhat sensationalist fashion – through the optic of American gangs.[9] 'Gang behaviour', affirmed the Polynesian Institute, 'shows manifestations in line with the distinct parallels of ... American urban development.'[10] Five years later, *Te Roopu o te Matakite*, an activist group that organized the pioneering Māori Land March of 1975, warned against the continued deracination of urban youth who would become '... a landless brown proletariat with no dignity, no *mana* [authority], and no stake in society. Like the Blacks in America, they will stand outside society and aggress against it.'[11]

Many Pākehā commentators parsed the gang problem through the narrative of New Zealand exceptionalism. For instance, Phil Amos, a Labour MP who had visited civil rights groups in the USA, was adamant that 'we have nothing to learn [from Americans] on how to live in society as a whole'.[12] One popular magazine took comfort in colonial stereotypes, suggesting that 'the easy-going temperament of the Polynesian may be all that will save Auckland from some future Watts-type explosion.'[13] Such responses weighted the onus of urban conflagration less on Pākehā racism and more on the pathologies of the Māori and Pasifika youth. But they were wilfully ignorant of the fact that the loose groups of Māori and Pasifika youth who comprised 'racial gangs' had in fact chosen their names – i.e. Nigs, Junior Nigs and Spades – from the racist expletives provided to them by Pākehā. Taura Eruera, a young Māori student activist, sought to dispel the comforting myths of exceptionalism and Polynesian pathology. Returning from a seventy-day study tour of minority communities in the USA, Eruera suggested that,

> we are always quick to assure ourselves that, compared to the USA, South Africa and Australia ... race relations in New Zealand are fine. As a comparative study this is true. But when we ... use this comparison as the basis for categorically stating that race relations in New Zealand are fine, we are kidding ourselves.[14]

In fact, Black Power rhetoric and thought had begun to infiltrate the prisons and education systems of Aotearoa NZ. And some even found it instructive for their own situation.

In the early 1970s racism was already part of the institutional bedrock of the New Zealand criminal justice system. Convictions of Māori were substantially higher than those of Pākehā, and Māori child offenders were twice more likely to receive prison sentences than Pākehā.[15] Similar to Black prison populations in North America, Black Power texts reached a captive audience. A newsletter written by prisoners and organized by a famous Pākehā non-conformist, Tim Shadbolt, devoted several pages examining the Black Panthers and Black Power. Following this exposition was an article written by an inmate agitating to 'stand firm and bit [sic] back at the pigs, as our coloured brothers in America are doing'.[16] Tellingly, the president of the King Cobras, a Pasifika gang, came out of prison brandishing Black Panther Bobby Seale's book, *Seize the Time*.[17]

Black Power literature was also picked up in some secondary schools. For instance, at Hilary College in Ōtara, a South Auckland suburb, some teachers began to tune their students into the contemporary global struggle against racism and imperialism from the Vietcong to the Sandanistas.[18] Continental and Diaspora African writers were also introduced, the history of Atlantic slavery was discussed, and some students began to follow Black Power politics with great interest.[19]

Similarly, interest in Black Power began to grow among university students, especially in the context of the passing of the Maori Affairs Amendment Act of 1967 that effectively made easier the compulsory acquisition and sale of putatively 'un-economic' Māori land held in freehold. Also in 1967, Jim Flynn, an American professor of political science and, at the time, chairperson for the USA civil rights organization, the Congress of Racial Equality (CORE), spoke to the Federation of Māori Students conference at Victoria University of Wellington. The topic of Flynn's speech was a comparative analysis of race and class in the USA and Aotearoa NZ undertaken by a non-New Zealander.[20] At Auckland University, another political science professor, Bob Chapman, introduced his Masters students to Black Power politics with some help from Flynn's essays.

One aspiring student of Chapman, Helen Clark, who would later become New Zealand Prime Minister and subsequently Administrator of the United Nations Development Programme, wrote a comparative essay for Chapman on the Black Muslims and the Jamaican Pan-Africanist, Marcus Garvey.[21] Atareta Poananga also attended Chapman's classes and became a great admirer of Malcolm X. She would later become (in)famous when, working for the Ministry of Foreign Affairs, she circulated a letter around the diplomatic core that chastised some of its Māori members by reference to Malcolm X's house/field negro analogy.[22] Syd Jackson was another Māori student of Chapman and read Eldridge Cleaver and Stokely Carmichael (whom he later met in person in Libya); he also studied African independence movements and sought to link their dynamics to the colonization of Oceania.[23]

The reception of Black Power by Māori and Pasifika youth radically undermined the exceptionalist narrative that outlawed any potential connection between anti-Black racism and anti-Polynesian racism. Some youth even started to consider that Black Power *was* relevant to Aotearoa NZ because white supremacy was a global system. A question thus crystallized: in what ways might and to what extent could Black Power express an indigenous articulation of radical, oppositional politics? This question was addressed most acutely by predominantly tertiary educated young Māori who congealed as a diverse group called Ngā Tamatoa.

Te Aute Old Boys versus young warriors

At this point we need to undertake a brief *whakapapa* of Māori student activism; specifically, we must retrieve the constitutive friction between reformist and radical strategies of pursuing *mana motuhake*. For this purpose, an important point of departure can be found in Te Aute College in Hawke's Bay, opened in 1854 by Samuel Williams, son of Henry Williams and head of the Church Missionary Society in Aotearoa NZ. Apirana Ngata was the college's most famous student who became the first Māori to complete a university degree in 1893, and indeed, the key scholar who pushed for Māori studies in university.[24] Ngata subsequently became the model Māori who worked in and through the institutions of settler colonialism in order to defend and forward *mana motuhake*, especially through the legal and economic consolidation of land holdings. Ngata's famous poem captures his strategy for attaining radical ends through reformist means:

> E tipu e rea i ngā rā o tōu ao
> Ko tō ringaringa ki ngā rākau a te Pākehā
> Hei orange mō tō tinana
> Ko tō ngākau ki ngā taonga a ō tīpuna
> Hei tikitiki mō tō māhuna
> Ko tō wairua ki te Atua
> Nāna nei ngā mea katoa
>
> Grow child in the days of your world
> Grasp with your hand the tools of the Pākehā
> As a means to support your body
> Keep in your heart the knowledge of your ancestors
> As a topknot for your head
> And turn your spirit to the lord
> From whom all things come.[25]

Ngata returned to Te Aute in 1897 to help in the formation of an Old Boys Association. Those who joined understood themselves to be working for a physical, mental and spiritual Māori renaissance along the lines laid out by Ngata, that is, to imitate the material achievements of Pākehā civilization but on Māori terms.[26] Eventually, members of the association would seek to make direct political interventions through the vehicle of the Young Māori Party.[27]

There was an inter-generational dynamic to Ngata's renaissance project, for at times the young educated Māori would find themselves in opposition to the practices of their elders. The Old Boys Association therefore directed young people to rethink and reassess – sometimes contentiously – the existing strategies for initiating a Māori renaissance.

In formal terms there were long gaps between these inter-generational discussions. A Young Māori Leaders Conference took place in 1939, and another only in 1959. In the latter conference, the youth took on a more pronounced role in setting out the issues of the day, which even at this time were dominated by the gathering pace of rural to urban migration.[28] Questions of leadership and the transmission of knowledge were also raised.[29] Nevertheless, Ngata's dictum remained by and large unchallenged: preserve the basic values of Māori culture – especially *aroha* and *manaakitanga* (affection and hospitality) – through a working understanding of Pākehā society.[30] All this would be challenged in the next conference that took place at Auckland University in 1970.

The 1970 conference addressed familiar problems of ongoing land alienation and the increasing urbanization of young Māori. Yet the disquiet and distance of the youth had reached new levels. Out of 100 delegates, 50 of which were actively participating, only 13 sat at the elders' table; and a 'sizeable number' of radical students shared the space with gang members and workers.[31] Perhaps the key point of inter-generational difference was the deracinating effect of urban living especially in terms of an intimate knowledge of Māori practices and Te Reo (language).[32] One group consisting of Syd Jackson (Chapman's student), Hana Te Hemara and Danny Harris (a former member of the Stormtrooper gang) criticized *kaumātua* (elders) for standing over the activities of the youth. Amplifying the complaints of the 1959 conference, Jackson et al. argued that what was really required of *kaumātua* was less active leadership and more transmission of language and culture to the urban youth.[33]

At the conclusion of the conference some of the Māori youth decided to create their own organization outside of the Te Aute tradition. With a membership open 'to Polynesians under 30',[34] Ngā Tamatoa functioned, in the main, as a pressure group consisting of educated urban Māori.[35] While Ngā Tamatoa cast their net of interests wide, it is fair to say that their predominant concern was the dislocation felt by a young generation many of whose families had memories and experiences of living in their *tūrangawaewae* (place of belonging) but who lacked that cultural immersion themselves. The challenge, in this environment, was to avoid becoming what Danny Harris described as an 'educated brown-Pākehā'.[36] Ngā Tamatoa tackled discriminatory legislation and also contributed to community services such as prison visits and food co-ops.[37] However, their prime aim was to build a bridge back to culture for dislocated youth by agitating for the teaching of Te Reo (Māori language) in primary and secondary schools.[38]

In the last chapter I noted that Māui's irreverence at any given order is not necessarily a modernist one. That is, Māui does not desire to destroy a traditional order, but rather seeks to wilfully rearrange its constituents in the pursuit of restitutive justice. In fact, if we dispense with the 'fatal impact' thesis it is not so clear where conservative reform ends and oppositional radicalism begins. And for those young Māori who claimed the radical banner, their elders would sometimes remind them that they were actually seeking to conserve their heritages by regenerating them in the present context.[39] In fact, these sentiments are evident in the selection of the name Ngā Tamatoa (the young warriors) itself, due to its 'indigenous appeal'[40] being also the title of the Māori battalion that had fought in the Second World War. Likewise, their motto, 'Tama tū tama ora / Tama noho tama mate' (stand up and live or lay down and die), captured the radical energy of Black Power but through a traditional *whakataukī* (proverb).[41]

While Ngata had sought to balance Pākehā means with Māori ends, the young warriors now saw their fluency in the Pākehā world as destructive and disabling of Māori ends: 'The Māori just wants to be what he was and is, a Māori! He doesn't want to be a brown skinned New Zealander. He is proud of his ancestors, and ancestral background, and he is proud of his customs and traditions.'[42] In radicalizing the Te Aute strategy Ngā Tamatoa sought to reclaim another political *whakapapa* of *mana motuhake*. Specifically, they aimed to reconstitute the student tradition along the lines of the often oppositional resistances practised by ancestors such as Hone Heke, King Pōtatau and Te Kooti.[43] Indeed, the personal *whakapapa* of some of the new warriors included these traditions. For instance, Hana Te Hemara's grandmother was a member of the old Kotahitanga (unity) movement, and she grew up surrounded by a critique of 'white greed and white aggression'.[44] To this end, Ngā Tamatoa made their key battleground Te Tiriti o Waitangi (the Treaty). But instead of using the Te Aute Old Boys strategy of tactful debating with their 'partners', Ngā Tamatoa set out to publically disrupt the national celebrations at Waitangi in 1971. In doing so they claimed that the method of 'courteous' engagement with the question of Te Tiriti (The Treaty) had been 'largely unsuccessful', and Māori patience was not 'limitless'.[45]

The response by elders was mixed. Pat Hohepa, an attendee of both the 1959 and 1970 leader conferences, described Ngā Tamatoa as the 'real Māori'.[46] And Hone Kaa, Anglican theologian and activist, later reflected that while Ngā Tamatoa were 'totally un-Māori', 'city Māori' and 'the children of policies of integration', they nevertheless 'became my teachers and the revisers of my history'.[47] This being said, Ngā Tamatoa's strategy of radical opposition drove a wedge between them and the majority of their elders. Witness, for example, the 1975 Land March to Parliament that started from Te Hāpua at the tip of the North Island. While Ngā Tamatoa, especially their female members,[48] had done much of the organizing for the march, the public face of the endeavour was respected *kuia* (elder woman) Whina Cooper. As the march arrived at parliament, members of Ngā Tamatoa, inspired by their aboriginal Black Power brethren and sistren across the Tasman Sea, erected a tent embassy in the grounds and refused to leave until substantive policy changes towards land governance had begun. Cooper distanced herself from these actions. Writing about Ngā Tamatoa to Matiu Rata, Minister of Māori Affairs, Cooper complained that 'they are an embarrassment to not only our Maori people but the government of today in that they have not the courtesy to wait for your reply'.[49]

An indigenous Black Power?

The attempts, at the turn of the 1970s, to retrieve a political *whakapapa* of *mana motuhake* impelled activists to ground with Black Power. I would argue that there are two reasons for this. First, Black Power in North America was predominantly the language of the youth living in racially fractured and majority white urban environments; many of them were one generation displaced from the rural South, the actual seedbed of the Black Power movement.[50] This urban context also seems to have partly muted the ideological impact of First Nations struggles on Māori activists, despite the two peoples enjoying personal exchanges at the time.[51] In a generational sense, then, young African-American radicals spoke more directly to the situation of Māori youth than many of the latter's *kaumātua* (elders).

But second, as I have noted, Black Power had entered into the public psyche of Aotearoa NZ specifically as a radical challenge to the exceptionalist narrative. In this respect, Black Power could easily be dismissed as foreign fanaticism influencing the pliable mind of Māori youth. Through this mainstream presumption it was all too easy to argue, by extension, that the idea of an oppositional politics *per se* was not indigenous but rather an inauthentic 'foreign' invention/invasion. For these reasons the grounding was necessarily contentious.

In fact, one group of Māori activists were directly concerned with addressing such assumptions and for this reason they sought to dismiss the idea that radical Māori were copying radical African Americans: 'the argument that Maori activism does not spring from "some original indigenous impulse" is quite untenable.[52] Citing the prophets Te Kooti, Rua Kenana, Te Whiti and T. W. Rātana, this group argued that radical Māori activism had a *whakapapa* that pre-dated 'European pressure-propagandist groups and twentieth century black activists'.[53] In other words, there was no need to import Black Power because oppositional strategies of *mana motuhake* already existed in the Māori past. These misgivings were no doubt inflamed by mainstream media, who had started to remix Black Power as 'Brown Power'. In 1968 John Rangihau, respected Tūhoe leader and academic, proposed a definition of Brown Power as, simply, the enactment of Māori culture itself.[54] But three years later, the Victoria University Students Christian Movement felt it important enough to hold their annual conference on the theme of Brown Power. Taura Eruera, chairperson of Ngā Tamatoa, attended and admonished those who spoke of Brown Power: 'these terms mean absolutely nothing to me ... the reports given haven't taken the time to understand Maori values or causes and a chain of sensationalism has begun'.[55]

Comparative questions as to the provenance, authenticity and applicability of Black Power in Aotearoa NZ were vociferously debated at the 1970 conference that gave birth to Ngā Tamatoa. Elders tended to ignore the question of Black Power altogether, having grown up 'in the marae situation whereas the young were reared in the city'.[56] And none of the delegates linked Black Power to the kind of *mana motuhake* that was practised on the *marae* (traditional meeting place). In other words, Black Power was effectively identified as an issue specific to urban Māori. Taura Eruera addressed the question of provenance directly, arguing that Black Power was inapplicable to the New Zealand situation where 'Māori have their culture and pride and knowledge of origins'.[57] But in contrast, several participants including Syd Jackson and Hana Te Hemara argued that Black Power could develop 'from conditions in New Zealand rather than from copying the movement in the USA' and that, as an ideology, it gave 'a sense of belonging' by helping to overcome 'the sense of alienation that develops in urban life'.[58]

Pat Hohepa had brought some Stormtroopers – a local Māori gang – to the 1970 conference who, when it came to voting, differentiated themselves from other participants by 'raised clenched fists – the American black power symbol'.[59] This was a crucial gesture which suggested that the apprehension of Black Power among those on the 'front line' was visceral and affective, and not just intellectual or comparative. Reflecting on its affective impact, one delegate reported that 'Black Power is to stop white power. Mention Black Power to Pākehā and they won't accept it. I mentioned it to one Pākehā and he said he would kill me'.[60] In this respect, the strategic importance of Black Power was generally acknowledged at the conference, with one delegate stating that 'Black Power will stop us being manipulated'.[61] After all, Black Power expressed a communal demand for self-liberation that did not ask for the permission of the oppressor to be pursued. And this illocutory effect was well recognized by those who would deploy Black Power rhetoric throughout the 1970s and even beyond.[62] Failure to address these demands could also be proffered as a threat – as Syd Jackson impressed upon the Race Relations Council annual conference in 1972.[63]

The more the government exhibited intransigence and active hostility towards social justice agendas as the 1970s wore on, the more activists sensed the possibility that society was heading towards a violent confrontation. The continued presence and growth of gangs – deracinated youth following an autonomous and mercurial leadership – testified to such a possibility. The 1977 Young Māori Leaders Conference focused expressly on these issues.[64] By 1979, Ranginui Walker, a leading Māori commentator, warned that 'Māori are now traversing the ground covered by Blacks in American more than a decade ago.' For Walker, the fatal shooting of a teenage boy, Daniel Houpapa, during a confrontation between police and the Mighty Mongrel Mob gang in 1976 had 'its American parallel with the Black Panthers'.[65] MP Mike Moore, later to become Director-General of the World Trade Organization, forcefully echoed these sentiments in a speech entitled the 'Time Bomb'.[66]

In this respect, perhaps the most important strategic difference between Ngā Tamatoa and their American Black Power counterparts was the abrogation of armed struggle. Some members of Ngā Tamatoa did occasionally express a desire to pick up arms, as the Oakland Panthers had already done: 'If Pākehā want war', warned Syd Jackson, 'we will pick up guns like our ancestors in Taranaki.'[67] Nevertheless, Ngā Tamatoa never seriously organized around armed insurrection, although one of their members, Vern Winitana, was accused of training gang members into shock troops at his karate classes.[68] But the key question was whether the gangs might become progressively politicized as social and economic conditions worsened. This possibility had always been in the minds of activists. For example, Syd Jackson suggested that gangs might 'work through the whole politicization bit and that's where the guts of the street movement will come from'.[69] Other young warriors argued that 'a lot of pseudo-criminal behaviour in the streets is [actually] a form of civil disturbance'.[70]

One gang even seemed to be experiencing such a political awakening. In 1970, Reitu Harris formed the Black Bulls, whose initial activities were to look after young Māori who had arrived in Wellington from the rural areas after the Department of Māori Affairs had closed its youth hostels.[71] On one occasion the Bulls went to confront another gang – the Mighty Mongrel Mob – over an attempted rape, and when the latter performed a *haka* (a posture dance) finishing with the taunt 'and who are you?' Harris replied on the spur of the moment, 'we are the Black Power'.[72] Later, Harris would explain that the name change was part inspired by the resistance movement in South Africa.[73] The inspiration is important to note, as will become clear soon enough.

Conclusion

I stated in the last chapter that knowledge cultivation is a circulatory process that necessarily interacts with a wider biotope, enfolding matter from other inhabitations. I also argued that the attempt to redeem the past does not only involve a binding together of the living and the ancestors but can also impel the binding together of different (post)colonized peoples in a project of restitutive justice – *tātou tātou*. Ngā Tamatoa practised this kind of knowledge cultivation. They broke from the Te Aute Old Boys strategy of partial accommodation with white power by reclaiming an oppositional strategy with an

indigenous pedigree. And their retrieval and cultivation of an oppositional *whakapapa* of *mana motuhake* necessitated a grounding with
Black Power.

In this chapter, then, we have witnessed the children of Tāne/
Māui and Legba meeting in the public-political realm. They have
met primarily via sociological-anthropological categories of difference,
comparative analyses, and in the shadows cast by sensationalist
mainstream apprehensions of the coming Black apocalypse. This
meeting has therefore been contentious and the binding together of
Black Power and *mana motuhake* has been somewhat weak. Yet it
seems that at least with some of the youth the grounding has been
deeper and the binding stronger than colonial media would allow or
presume. So let us now follow these inclinations and, while staying in
the same time period, shift our analysis from comparisons with Black
Power to identifications with Blackness.

The Rise and Fall of Political Blackness

Introduction

Blackness was a mode of being that Black Power activists in the USA sought to recover and sanctify in order to confront a viscerally and institutionally racist settler state. In this chapter we examine the political identifications with Blackness that emerged in another racist settler state – New Zealand. In pursuit of restitution for colonial injustices, the identification with Blackness provided for a deeper binding between the children of Tāne/Māui and Legba. Along with Māori we must now add to this journey their *tuākana* (elder siblings), the Pasifika peoples – especially those from islands that the New Zealand state enjoyed some prior imperial relationship with – who had also arrived in urban areas in increasing numbers during the 1960s.

In this chapter, we shall first witness how young Pasifika activists learnt similar lessons to their Māori cousins in Ngā Tamatoa regarding Black Power, yet cultivated, through the activities of the Polynesian Panthers, a closer political identification with Blackness. We shall then turn to the high point of confrontation during this period, the anti-Apartheid resistance to the tour by the South African Springboks rugby team in 1981. With regards to this resistance we shall retrieve a *whakapapa* of colonial administration that binds South African Apartheid to breaches to Te Tiriti o Waitangi (The Treaty). And through this retrieval we will be able to glean why some Māori would begin to politically identify with Blackness. Subsequently we shall focus upon the Black Women's Movement that spanned this time period and that sought to bring political identifications with Blackness quite literally home. We shall finally witness the abrupt breaking of these anti-colonial connections.

The Polynesian Panthers

Most parents of the youth who would join the Polynesian Panther Movement had migrated from the islands with an assumption that Aotearoa NZ was the place to 'get ahead'.[1] Upon arrival in Auckland and other towns across the north and south islands, parents encouraged their children to assimilate in order to enjoy the benefits of New Zealand society. However, the desire to enter into a majority Pālagi[2] society as an equal tended to foster insensitivity to the prior and continuing dispossession of Māori. Among many parents and elders – both Māori and Pasifika – this conjuncture of labour exploitation and land dispossession played into a 'divide and rule' mentality.[3] However, visceral racism, with its global anti-Black grammar, had a perversely democratizing impact on the quotidian experiences of Māori and Pasifika youth. For instance, buses to Ponsonby (the inner-city neighbourhood of Auckland where many Pasifika peoples resided) were labelled the 'Congo run'.[4] And at school, under the colonial gaze, Māori and Pasifika youth were all lumped into the same subaltern category of Polynesians. Indeed, those Pasifika youth who were born in Aotearoa NZ, and therefore sported a Kiwi accent, were often assumed to be Māori.[5] Inevitably, the assimilatory pressures felt by Māori started to affect Pasifika communities too and, likewise, their youth pushed back.

Unlike Ngā Tamatoa, the constituency of the Polynesian Panthers was largely (but by no means entirely) Pasifika and non-tertiary educated. Its initial core group was composed of ex-members of a Pasifika gang, the Nigs. Chairman Will 'Ilolahia was the only member to attend university. And while his encounter with Black

Power came during his university studies, it was his fellow gang members who provided 'Ilolahia with his 'real education'.[6] Meanwhile, family members and friends who had left school to work as seamen returned regularly with Black Power literature and information from the outside world.[7] Inspired, 'Ilolahia encouraged his gang mates to make a principled decision to do something more for their immediate community than hanging on the corner. However, they could not call themselves the Black Panthers because a broad association of Māori and Pasifika gangs, which included some of their brothers, had already taken that name. Hence the Polynesian Panther Movement (PPM) was inaugurated in June 1971.[8]

Initially the Movement was apprehended simply as a kind of acceptable gang.[9] However, the Panthers strived to be something more. They enthusiastically adopted the Black Panthers' Ten-Point Programme of freedom, equality and social justice so as to teach Pasifika families how 'to survive in the system'.[10] The Movement even professed to be 'the New Zealand response to the Black Revolution'.[11] Structuring themselves in the same micro-nation format as their US counterparts with various ministerial portfolios,[12] the Polynesian Panthers echoed Malcolm X's organizational mantra of Black Power: 'we cannot have black and white unity until we have black unity'.[13] The Panthers were especially concerned with both dividing lines among Pasifika peoples of various islands as well as between Māori and Pasifika. Blackness as a Polynesian identity was the solution to colonial divide and rule.

The Polynesian Panthers focused their practical efforts on grass-roots activities (some in partnership with the Peoples Union, their Pālagi equivalent in the inner-city suburb of Ponsonby) including: organizing prison visit programmes and sporting and debating teams for inmates, providing a halfway-house service for young men released from prison, running homework centres, offering interest-free 'people's loans', legal aid, and organizing food banks that at one point catered for 600 families. The Panthers also employed one of their core Māori members, Miriama Rauhihi-Ness, as a full-time community worker.[14]

But while community welfare was the major activity of the Panther Movement, survival was a strategy, not a goal; for their aims were directly political: to eliminate the visceral and institutional racism and exploitation that accompanied assimilation policies. These politics were evident from the beginning of the Movement and took the form, for instance, of protest marches against Vietnam wherein slogans from Muhammad Ali were remixed for the Oceania context: 'no Vietnamese ever called me coconut'.[15]

After a couple of years the Movement somewhat contentiously became a fully fledged Party. While the community initiatives continued, more focus was placed on political education and mobilization of the people.[16] With the adoption of a vanguard identity more direct forms of confrontation with the racist and exploitative power structure ensued. As both their American and Australian Black Power counterparts had done, the Panthers helped to run a PIG patrol that shadowed police patrol cars in order to pre-empt raids on predominantly Māori and Pasifika drinking establishments.[17] In their legal aid activities, the Panthers were supported by a lawyer and future Prime Minister, David Lange. The Panthers also stood up against so-called 'dawn raids' whereby the police specifically targeted the homes of 'Polynesians' (sometimes including Māori and Pasifika citizens) in a racist government campaign against overstayers.[18]

The Polynesian Panthers were not Oceanic subalterns. They did not simply copy the ten-point programme of the Oakland Black Panthers and extend it into Oceania. Instead, and despite very tenuous material linkages, the Polynesian Panthers' grounding with their African-American cousins facilitated a binding of colonial New Zealand presents back to decolonial Oceanic pasts.

This process was visibly marked by the way in which Pasifika aesthetics combined with African-American when it came to the Polynesian Panthers' dress code: men would wear 'cultural shirts' along with the standard black dress, while women would wear 'cultural dresses'.[19] Furthermore, while members were advised to read *Seize the Time* and *Autobiography of Malcolm X* they were also encouraged to 'read on our culture, to give us something to identify with'.[20] The various independence movements of Oceania (including those of Māori) featured heavily in the Panther psyche, as well as opposition to French nuclear testing in the region.[21] Indeed, as was the case with some members of Ngā Tamatoa, anti-colonial struggles were already woven into the personal genealogy of some Panthers.[22] More importantly, Oceanic pasts formed the living cultural matter that politicized Pasifika youth as they started to engage with Black Power. Take, for instance, Tigilau Ness – the Polynesian Panthers' minister for culture. His radicalization occurred after he was suspended from school for refusing to cut his afro. Ness was singled out, despite Pālagi 'surfer' students being allowed to keep their hair long. But while the afro aesthetic owed much to Black America, the actual practice of the eldest boy growing out their hair came from his Niuean heritage.[23]

Ngā Tamatoa had demonstrated a qualified irreverence to the given order represented by Te Aute Old Boys. The Pasifika children of Māui demonstrated likewise. Rather than cut the threads of their Pasifika heritage so as to become model New Zealand citizens, the Panthers wanted to manipulate the arrangements of migrant communities to better survive in Aotearoa NZ. Indeed, particular Pasifika values intentionally informed the organization and operation of the Panthers. For example, the practice of according respect to elders due to their demonstrated leadership featured in gangs such as the Nigs and followed through into the Panthers.[24] At the time, 'Ilolahia even considered this respect to be a 'revolutionary thing' because 'there's all this European shit breaking up the [Polynesian] family unit'.[25]

But unlike Ngā Tamatoa, the Panthers, as radical children of Island migrants, had no established Te Aute Old Boy tradition to contend with. In fact, Pasifika elders were struggling to reproduce their hierarchies of affiliation and attendant cultural practices in Aotearoa NZ. Nonetheless, the Panthers still had to grapple with a similar inter-generational tension to that faced by Ngā Tamatoa. Indeed, some Pasifika elders had started to argue that their rebellious youth were compounding their communities' problems by undermining the accommodationist strategy of engaging with the Pālagi majority.

All these tensions are clearly exposed in the Panthers' provision –
along with the Citizens' Association for Racial Equality (CARE) – of
homework centres designed to promote 'Polynesian culture' and to
encourage parents to participate in children's welfare and education.[26]
But such after-work-hour activities impacted directly on the time
that families would usually spend at their church. Pasifika churches
in Aotearoa NZ commanded such a large share of community time
because they functioned to retain the cultural practices (including the
use of language) that migrant parents had had to leave behind. The
Panthers recognized precisely this point that churches did 'a lot to
preserve the communalism that exists back in the Polynesian islands'.
And because of this, church leaders commanded significant respect.[27]
However, for the sake of community survival, the Panthers were now
asking their parents to commit to alternative activities after the work/
school day.

These inter-generational tensions manifested most acutely through
gender dynamics. Many young women at the time had to work outside
of the home, even if they had families.[28] (In fact, Rauhihi-Ness, the
Panther's full-time social worker, had first come to the movement's
attention through the strike that she had organized with Pasifika
women over pay conditions.[29]) For some women the Panthers provided
a social and purposive space outside of the home, church *and* workplace
wherein they could take active part in the struggle against inequality
and discrimination and stake their own claim in wider society. It is
true that in this space Panther men often ridiculed women's efforts.
But Panther women collectively confronted these internal discrimina-
tions.[30] Inevitably, the audacity of the Panthers' confrontational pursuit
of social justice, combined with the radical space opened for 'feminist'
impulses, led to some churches discounting the Party as 'Fia Pālagi
communists' – agents of ungodly outsiders.[31]

In many ways, then, similar contentious dynamics informed Ngā
Tamatoa and the Polynesian Panthers' grounding with Black Power.
However, the Panthers had to contend with one further challenge that
perhaps required a political identification with Blackness more so than

many of their Māori counterparts. As I noted previously, the *tēina* (junior)/*tuākana* (senior) relationship is a fundamental structuring principle of *whakapapa*. Pasifika people are considered the *tuākana* (senior) line to Māori, the *tēina* (junior), in so far as Māori migrated from the Islands to Aotearoa NZ.[32] Yet at the same time, Māori are the *tāngata whenua* (peoples of the land) in Aotearoa NZ and Pasifika peoples are, strictly speaking, *manuhiri* (visitors). Situated within this network of relations, the Polynesian Panthers' programme of community survival was necessarily dependent upon and bound up in Māori *mana motuhake* (self-determination).

In order to pursue social justice while honouring these complex relations, the Panthers creatively reinterpreted Huey Newton's notion of 'revolutionary intercommunalism'.[33] For Newton, co-founder of the Oakland Black Panthers, revolutionary intercommunalism was a notion that developed out of a shift in his understanding of the global role of the USA. As an imperial military and economic power, Newton came to realize that the USA consistently undermined the self-determination of peoples. In light of this realization his earlier conceptualization of African Americans as an 'internal colony' could no longer hold, and he replaced it with the idea of dispossessed (lumpen) communities. Newton believed that it was in this state of mutual dispossession that African Americans, Vietnamese and all colonized peoples could connect as the world's lumpen-proletariat.[34]

'Ilolahia, chair of the Polynesian Panthers, provided a different interpretation of Newton's concept. He was confident that Māori and Pasifika youth shared the same problem: racism. However, in identifying as a united front of Polynesians, 'Ilolahia was clear that Māori could not 'lose their *Māoritanga* [culture] and replace their Maoriness'.[35] 'The solution to our predicament', declared 'Ilolahia, 'lies in UNITY through DIVERSIFICATION, and not UNIFORMITY'.[36] Hence, strategically, the land issue was to be strictly led and determined by *tāngata whenua*, i.e. 'Māori Polynesians', although *manuhiri*, especially 'non-Māori Polynesians', should 'take a stance of solidarity and support'.[37] Following this logic, the Panthers took a supportive role in some of the seminal Māori struggles over land dispossession in the 1970s including the great Land March of 1975 (wherein they acted as security as it passed through Auckland) and the occupation of Bastion Point in 1978.[38] Conversely, racial discrimination and exploitation over housing, education, the courts, work and employment were issues that *all* Polynesians owned,[39] and here the Panthers often took leading roles. Tellingly, 'Ilolahia's strategy was announced in Rongo, a multilingual news magazine jointly published with Ngā Tamatoa and other Māori and Pasifika radicals.

'Ilolahia's revolutionary intercommunalism formed part of a wider aspiration among Polynesian Panthers to cultivate a global infrastructure of anti-colonial connectivity. Beyond Aotearoa NZ, the Panthers hoped for an Australasia–Pacific common front, a Black Power collectivity that also included indigenous peoples generally considered *not* to be Polynesian (i.e. the peoples of Australia, Papua New Guinea and the New Hebrides).[40] Beyond that, they looked forward to a united Black Power front composed of all oppressed peoples in the 'world struggle'.[41]

In sum, the Polynesian Panthers sought to redeem the *tuākana/ tēina* relationship between Pasifika and Māori by mobilizing Blackness as a political identification through which to bind together the diverse yet related peoples of (post)colonized Oceania in a global anti-colonial project of restitutive justice.

The coming of the Springboks

But what of Māori? Was there any political imperative that required the *tāngata whenua* (peoples of the land) not just to compare themselves with Black Power but to identify with Blackness? To answer this question we must now shift geographies and narrate the constitution of colonial ties and anti-colonial resistance between South Africa and Aotearoa NZ, and specifically, between Apartheid and Te Tiriti (The Treaty).

In the first instance, such a *whakapapa* binds Aotearoa NZ and South Africa together as British dependencies that share a long history of administrative relationships. George Grey, for instance, served as governor of both colonies. Grey did much to set the structures of white supremacy in South Africa, while in Aotearoa NZ he launched the invasion of the Waikato against the Kīngitanga (Māori King Movement).[42] These administrative relations are long standing. For example, in Aotearoa NZ Apartheid categories were deployed in inter-state relations as late as 1970 in order to facilitate a rugby tour of South Africa when the status of 'honorary whites' was accepted for Māori players on their behalf by the Māori Council. However, the *whakapapa* that I am retrieving also binds the two settler colonies together through anti-Apartheid agitation. Indeed, the disavowal of ancestry that accompanied the status of 'honorary whites' was decried by the Māori Women's Welfare League.[43] Subsequently, Vern Winitana, Ngā Tamatoa member, turned down the opportunity to tour South Africa as an All Black.[44]

The first national protest over the sporting relationship between South Africa and Aotearoa NZ took place as far back as 1936/7 and was driven by two Māori, Te Puea Herangi and Tai Mitchell.[45] Soon afterwards, members of the Māori Battalion experienced racism from white South African soldiers during the Second World War, and this was not to be forgotten.[46] After having led a motion of 500 Māori to oppose another Springbok tour in 1972, the Māori Organization on Human Rights wrote in their newsletter: 'Kiwis who fought against Hitler remember: we are against the Nazi master race theories that led to the massive violence of World War Two with the organized murder of 6 million Jews – and to the present day rule of Apartheid law in South Africa.'[47]

When in 1981 the Springboks were welcomed, as per protocol, onto Poho-o-Rawhiri *marae* (meeting place), just before their first game at Gisborne, a small group of Māori sought to deny entrance to the visitors. A great-great grandson of Apirana Ngata was part of the protest. He recalled that East Coast Māori formed the bulk of the

Māori Battalion and that during the war they were initially barred from entering Cape Town while white soldiers were permitted. 'Perhaps we are too hospitable', pondered the grandson; 'I think if Hitler was alive we would welcome him.'[48]

This *whakapapa* retrieves the intimacy with which the anti-apartheid struggle was bound to the struggle for *mana motuhake*. The tensile strength was provided by the apprehension among Māori that support for apartheid desecrated Te Tiriti (The Treaty). For instance, in 1960 a petition against the forthcoming Springboks tour was launched by Bishop Wiremu Netana Panapa that charged the sporting relationship with breaching the principles of Te Tiriti with regards to protection and equal treatment of Māori.[49] By 1972 the second national branch of Ngā Tamatoa had issued a statement of aims opposing 'white racism at home and abroad', while seeking ratification of the spirit of Te Tiriti.[50]

The issue of immigration policy was also included in the 1970s struggles against sporting relationships with the apartheid state. In this respect, activists were recalling, once more, the *whakapapa* of colonial administration that bound South Africa to Aotearoa NZ as settler colonies wherein the 1897 Natal Act in South Africa inspired both Australia and New Zealand's *fin de siècle* racist immigration acts.[51] Some Māori activists protested that the immigration policies of the New Zealand state threatened to destroy the *tēina/tuākana* relationship between them and Pasifika peoples. In fact, the Kia Ngawari youth club of Wellington directly likened the 1970s 'dawn raids' against suspect 'Polynesians' to the South Africa group area act of 1950.[52] Ngā Tamatoa, in pledging to support the 'Black freedom fighters in South Africa', also pledged to overthrow 'New Zealand's present racist regime' so as to support the right 'of all pacific island peoples to free and unrestricted entry'.[53]

For all these reasons, Māori and Pasifika activists were especially critical of the majority of Pākehā anti-Apartheid activists who, having imbibed the exceptionalist narrative of New Zealand colonization, failed to make the global connection between the mores and laws of the two settler colonies, especially with regards to land dispossession, a racist division of labour, and de facto second-class citizenship.[54] The appropriation by many Pākehā anti-Apartheid activists of Steve Biko as symbolic of apartheid violence was especially galling. Biko, the leader of the Black Consciousness movement, had been murdered by the South African regime on 12 September 1977. At a protest meeting during the beginning of the 1981 tour Donna Awatere sought to bring Te Tiriti onto the agenda and was met with 'what's that got to do with it?' by a Pākehā attendee. 'What hurts most', Awatere conceded, 'is that they make a monument of Biko. But how many turned out when Daniel Houpapa was murdered?'[55] In Awatere's understanding, Biko's Black Consciousness could not be – and should not have been – segregated from the pursuit of *mana motuhake* and the honouring of Te Tiriti.

Consonant with the *whakapapa* that I have retrieved above, Māori protestors by and large framed apartheid as a global form of settler-colonial governance. For instance, on the eve of the 1981 tour, Whetu Tirikatene-Sullivan, MP for Southern Māori, suggested that 'many Maori people in this country have had a taste of Apartheid attitudes here at home'.[56] Some even began to identify themselves with the African sufferers of apartheid. Hone Harawira argued the point on behalf of the Māori Peoples Liberation Movement: 'We are as much slaves as [South African Blacks] are, a little better paid, and a little better housed of course – but slaves to the cause of imperialism nonetheless.'[57] This was less a case of comparing natives to negroes, browns to blacks, and more a case of politically identifying with Blackness against shared colonial injustices.

This incipient or actual identification is what differentiated the level of Māori militancy from that of most (but not all) of their Pākehā counterparts. While for most Pākehā the campaign was focused on combating a foreign evil, Māori and Pasifika activists sought to arrest the encroachment of this evil upon their children's future.[58] For this reason, Māori and Pasifika groups planned their activities with a much more military mindset and deeper intensity of confrontation than the predominantly Pākehā-run anti-tour organizations. And these militant plans were rarely conveyed to Pākehā marshals.[59]

A police unit called the Red Squad had been trained to forcefully confront protestors and they had been armed, for the first time in Aotearoa NZ policing history, with long batons imported from the United States where they had been designed to ruthlessly quell the predominantly Black urban uprisings of the 1960s and 70s. Māori and Pasifika activists in Auckland took the initiative to create a counter-organization, the Patu Squad. *Patu* can be glossed as to strike; in noun form, the word indicates a club. The Patu Squad studied the formations of the Red Squad and developed counter-tactics.[60] Armour that could deflect the long baton blows was manufactured, predominantly at home, although machinery at car factories was occasionally utilized.[61]

There had existed a 'military wing' of the Polynesian Panthers that sometimes undertook direct actions just on the other side of legal.[62] Will 'Ilolahia, former chair of the Panthers, drew upon these past experiences to organize a special military wing of the Patu Squad, populated by some of the best fighters from gangs.[63] Members of different gangs marched together at anti-tour protests, and many were on the front line of confrontations with the police, but would drop back as soon as the cameras came closer.[64] It should not be forgotten that Pākehā activists were often in the front lines alongside Māori and Pasifika.[65] Nevertheless, at the end of the last march of the tour in Auckland it was mostly Māori and Pasifika that remained, ready to physically confront the police.[66] At one point, gang leadership marshalled fleeing protestors to regroup and successfully counter-charge the police.[67] Was this evidence of the political awakening of gangs that had long been feared as the arrival of Black anarchy?

The differences in militancy between Māori, Pasifika and Pākehā protestors also produced different consequences, and this is especially the case with regards to policing and the criminal justice system. Riot police, armed with the new batons, frequented drinking establishments known to have a 'black presence'.[68] Women were not spared from the baton, especially if they congregated at a known Māori and Pasifika activist community centre.[69] In fact, the police squad that was responsible for publically drawing the first blood of protestors in Molesworth

Street, Wellington, also visited Takapūwāhia Pā in Porirua in a similarly violent fashion but out of the glare of city headlines. Ostensibly, they had been tasked with tackling the smoking of Marijuana by groups of Māori youth who had become interested in the RasTafari faith.[70]

Meanwhile, although many Pākehā took part in the confrontations, arrests for more serious charges of riotous destruction overwhelmingly targeted Māori and Pasifika activists – both male and female.[71] A number of defence funds were set up in response.[72] As 'Ilolahia and Hone Harawira went on trial in Auckland facing serious jail sentences, outside the court supporters shouted 'white justice, black oppression!'[73] The sentences were only quashed because, with the help of Halt All Racist Tours (HART) and veteran Māori activist Titewhai Harawira, Desmond Tutu (visiting on church business) was sequestered to make a personal appearance in court wherein he testified graphically as to the realities of living under Apartheid.[74] Nevertheless, upon leaving court, 'Ilolahia was informed by police that they were still out to 'get him'.[75] Both 'Ilolahia and Eruera Nia, a founding member of Ngā Tamatoa in Wellington, were so disgusted with the state's response to the Springbok tour that they left Aotearoa shores (with 'Ilolahia only returning many years later).[76] Tigilau Ness, culture minister for the Polynesian Panthers, was not so lucky and in a separate trial received a substantial jail term.

Inevitably, the protests affected Pākehā activists too. Mitzi Nairn, a leading Pākehā figure in these movements, suggests that Pākehā-led anti-racist campaigns started in earnest only after the Springbok tour precisely because the state response made domestic racism unavoidably visible. What is more, middle-class Pākehā had now witnessed first-hand the marshalling skills of Māori and Pasifika on the front line, as well as their deeper investment in the struggle.[77] It therefore became far more difficult to categorize these youth as 'happy-go-lucky' Polynesians or pathological vectors of urban society. At a recent thirty-year commemoration lecture, John Minto, a key Pākehā anti-apartheid activist, acknowledged that the displacement of racism onto foreign issues was a 'valid criticism' of the anti-apartheid movement.[78]

What was clear at the time, though, was that the tour had split Aotearoa NZ straight down the middle. One poll undertaken at the height of the confrontation reported that 49 per cent of the respondents believed that the Springboks should not have come and 43.5 per cent believed that the tour should stop immediately.[79] Pākehā families were internally divided, sometimes violently,[80] and so too were Māori and Pasifika privately and publically, with Māori policemen sometimes being called 'house niggers' and 'uncle Toms'.[81] Church constituencies also suffered, with those who supported the protests sometimes receiving unprecedented criticism and anger from their congregations and superiors. In fact, many priests and pastors involved in the protests subsequently abandoned the institutional church.[82] But above all, the multiple confrontations that took place over the tour intensified the terms of engagement with Blackness.

From Blackness to *taha Māori*

In Great Turtle Island (North America) the central aim of Black Power had been to unravel the dependency on white beneficence and instead build self-reliance within Black communities. Merata Mita, Ngā Tamatoa member and director of the documentary of the Springboks protests, recalls that the confrontations over the tour effectively vindicated self-determination strategies cognate to Black Power by forcing Māori to realize that 'if we waited for them [Pākehā] to grow up it wasn't going to happen'.[83] Mita points out that the Te Reo (Māori language) immersion schools movement shifted gears in the aftermath of the tour as did *mauri ora* (spiritual wellbeing) health projects, nowadays known as *whānau ora* (family wellbeing).[84] There were other effects, too. After the tour a number of Māori activists returned to their *tūrangawaewae* (places of belonging), often bearing deep scars from their urban struggles, in order to ground for extended periods of time with their peoples in their *tūrangawaewae*. In 1984, a gathering at Ngāruawāhia – the home of the Kīngitanga (Māori King Movement) – was convened, called by Māori for Māori in order to find common cause in Te Tiriti (The Treaty).[85] And while the Māori Land March had helped to put in place the Waitangi Tribunal in 1975, it was only after the Springboks tour, in 1985, that its mandate was extended retrospectively to encompass the colonial history of land dispossession since 1840.

Therefore the Springboks tour confirmed the sagacity of updating the Te Aute tradition with a more oppositional approach to *mana motuhake*. But while these radicalizations had been contentiously compared to Black Power, the engagement with apartheid, especially for Māori, was far less framed by comparison and much more cultivated through a *whakapapa* of *mana motuhake*. This was why the tour had to be stopped: the breaches to Te Tiriti were proof that apartheid was alive and well in Aotearoa NZ also. And through this *whakapapa* some Māori began to mobilize Blackness as part of their political identification: 'be proud, be strong, be black', proclaimed the Waitangi Action Committee.[86] As we have witnessed, the Polynesian Panthers had already demonstrated a close identification to Blackness; they were, after all, non-indigenous migrants to the urban areas in somewhat the same fashion as African Americans. Crucially, the anti-tour protests channelled most of these Māori and Pasifika activists into the front line. What is more, some of these activists were also key participants in the Black Women's Movement. And it was this Movement that worked through the political identification with Blackness most intensely and intimately.

The Black Women's Movement that coalesced around 1978–9 was in part a response to the sexism that women had long experienced in the activist movements of that decade.[87] It was also made necessary by the inability of the wider feminist movement to accept that white supremacy was part of the foundation of patriarchy. For Māori women the Movement sought to recover a radical feminist *mana motuhake* that could be distinguished from the more ameliorative work of the Māori Women's Welfare League (cognate in many ways to Ngata's Te Aute Old Boys tradition).

For the members of this Movement 'Black' did not so much signal
a sociological content but much more a political intent along the
lines of Steve Biko's understanding of Black Consciousness, that is,
an intentional politics of positive identification in solidarity against
the white power structure.[88] For instance, Zena Tamanui, an activist
based in Ōtara who attended the first Black Women's *hui* (meeting)
at Ngāti Ōtara marae in September 1980, argued that the term 'black
women' encapsulated 'the common bond of being the lowest, the most
oppressed: the only ones to lead the revolution'.[89] In this way, 'Black'
once more re-politicized a broad Oceania identity just as the 'revolutionary intercommunalism' of the Polynesian Panthers had done, with
the effect that Black women could now be said to include 'Māori,
Pacific Island and other Black women'.[90] In fine, Blackness delineated
for the Women's Movement a radically autonomous but united space
of struggle against colonial rule. Along these lines the Black Manifesto
of the first *hui* (meeting) proclaimed: 'A black woman taught by
whites how to be white learns to hate her blackness … [and] prefers
to be brown so she can feel comfortable and close even closer to being
white.'[91] Even Brown Power was a sell-out. Only 'the blanket of black
skin' could act as 'a *whāriki* – a cloak of dignity'.[92]

The Black Women's space of protest was not only public but
avowedly personal. Foci on health, domestic violence and sexuality
at *hui* (meetings) brought the effect of colonial rule – in its patriarchal and racial manifestations – quite literally home. The Movement
specifically bemoaned practices that could be conceived of as 'white
integration/infiltration' or the actions of 'house niggers'. And it was
also in the home where the Movement confronted this infiltration
most contentiously as it undertook a critical assessment of inter-racial/
ethnic personal relationships. The issue had, in fact, been brought
up by some women at an Ngā Tamatoa national *hui* in 1976, leading
to intense confrontations with some male members who had white
female partners.[93] A few years later, the Māori Peoples Liberation
Movement made it policy that members could not engage in inter-
racial relationships.[94]

Over the period of 1981 to 1983, sexuality and 'Māori sovereignty' were consistent themes at *hui*.[95] But then, in 1983, a first national *Māori* – and not *Black* – women's *hui* was held at Otaua marae.[96] Reflecting on the second *hui* of this kind in 1984, Ripeka Evans explained the shift in identification from Black women to Māori *wahine* (women) as a 'need to reclaim our taha Māori (Māori side)'.[97] The shift was contentious and, for some, traumatizing. Indeed, by 1983 the Black Women's Movement had begun to implode. Lines of demarcation had been drawn inside Blackness – ethnicity first, regarding intimate relations between Pasifika and Māori, and sexuality second, between men and women.[98] After this moment individual activists might still acknowledge their Blackness;[99] however, Blackness was no longer a central political term used for radical identification, solidarity and mobilization. Instead, lines of agency, guardianship and accountability were re-clarified into Māori, Pasifika and Pākehā, although, of course, multiple forces interacted and contended within these lines.

From 1970 onwards Black Power had become implicated in a publically articulated strategy of radical opposition to settler-colonial rule. Because many key activists in the Black Women's Movement played leading roles in the Springbok protests, I would argue that political identifications with Blackness peaked around 1981 to 1982 followed by its rapid denouement. In effect, while Black Power was seminal to the rebirth of radical strategies of *mana motuhake*, the very terms of these strategies also required the shedding of Blackness as political identification for the retrieval and renewal of ancestral identifications. Black Power had done what it needed to do. Apparently, the relationship between the children of Tāne/Māui and Legba was to be a temporary one, born and dying in a particular conjuncture.

Conclusion: Towards and away from identity politics

The children of Tāne/Māui have reached out to Blackness, and this Black matter has catalysed a binding back to their decolonial pasts in the context of racist and colonial urban presents. So is it necessarily a problem that, in this process, the 'blanket of black skin' was discarded for a more fitting Māori *whāriki* (cloak of dignity)? In addressing this question I want to turn our attention to Zena Tamanui's retrospect on the Black Women's Movement. In her assessment, the process of re-identification that the Movement undertook was driven by a power that lacked *aroha* (love, sympathy, empathy).[100] Power absent of such a binding force inevitably categorized and segregated peoples, whereas power exercised through *aroha* could have re-related them to themselves *and* the world.

Is there something lost in the mobilization of a loveless power, even in the pursuit of decolonization? In Aotearoa NZ this period of tumult within Māori activism was immediately followed by the sudden inauguration of neo-liberal governance in 1984. In many ways, neo-liberal governance has since sought to assimilate indigenous identity so that 'Māori' becomes only an adjective that describes the outward appearance of the instrumental interest-maximizing individual of market lore.[101] Some of the elder activists who I have spoken to bemoan this emergence of an 'identity politics' stripped of decolonizing agendas and social justice sensibilities, and personalized in a cadre of what one elder terms 'power Māori'. We must certainly be careful not to casually dismiss these political changes as entirely disabling to Māori (and Pasifika) peoples. Nevertheless, it is fair to say that since the mid-1980s the state has sought to coopt the Māori Renaissance as well as the broader multiculturalism of 1970s Māori, Pasifika (and even Pākehā) activism so as to continue colonial practices of land expropriation and resource extraction most recently evidenced in the debacle over the Foreshore and Seabed Act.[102]

But Black Power was never simply identity politics.[103] Its aims were not only to set Black men free to compete as individuals in the marketplace and halls of government. Among Legba's children, whether in South Africa, Louisiana or Oakland, Black Power also sought collective re-humanization against the categorical segregations generated by colonial science so as to refocus struggles upon the self-determination of a beloved community. In fact, the Black Power movement never significantly detached itself from the *agape* (unconditional love) promoted and practised by the civil rights movement.[104] Blackness was an investment in Black love; its power, at heart, was a soul power. Moreover, lest we forget, the mantra of the Oakland Black Panthers was 'all power to the people', not 'all power to the Black people'. In other words, the liberation of Black peoples was crucial not only in and of itself, but because it would also augur the destruction of a wicked global *system*. In short, Blackness – as Black love – taught how to know oneself and *whakapapa* to the world. And so, returning to the relation between the children of Tāne/Māui and Legba, I want to retrieve another pathway through their 1970s groundings that did not converge with neo-liberal governance to subsequently mestatize into identity politics.

At the 1970 Māori Leaders conference Taura Eruera, the first chair of Ngā Tamatoa, had argued that Māori could already lay claim to a *whakapapa* of radical oppositional politics and therefore should be wary of cultivating deeper relations with Black Power. In early February 1971, Eruera wrote to a Pākehā church minister, Don Borrie, during a seventy-day tour of minority communities in the United States. Eruera's visit to San Francisco and Berkeley coincided with the arrest of Angela Davis and a concerted effort by government to fracture and destroy the Black Panthers. Nevertheless, Eruera admitted to Borrie that he was much more interested in the struggle of Chicano peoples and First Nations. This, Eruera suggested, was for two reasons:

> there are more parallels and comparison between us and the Indians/ Chicanos and probably because I sense, rightly or wrongly, that the latter accept me more readily than the negro which is understandable I guess. No sweat with me – they have their problems and they are the ones to solve their own problems.[105]

And yet Eruera immediately went on to retell a meeting with quite a different outcome:

> But I think that the highlight of San Francisco was a church service, conducted by a Rev Cecil Williams, a black, at a church called the Glide Memorial. It was absolutely fantastic. It was just like Jumping Sunday [an outdoors event in Auckland], complete with light shows and rock groups, a chorus like something straight out of Hair both physically and vocally wise, and people everywhere. Everywhere man, in the exit doors, in the exit stairs, in windows, aisles, in all the seats on both floors. All the songs were contemporary ones that are applicable to any religional context rather than being hymn type ones, complete with rock backing. And everybody sang and danced. And at the end of each song everybody gave peace signals, power salutes and everything else – expressing themselves as they wished … Fantastic man … It was a truly glorious though unbelievable event that nearly reduced me to tears for I have never seen such a mass participatory session since my brother's tangi [funeral].[106]

'Natives' and 'negroes' fail to bind together because they are created precisely as colonial-sociological categories of segregation, of subalternization. They serve global systems of colonial extraction. Their identities do not disturb but confirm colonial governance. But where these categories fail to connect, affective, aesthetic and religious experiences exceed and subvert colonial governance. They can even provide for a crossing over so that Tāne/Māui and Legba can be gleaned walking together in the uncolonized spiritual hinterlands, ready to confront colonial injustices in solidarity. We are heading in this direction, away from identity politics, towards a deeper identification, perhaps even collective inhabitation. So in the next two chapters we shall turn away from the public-political arena of the manifest world in order to examine the grounding of the children of Tāne/Māui and Legba as they cultivate soul power through theological reasonings and artistic performances.

4

Black Liberation Theology and the Programme to Combat Racism

Introduction

Black liberation theology addresses the question as to how one can claim to have knowledge of God. James Cone provides an answer by politicizing revelation as a process emanating out of suffering and injustice: 'God comes to those who have been enslaved and abused and declares total identification with their situation, disclosing to them the rightness of their emancipation on their own terms.'[1] For the children of Legba, the experience of the oppressed becomes God's experience, hence knowing God is to participate in liberation and thenceforth to determine, phenomenologically, that 'we must become black with God!'[2] With regards to the Christian tradition, Black theology displaces the white supremacist interpretation of the Bible story; exodus, enslavement, revelation and, above all, redemption, become the prophetic cornerstone of Black liberation.[3] This theological position was mobilized in the 1960s in order to testify to the right-eousness of the Black Power struggle, thereby contributing to a broader global re-politicization of Christianity. But although the coining of the term is more recent, I would situate Black liberation theology within the traditions emanating from the 'invisible institutions' of the plantation. As a contemporary articulation of the long-practised sciences of Legba, Black liberation theology seeks the uncolonized spiritual hinterlands wherein dehumanized sufferers can find their agents of sanctification and redemption.

Moana Jackson, a notable Māori lawyer, defines one of the key effects of colonialism as 'creating a suspension of disbelief which requires that those from whom power is to be taken have to suspend their own faith, their own worth, their own value and sense of goodness'.[4] Jackson is articulating the wound that colonial science inflicts upon what we have discussed as 'deep relation'. In this chapter we shall follow Black Power as it articulates on a deeper plane as soul power, that is, as liberation of souls from dehumanization at the hands of colonial science. For the children of Legba, the statement that God is Black is made precisely to address Jackson's points as to the effect of colonialism, especially, the dehumanization of enslaved peoples through the automatic testimony provided by their skin colour.[5] This dehumanization effectively outlawed any attempt to *whakapapa* oneself and community back to the seedbed of creation. The greatest colonial crime of dehumanization, then, was de-sanctification, i.e. to segregate all the way down.

In 1968 the World Council of Churches (WCC) assembled at Uppsala in order to respond to church involvement in the anti-racist and anti-colonial struggles that had spread around the globe. Martin Luther King Jr was to be the opening speaker. His assassination just two months prior underlined the urgency of the meeting, the agenda of which was set out by James Baldwin's passionate speech entitled 'White Racism or World Community'. The assembly affirmed that racism was a 'Christian heresy'. And in the following year the WCC set up its Programme to Combat Racism (PCR) through which 'new relationships' – practical as well as theological – could be created between the churches and those peoples suffering under racial and colonial discrimination.[6] Among such situations, declared the WCC Central Committee in 1969, were 'those of the aborigines in Australia, the Māori in New Zealand, the black majorities of southern Africa, the Indians, Afro-Americans, the coloured immigrants and students in the UK and continental Europe'.[7]

In the early 1970s, some theologians believed that Black liberation could be mobilized to decolonize Christianity in Aotearoa NZ, and that becoming Black with God might help to liberate Māori and Pākehā souls. The WCC's Programme to Combat Racism was their vehicle. In what follows we will witness another contentious grounding with Blackness, but this time through the theology of liberation. Here, the children of Arcadian Hermes will also have a part to play.

Pākehā privilege and the Church

In 1968 Don Borrie, the Pākehā theologian that Taura Eruera would later write to, travelled to the United States to undertake a post-graduate degree with Preston Williams, the Martin Luther King Jr Professor at Boston University.[8] During his studies King Jr was assassinated and Borrie witnessed the shift in popular sentiments towards Black Power. Borrie became part of a crisis team organized by the Presbyterian Church and assigned to the inter-racial council based in St Louis. There, he met Chuck Cohen, a Black Baptist minister who worked closely with children from the ghettoes under the dictates of his Black liberation theology. For these subversive activities Cohen was at one point chained to his hospital bed, while Borrie – white, middle class and a foreigner – could walk around with entire freedom.

Such experiences provoked in Borrie a need to address the white privilege that he enjoyed. It was clear to him that to depend upon reform directed by whites was simply an act of deferral. And yet it was just as clear to him that it was delusional, as a white churchman, to mimic the activities of Black liberation theologians. What ethical and political relationship to Black liberation could and should a white clergyman cultivate? This was the question that Borrie pondered as he flew back to Aotearoa NZ via the South Pacific islands. Arriving home, it was clear to Borrie that, there, white racism manifested specifically as Pākehā (European settler) privilege. Borrie would have to force his church to address head on its complicity in colonial injustice and to disassemble the Pākehā domination of leadership and agenda setting.

In April 1970, Boudewijn Sjollema, the first director of the PCR, wrote to the National Council of Churches in New Zealand concerning the possibility of a team visit to the region.[9] Borrie, now General Secretary of the New Zealand Student Christian Movement, seized the moment. Replying to Sjollema, Borrie warned of the tendency for Pākehā to refuse to admit the existence of any problem; he also underlined the importance of including Māori representatives in any future planning.[10] Later in the year Borrie wrote again to Sjollema, noting the rapid rise in race consciousness among Māori and Pasifika activist youth as well as the new confrontations that were brewing over sporting relations with South Africa.[11] Borrie warned that Aotearoa NZ might have to go through the same polarizations evident in the United States before reaching more equitable arrangements. To address these issues Borrie informed Sjollema that the New Zealand Student Christian Movement was planning a conference on 'Power, Justice and Community' and that an American in attendance might be very valuable. Geneva sent the new General Secretary of the PCR, Rev Charles Spivey Jr.

Spivey arrived in Geneva from New York City where he had directed the 'Crisis in the Nation' programme of the US National Council of Churches. The Crisis was a response from Black church leaders to the lack of political engagement by white church structures with the uprisings that had peppered the urban landscape of the USA, starting with Watts in 1965.[12] Like his father, Spivey was an African Methodist Episcopal (AME) minister and a keen advocate of social justice.[13] The AME had emerged out of the Free African Society, a mutual aid organization begun in 1787 to promote the self-determination of free Black peoples in and around Philadelphia. Richard Allen, one of the founders of the Society, resolved to put an end to the racial segregation practised in the Methodist churches by forming an independent church that would also carry on the aims of the Society.[14] The AME was perhaps the first body in North America, outside of the 'invisible institutions' of the plantations, to publically promote what would eventually be known as Black liberation theology.

Spivey touched down in Aotearoa NZ in late November 1971 and during his visit met a diverse array of people: conservative, moderate and radical white laity, government officials (especially the minister of Māori affairs), civil society organizations such as the Race Relations Commission and various anti-racist sports groups, key Māori figures including MP Whetu Tirikatene-Sullivan (a member of the Rātana faith), the Māori Women's Welfare League, and the Māori Queen – Te Atairangikaahu. Spivey also grounded with Māori student and faculty groups, and with Māori and Pasifika radicals including Ngā Tamatoa, the Māori Organization on Human Rights (MOOHR) and the Polynesian Panthers.[15] Tigilau Ness, a Polynesian Panther, remembers himself and Hana Te Hemara from Ngā Tamatoa attending one workshop with Spivey that involved role-playing activities designed to sharpen participants' understandings of the 'White Male Club'.[16] Spivey also undertook two television interviews for mainstream audiences. He acknowledged the 'increasing ferment' within Māori youth groups, and was disappointed with the National Council of Churches' prevailing lacklustre attitude to discrimination against Māori.

In general, Spivey argued that racism in Aotearoa NZ was engaged with mostly within the domain of international sports. And he noted that his attempts to bring up the notion of domestic institutional racism were dismissed as American ignorance of the exceptionalism of New Zealand society.[17] Journalists who followed Spivey's engagements reported that 'he is striking few sympathetic chords when he hints that white racism could exist in New Zealand'.[18] Pathologizing Black Power as bloodthirsty race revenge, the mainstream press asked Spivey if he supported the 'violent' strategies of the Black Panthers. Spivey replied that 'violence arises in situations where people have no other alternatives'.[19] In response, the congregation of Karori, a predominantly white suburb of Wellington, demanded that the Bishop of Wellington dissociate the church from the PCR.[20] Indeed, many of these reactions from Pākehā were generated by concerns that the WCC was endorsing violence as a necessary means for liberation in the various anti-colonial struggles that raged at the turn of the decade.[21] Perceptively, Miss

Althea Campbell, a Pākehā missionary resident in Kenya, suggested that the Pākehā outcry was in fact to do with racial concerns over the safety of white settlers in the context of liberation struggles. Where was the general outcry when black and brown people were killing themselves, Campbell asked?[22]

Alternatively, Spivey gained far more support from Māori and Pasifika activists with which he enjoyed fruitful groundings. Witness, for example, a letter from Tom Poata of the Māori Organization on Human Rights to Spivey sent after his visit: 'your forthright comments on white racism during your visit here were very heartening to many Māori'. Poata also noted that Spivey's critical comments on land ownership were especially well received.[23] Spivey seems to have shared useful strategies with activists during his groundings with them. When asked by media what their role might be in the event of a race riot, one Ngā Tamatoa member commented on the creation of urban cadres: 'it's something that Algerian [sic] Frantz Fanon and American Dr Charles Spivey are both good on'.[24] Spivey even attempted to connect Māori and Pasifika to global liberation networks and on at least one occasion funded Māori participation in international symposia on Third World women's struggles.[25] Subsequent to Spivey's visit, some small funding was initiated by the PCR to support Ngā Tamatoa and the Polynesian Panthers.

Borrie was keen for Spivey to return for a longer visit in order to 'make more extensive and deeper contacts with Māori and Pacific Island people'.[26] Yet Spivey's visit had troubled the church waters and a vigorous debate began over the utility and ethics of Black liberation theology especially when applied to Māori/Pākehā relationships in Aotearoa NZ. In this way, the same issues that were being debated regarding the public-political use of Black Power also found their way into church politics. At the time of Spivey's visit, A. Gnanasunderam, a theologian from Sri Lanka, was the secretary for the Church and Society Commission of the National Council of Churches. Gnanasunderam orchestrated a debate on precisely these issues between himself, Spivey, Borrie and Paul Reeves, the Māori Bishop of Waipou (and future

Governor-General of New Zealand). The issues manifested by Spivey's groundings continued in these letters. And through them we can draw out some key contentions concerning the suitability of Black liberation theology as a salve to Pākehā privilege and a catalyst for *mana motuhake* (self determination).

Gnanasunderam seems to have accepted the popular 'exceptionalist' narrative of Aotearoa NZ race relations that activists such as Ngā Tamatoa were busy trying to dismantle. For example, he explained to Sjollema on the eve of Spivey's visit that 'the Māori are in a different position to that of the Indians in America and the Aborigines in Australia. In spite of the subtle form of white racism present, most of the Māori today would be offended if they are referred to as a "racially oppressed" people.'[27] Gnanasunderam suggested that the hostile response of many Pākehā to Spivey was because of the specifically American sensibility through which the latter had communicated the politics of race.[28] To this assessment Spivey replied that Gnanasunderam was being far too generous, and that the 'lack of understanding' was, in fact, a manifestation of the 'real racism' that lay 'just under the surface.'[29] Additionally, Spivey defended Borrie's programme of confronting Pākehā with their own white privilege using the methods garnered from his American sojourn while acknowledging that there could be no 'ready made approach to New Zealand racism coming from outside.'[30] (In fact at this point Spivey was sending readings on methodology and research to Syd Jackson of Ngā Tamatoa with the precaution that these materials were 'US centric'.[31]) Nevertheless, the key point Spivey wished to impress upon Gnanasunderam was that even in the absence of slavery one had to still account for the 'white superiority/black inferiority' attitude that prevailed in Aotearoa NZ.[32]

In order to facilitate this dialogue further, Spivey sent Borrie, Gnanasunderam and Reeves a copy of Robert Terry's writings on white racism. Terry, at the time, was the director of the Detroit Industrial Mission. Influenced by the current crises, Terry sought to channel discussions held by the Mission into a critique of the structural racial division between white managers and black workers. Facing Black Power,

Terry asked the white managers: 'what does it mean to be white today?'
Much of his answer referenced the constant deferral of white privilege,
that is, the privilege not to have to think in terms of – or talk about –
racial identity.[33] Alternatively, Terry encouraged whites to 'explore new
meanings and anti-racist ways to be white while still recognizing that
whiteness accrues unearned benefits to whites in a white racist society'.[34]
Standing against racism and social injustice therefore required 'aggressive
action to redistribute power, create open resources and institutions, and
affirm cultural pluralism'.[35] Rather than feeling guilty about their institutional privileges, 'new whites' would need to cultivate a positive sense of
self and direct that energy to tackle the core of the problem.

Gnanasunderam agreed with Terry's fundamental point that
'old' white consciousness was the basic problem to be overcome.
Nevertheless, Gnanasunderam still worried that this admission might
encourage binary thinking and violent confrontation, both of which
he seems to have uncritically identified with Black Power. 'It is not
possible', confessed Gnanasunderam to Spivey, 'for me as a coloured
person to accept it entirely as a white problem': non-whites would
have to take some responsibility too.[36] Reeves, the Māori Bishop
of Waipou, concurred with Gnanasunderam, protesting that Terry
'literally says things in terms of black and white'.[37] Reeves drew upon
another well-worn trope of New Zealand exceptionality to contest this
framework, namely, that colonial conflict was being resolved peacefully
and progressively in the bedroom with the production of a sizeable
'mixed-race' population.[38] In response, and pre-empting some of the
contentions that would soon be raised by the Black Women's Movement,
Spivey argued that Reeves' position ignored the uneven grounds of
inter-mixing. Which cultural complex, Spivey asked, was actually
defining 'the standards of success, achievement, cultural, ethical and
moral values, beauty etc?'[39] Was there an unspoken aspiration towards
whiteness in the trope deployed by Reeves? In the US, reflected Spivey,
the Black Power movement had rejected this aspiration to 'pass' in
white society: 'in a sense, those who pass are dead, dead to anything
Black';[40] and to anything Māori?

These discussions demonstrate that the provenance of Black Power was interrogated just as much in the Church among theologians as it was in the street among activists. But in many respects, the theological stakes were higher than the political in so far as identification with Blackness sought to re-sanctify a people who had been forcibly segregated from God. To become Black with God: there lay the energy store for soul power and the compass for Black Liberation. No wonder, then, that contentious questions as to the provenance of Black Power emerged in theology as much as they had in the protest politics of Ngā Tamatoa. Did Black liberation theology require the consumption of African-American soul without any cultivation of indigenous *wairua* (soul)? Would Black liberation theology reproduce precisely the 'suspension of disbelief' in one's indigenous spirituality that Moana Jackson attributes to colonialism? And if this was the case, would the pursuit of a 'new white' (American) identity by Pākehā churchmen simply be reproducing the same problem? In short, how might specifically *Aotearoa* liberation theologies be cultivated?

Aotearoa liberation theologies

Reeves' core concern with Black liberation theology was less its provocation that to know God is to participate in the Black struggle and more the under-examined methods of acting upon this theological shift, especially in pursuit of *mana motuhake*. Reeves suggested that Borrie's impetuousness in leading the groundings with Spivey instead of working with a Māori partner was a sign of his own complicity in the 'Pākehā veto'.[41] Borrie, for his part, acknowledged these criticisms.[42] Indeed Reeves was well aware of the continuing paternalism of the Pākehā-run church, and even defended Spivey's employment by the WCC against the 'liberal white opinion' of the National Council of Churches.[43] In this respect, Reeves was a true son of Māui: he sought rearrangement of the Church on Māori terms and in Māori spaces.[44]

The problem for Reeves was that radical Māori activists were already driving forward this rearrangement: at that time, Pākehā Christians of an activist bent were being taught how to shift their framework from the 'Māori problem' to the 'Pākehā problem' by Hana Te Hemara of Ngā Tamatoa.[45]

Te Hemara's shift in frameworks, cognate to Borrie's, connotes a shift in political and theological identification – from a generic white (American) to a *settler* (Pākehā). And this shift gives rise to a question: was it possible for Pākehā to cultivate their own liberation theology appropriate for Aotearoa NZ? Following this line of inquiry, let us now turn to the other side of the exchange – a trip by Borrie and a contingent of three other Pākehā as well as Gnanasunderam to the USA under the auspices of Paul Schulze, Director of the Centre for Social Change in Oakland, and Terry of the Detroit Industrial Mission.

In Borrie's assessment, the visit cultivated a new white consciousness among its Pākehā participants, especially in terms of the revelation, contra the exceptionalist narrative, that white racism was part of a 'global reality' and that Pākehā paternalism did not sit outside of this reality.[46] Rev John Grundy was also part of the trip and subsequently reflected upon the Pākehā tendency to apply anti-racist activities mainly to foreign situations – especially to the sporting relationship between Apartheid South Africa and New Zealand. This, Grundy supposed, was a way for Pākehā to avoid complicity in similar structures of inequality at home.[47] The trip also addressed Reeves' concerns that a radical agenda for anti-racism in the Christian ecumene should proceed in ways that were accountable to Māori.[48] While in Detroit, the visitors studied Terry's methods in developing new white consciousness. And one particular practice stood out, namely, the presence of a Black "monitor" in workshops run by and for whites. The principle applied in this case was that whites must accept not just responsibility for their own trans-formation but also accountability in the process, so that 'where others are affected, they need to be consulted at every stage of planning'.[49]

Subsequent to this visit a planning committee was charged with developing an anti-racism training programme for Pākehā under the auspices of the PCR.[50] As plans were being slowly developed, Paulo Freire visited Auckland to promote the strategies of learning that he had outlined in *Pedagogy of the Oppressed*. To diverse constituencies – Māori, Pasifika and Pākehā – Freire suggested that each had a complementary agenda, and that the act of working together, in a context of significant power imbalance, was often most meaningfully achieved through a co-intentionality of discrete agendas and projects.[51] Freire's suggestion accords to the binding skills of Tāne/Māui, which do not seek to collapse domains but, rather, to make their agents and energies traversable in the pursuit of restitutive justice. Hence, Freire's strategy addressed Reeves' concerns and also supported the lessons learnt at the Detroit Mission.[52] A planning committee was put together in late 1973 with the aim of training 50 Pākehā that would facilitate the engagement with 'white racism as a white problem'.[53] By 1974, however, the project had run into inertia on multiple fronts and was temporarily sidelined.

Meanwhile, around the time that Spivey was making an impact in Aotearoa NZ, Bob Scott, a Pākehā Anglican, travelled to South Africa to participate in a University Christian Movement (UCM) conference that was also being attended by Steve Biko. On the first evening that Scott spent in Johannesburg, he attended a South African Soccer Federation reception where he was introduced to the Black Consciousness movement and its critique of white paternalism.[54] Soon afterwards, Scott attended the UCM conference, where, on the first day, resolutions of dissolution were passed. By evening time, Scott was the only white who had remained and was witness to the telling of stories by Blacks about white racism. Scott was daunted at the scale of the struggle that he was witnessing.[55]

At this point, Biko personally took Scott for a grounding session and explained that what Black people required from white people was not sympathy but anger over the debilitating effect that white supremacy had upon whites themselves. Biko told Scott that they could never be sure that whites would stick with them for the duration of the struggle. However, if whites were angry themselves they would be personally invested in the issues and could be counted upon. Biko suggested that to be committed and accountable to the struggle in this way rendered Scott's prime task as 'working with your community, not ours'.[56] When Scott protested that he knew too little to undertake this work, Biko replied that 'what you're hearing gives you enough to start'.[57]

As I noted in the last chapter, it was only in the aftermath of the Springboks tour that the majority of Christian anti-Apartheid activists would sense the need to address the race question not just as a white problem but as a *Pākehā* problem – i.e. as a problem of colonial settlement in Aotearoa NZ.[58] In the early 1980s Scott, with help from Māori Anglican and WCC member Hone Kaa, finally managed to put the 'new white consciousness' agenda to work in a series of anti-racism workshops.[59]

In these ecumenical workshops that spanned 1982 to 1987 the directions for Pākehā attendees were as follows: first, you must know that you are not cultureless, but carry a particular culture of individualism, a culture that is embraced and privileged in the mainstream institutions of society; and second, you must know your own history, not the sanitized history of the Commonwealth, but rather the history of colonial dispossession that, like it or not, you – and your culture – are implicated in and benefit from.[60] Cognate to the protocols of the Detroit Mission, a Māori monitor would always be in attendance.[61] (Scott often worked with veteran Māori activist Titewhai Harawira.[62])

Pedagogically, the workshops proceeded by encouraging Pākehā participants to write as much history as they knew on a white paper above a line that divided the sheet in half. In almost all cases this took shape as a sanitized history of settler colonialism: of discovery, development, gentlemanly disagreements and honourable battles, of reasonable assimilation and the triumph of civilization. Afterwards, the facilitator, with support from the Māori monitor, would fill in the other half of the story under the line as a counterpoint: a history of prior discovery and indigenization, of incursions, dishonourable agreements and genocidal war, dispossession and racial oppression.

In the spirit of Freire, through the mandate of Biko, and inspired by the practice of Terry and Spivey, the workshops aimed to be positively therapeutic and to empower Pākehā with the personal accountability to tackle a white supremacism that, while global in extent, started with its detrimental effect upon them as Christians who sought to live in good faith. Nonetheless, the challenge of building a new Pākehā consciousness should not be underestimated. White theology was, after all, built upon categorical segregation as much as anthropology had been. The native could not ground with God; she might only enjoy a vicarious attachment to creation through a biblical *whakapapa* that was owned by whites. And yet, the white laity had never placed themselves personally within this *whakapapa*. Indeed, they could not do so: their personal investment in the story began with Jesus, not with the patriarchs and matriarchs of the Old Testament; their missionary licence (and we shall return to this in later chapters) tasked them with proselytizing the Good News of the Son and not the outstanding legacies of his ancestors. This preference for brand new beginnings promised by the Son theologically mirrored the settler-colonial practices of making 'god's own' land anew.

A fundamental rule of the anti-racism workshops stipulated that participants were not allowed to address statements or questions to the monitor because to do so would deflect the responsibility for change away from Pākehā.[63] However, during one workshop the head of the Salvation Army broke protocol and asked the Māori monitor, Hone Kaa, where Adam and Eve fitted in to the Māori creation story: had not the whites brought this biblical story with them? For 20 minutes Kaa proceeded to recount a detailed *whakapapa* (similar to that of Māori Marsden that I rehearsed previously) that bound manifest and spiritual domains together so that he could personally walk a path from himself, through his ancestors, back to creation. Kaa then asked his inquisitor, 'What's your creation story; where are you from?' Kaa had deftly exposed the spiritual and theological challenge of building a new white consciousness in the settler context of Aotearoa NZ: in order to master the manifest domain, the settler had to segregate himself from creation. Fundamentally disturbed, the Pākehā attendee left the workshop.[64]

Kaa's *whaikōrero* (speech making) reveals the rich binding skills inherited by the children of Tāne/Māui. In fact, Gnanasunderam had long been aware of the living heritage of Māori cosmologies, and was interested in comparing the indigenization of Christianity by the Māori prophet T. W. Rātana with that of African independent churches.[65] In 1974 Gnanasunderam wrote a discussion piece wherein he noted that theologies of liberation might differ in terms of their context, meaning and purpose between continental and diasporan Africans. And if Black liberation theology was being diversely cultivated even among the children of Legba, then surely the children of Tāne/Māui would have to intentionally cultivate their own spiritual *whakapapa* of liberation.[66]

T. R. Tahere, a pastor from South Hokianga, was one such church member who, it seems, picked up this calling in 1971. Initially accepting the mainstream apprehension of Black Power as a violent departure from the peaceful civil rights movement, Tahere was worried that the same mutation might take place in Aotearoa NZ through the likes of Ngā Tamatoa. As an antidote, Tahere wished to undertake study in the United States on the supposedly opposing gospel to Black Power administered by Martin Luther King.[67] Tahere himself came from an Ngāpuhi family with a long tradition of leadership and had been actively involved in social justice issues, such as improving substandard housing for local Māori.[68] Through the WCC, Tahere received a scholarship at the end of 1971 to study at Colgate Rochester Divinity School. Tahere also met Spivey during his studies there and discussed with him further research projects in Oakland. A couple of years later Gnanasunderam commented on Tahere's American sojourn and its effect:

> like many of the Māori clergy, [Tahere is] sensitive about their culture
> with a deep desire to serve their people, but quite happy to work along
> with the white clergy on white norms. They are polite to them even
> in matters affecting their people … [But] his studies have given him
> a deeper awareness of the real needs of the Māori people and he now
> writes in terms of empowerment of his people.[69]

Henceforth Gnanasunderam proposed that Tahere could even act as a bridge between the elders and the young radicals.[70]

This episode suggests that, rather than learning how to consume another's beloved community, Tahere's grounding with Black liberation theology through the networks of the WCC cultivated a radical renaissance with his own beloved. Tahere was not the only one to renew his soul power; the spirit was abroad across the islands. Indeed, Hone Kaa's commentary to the Pākehā attendee at the anti-racist workshops might have been partly enabled by a WCC conference that he attended in 1976. There, Kaa and others met with the Black Mauritius Catholic priest Filip Fanchette (an associate of Paulo Freire) who, in closed session, led them to face the fact that they were 'house niggers'.[71] Fanchette also heavily influenced Zena Tamanui, a key member of the activist group Whakahou, some of whose *tīpuna* (ancestors) had already cultivated 'Māori understandings of Jesus'.[72] Whakahou had both Pasifika and Māori members and enjoyed close links with the Polynesian Panthers. Alec Toleafoa, a Panther, later became a minister and today works on cultivating a Christianity indigenous to Oceania. Toleafoa argues that the special relationship between brother and sister, prevalent in many Oceanic cultures, was done great damage to when missionaries proselytized that only one beloved relationship was allowed – to a Jesus that they claimed to be the sole avatars of.[73] This is surely one of the deepest colonial cuts in need of repair: to segregate a people from creation, thereby commanding them to surrender their souls to the master's son.

These were the new cultivations of Aotearoa liberation theologies – indigenous and also, as in the Pākehā case, endogenous. And I would suggest that the groundings with Black liberation theology were influential in these rejuvenations of soul power. But what of the children of Legba: how did these theological groundings affect their soul power?

During his second trip to Aotearoa NZ, Spivey attempted to deepen his relationship with *Te Ao Māori* (the Māori world) beyond its urban settings. He spent time with Māori in their rural areas and engaged with indigenous biblical faiths, visiting the small town at Rātana

Pa as well as members of the Ringatū church around Whakatane through a respected intermediary, Norman Perry.[74] Spivey's register of Black Power was somewhat lost on many rural people's ears;[75] nevertheless, he himself was enamoured of the Māori prophetic faiths, especially Rātana and Ringatū, and hoped for further interaction in the future.[76] Spivey's experience of these rural wellsprings affected him greatly. Writing to Roka Paora Tekaha – future co-editor of the Ngata Dictionary – he reflected:

> Your deep sense of roots, from which you cannot be removed, your sense of being part of a living vital ongoing tradition coupled with a quiet certainty and security is greatly to be admired. These qualities are not found often enough where I come from – among Black people in the United States. Perhaps it is due in part to the fact that you live breathe and stand on your land, yours, your fathers' and your fathers' fathers.[77]

Visiting Aotearoa NZ through the PCR scheme the following year, a group of African American churchmen – including another AME Bishop, Vinton Anderson, and Al Ragland, director of the Chicago Conference on Religion and Race – had a similar experience. They also picked up on how the binding skills provided by Tāne/Māui had enabled indigenous culture to defer a total uprooting visited by settler colonialism.[78] Presciently, Ragland had already been introduced to the suffering of First Nations in Alaska where he had served as a medical technician in the US Army and had developed a working relationship with the American Indian Brotherhood.[79]

Conclusion

The children of Tāne/Māui and Legba are grounding through liberation theology and the children of Arcadian Hermes are learning to participate, but not as colonial masters. The theological challenge of identifying with Blackness has compelled Pākehā to re-examine and even dissolve their colonial privileges for the sake of their own souls. No longer Britannica, from whom all meaning must derive, they are striving, as Sartre had, to witness and appropriately support a liberation struggle that is being planned around campfires that are not their own. The same challenge has led some Māori to connect the liberation of their souls to the radical struggle for *mana motuhake* in the political realm. Through this connection they will also bind back to their decolonial pasts utilizing indigenous prophetic *whakapapa*, an enterprise to which we shall turn soon enough. Meanwhile, Black theologians have come to spread a Black love of liberation, and have found indigenous resources that are instructive – even awe inspiring – to their own cause. These theological groundings have not been undertaken on the thin grounds of comparison but rather through identification with the godhead, the seedbed of creation.

Black power has become soul power. The theological identification with Blackness – becoming Black with God – has quickened a retrieval of the sanctity of ancestors in the story of creation. And so we have moved closer to the spiritual hinterlands. But we are not there quite yet. For between theology and the liberated spirit there stands art, the quotidian theology of the sufferers. Art is the binding skill practised by those who do not occupy a privileged place in the laity, yet who nevertheless wish to pursue the ethos of humanity, that is, the cultivation of deep relation for the sake of restitution. Take, for instance, Eruera Nia, a founding member of the Wellington branch of Ngā Tamatoa. Nia recalls how his ancestors in Taranaki densely encoded their experiences of land dispossession and their wisdoms of creative survival through *karakia* (chants) and *waiata* (songs). Black radical thinkers helped Nia to decode them for mobilization in present-day struggles.[80] We now turn to an arts project that intentionally sought to provide just such a key: Keskidee Aroha.

Keskidee Aroha: Walking Out of Egypt Land

Introduction

In 1972, Harry Dansey's play *Te Raukura* was performed at the Auckland festival. While the drama was historical, set in the wars over land expropriation in 1860s Taranaki, the play consciously spoke to the activist context of the early 1970s. At one point, the following dialogue occurs:

> *Koroheke*: … We come now to Te Morere, known to the Pākehā
> as Sentry Hill, on which the Pākehā had built a fort within the
> ancient Ati Awa land and thus in constant challenge did it stand,
> a taunt to Māori mana, pride and worth.
> *Tamatāne*: (groans) Oh save us from Poetry![1]

The figure of Koroheke (translated literally as 'elderly man') can be said to embody the Te Aute Old Boy's model of tactful engagement with Pākehā governments, while Tamatāne (boy) represents the radicalization of this engagement. In fact, Tamatāne was originally played by Syd Jackson of Ngā Tamatoa.[2] Tamatāne storms off stage before the end of the play leaving the comforting reconciliatory words of Koroheke to the Pākehā somewhat haunted by his absence.

A number of commentators have drawn attention to the 'theatrical' oratory and performances that have traditionally taken place on the *marae ātea* (the cleared space where visitors are encountered).[3] But in the early 1970s young Māori who sought to dramatize anew the anti-colonial struggle found it difficult to employ existing Māori cultural mediums, the infrastructure for which was often lacking in everyday urban life. Meanwhile, the mediums that urban Pākehā used were alien to Māori.[4] And plays such as Dansey's were quite unusual. In this context some activists looked to the children of Legba for artistic inspiration and organized to bring over Keskidee, a London-based Black theatre troupe, and their associated RasTafari musical band, Ras Messengers.

The rationale for this project can be found in the combination of factors that impacted acutely on Māori and Pasifika communities in the latter 1970s, namely, increased institutional racism, economic cut-backs and job losses. On top of this, a decade of radical activism had reaped few substantive rewards. Like many activists, those who organized the tour of Keskidee and Ras Messengers looked towards a 'looming confrontation' after the 'moment of truth' (1969–72) had subsided.[5] Dansey's play is important to remember in this respect because, while activism had heretofore primarily worked on the 'body', i.e. housing, employment and street-level organization, now was the time to work on the 'soul'.[6] The organizers of Keskidee Aroha believed that confrontation required cultural renewal through a decolonial agenda. And for this purpose, identification with Blackness through an artistic register might serve as the 'catalyst'.[7] We shall now witness how this catalyst was introduced and with what consequences.

Decolonizing theatre

By the mid-1970s, songs of distant island sufferers started to pervade the airwaves in Aotearoa NZ. The music was called roots reggae and one artist especially, Bob Marley, spoke in a language that was both radical and redemptive. The sufferers of Aotearoa NZ were paying attention. In 1977 Denis O'Reilly, an Irish Catholic member of the Black Power, a predominantly Māori gang, took note and obtained a

Commonwealth Youth Fellowship to travel to Jamaica charged with the mission to 'bring Bob back'.[8] O'Reilly did not find Marley at home. Subsequently he travelled to London via Ottawa and, after visiting a number of organizations including the Ethiopian World Federation, was directed by the Interaction Centre to seek out Keskidee.

Keskidee is a small Guyanese bird renowned for its resilience in unforgiving environments. Oscar Abrams, one of the founders of the Keskidee Centre, had articulated its purpose in the form of a motto: 'a community discovering itself creates its own future'.[9] While the Keskidee Centre often acted as a forum for Third World liberation politics it also tackled a diverse array of local needs from education on legal rights to courses in cookery, painting etc.[10] The Keskidee Centre was initially designed to help African-Caribbean youth connect to the cultural resources of their parents, resources that they had become at least partially alienated from in London.[11] This binding back across the ocean to island cultures of creative survival was intended to fortify the youth when living as a minority in a viscerally and institutionally racist society. The Keskidee mandate therefore spoke quite intimately to the inter-generational context that we have witnessed in Aotearoa NZ wherein disaffected and alienated youth came from the families of internal Māori and external Pacific 'migrants'.

By the time that O'Reilly visited, the Keskidee Centre had also become the central site for the development of professional Black theatre in the UK with a distinctly agitprop agenda of reflecting the gamut of Black Power struggles. The pursuit of social justice alongside the promotion of the arts was not always harmonious. Indeed, the professional aims of the theatre arm somewhat clashed with those of community service, and I shall return to this point later.[12] Nevertheless, O'Reilly was extremely impressed with the force and substance of Keskidee's theatrical productions and upon returning to Aotearoa NZ resolved to bring the troupe over on tour.

For this aim the Keskidee Aroha collective was initiated (*aroha* can be glossed as love, sympathy, affection). The national collective included stalwarts of the decade's political struggles such as members of the Polynesian Panthers and Pākehā community activists, while the regional collectives included members of Ngā Tamatoa and an array of more local community organizations. Funds were in the main provided by the Queen Elizabeth Arts Council, the Calouste Gulbenkian Foundation and – controversially – from the Department of Internal Affairs. (The project was supported by the Prime Minister of the time, Robert Muldoon, who enjoyed a working relationship with the Black Power gang but was much maligned by most activists.) We should note that funds were also raised by various gang members and other disadvantaged youth.

Marking a return to 'social and cultural action', the Keskidee Aroha national collective conceived of their project as a means to 'nurture the soul'.[13] The collective proposed that their 'soul train' had to be joined by workers, 'womin', gangs, Māori, Pasifika and Pākehā youth who were all willing to struggle for liberation as part of a global journey. While 'soul', at this point in time, had a particularly African-American provenance in popular culture, the national collective associated it with the deeply significant Māori word, *wairua*.[14] In this respect they sought to dispel the 'cultural cringe' that accompanied much of the artistic products of Pākehā.[15] Let us recall, at this point, the *Graphic*'s imperial world map and its division of peoples into active metropolitan culti-vators of knowledge and passive producer/consumers of other peoples' knowledge. The 'cringe' marked an acceptance of this creativity map, even by Pākehā. Alternatively, the national collective proposed that 'the resources we need to build relevant human structures can be found in the many traditions of culture and human commitment that lie un-used in our present one value system'.[16]

At stake, then, was the formation of a new publically enunciated art that had heretofore been captured by both the paternalism of Pākehā culture and the Te Aute Old Boys' sensibility of strategic accommo-dation. In these conditions, reasoned O'Reilly, an alternative catalytic force would have to be introduced in order to publically 'decolonize' art and cultural education in Aotearoa NZ.[17] Writing to the Queen Elizabeth Arts Council for support, O'Reilly argued that the 'West

Indian' was an extremely appropriate catalytic agent with which to bind creative souls back to the traditions outlawed by settler society.[18] Similar to Māori and Pasifika youth, African-Caribbean peoples had been 'plucked from one environment and settled in a new land'. They, too, were 'conscious of their roots and aware of their present cultural nakedness'. Yet they had also been able to develop 'contemporary cultural forms' from the traditions that they had managed to 'hold onto'.[19] In this respect, Keskidee seemed to exemplify a successful binding of the colonial present back to decolonial pasts in the pursuit of Black liberation, and one that might catalyse a similar process by the sufferers of Aotearoa NZ.

The vision of the proposed tour was in many ways exemplified in one of the plays that Keskidee had been performing in London – *Lament for RasTafari*, written by Edgar White. The play's main protagonist is Lindsay, a young Jamaican who, in his sojourn in London and subsequently New York, encounters racism and its destructive social, economic, psychical and spiritual effects. Lindsay eventually manifests as a RasTafari mystic and proclaims redemption by way of return to the Promised Land:

> *Juju Man*: … But I going to burn down Babylon, get out me way I
>   have wings …
> *Chorus*: Armageddon. Call the tribes.
> *Juju Man*: … Walking you through Egypt land. The thirteenth hour.
>   Give them music to walk.[20]

Let us bring the protagonists of Dansey and White's plays together: Legba (Juju Man) is speaking to Tāne/Māui and emboldening the young sons and daughters of the latter (Tamatāne/Tamāhine) to cultivate a radical redemption that had not been managed so far by Koroheke (the old man).

In March 1979, Tigilau Ness, Polynesian Panther and member of the national collective, spent some time in London at the Keskidee Centre finding out about the artists' environment and preparing them for the tour. Before departing on this trip, Ness expressed in visual form the grounding that the national collective hoped for (see Figure 5.1). Within a protective womb, Ness drew the figure of a coconut tree that 'relates to the peoples of the West Indies, Jamaica, and the South Pacific'. The fronds of the tree were drawn in the style of *kowhaiwhai*, a traditional pattern of Māori carving but which also symbolized 'the Dreadlocks of RasTafar-I relating to the ancient African roots of Keskidee'. Ness depicted the roots of the tree also in the style of *kowhaiwhai*, but here they symbolized 'the Māori roots in which Keskidee Aroha has grown up out of Roots to which I an' I in-a-New Zealand bilong [belong]'.[21] Ness's motif expresses not just an aesthetic identification with Blackness, (although it does that too), but more so, an inhabitation of Blackness yet on indigenous grounds.

In any case, the motif certainly presents a counter-aesthetic to the *Graphic's* imperial world map. This being said, it should be remembered that the peripheral characters of that map were composed of

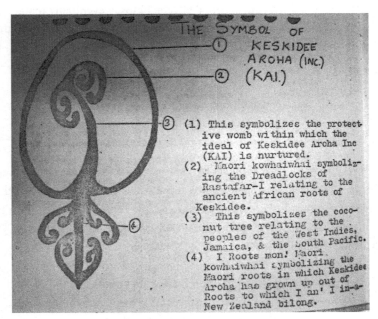

Figure 5.1: Tigilau Ness's symbol of Keskidee Aroha

both settlers and colonized peoples. And within the national collective there were Māori, Pasifika and Pākehā members. These relationships required constant efforts at decolonization similar, we might say, to those that were pursued through the Programme to Combat Racism. In fact, at one point in the organizing of the tour, Pākehā members were briefly ejected from the national collective. Nevertheless, it seems that the geo-political hierarchy of core/periphery lay on top of this contentious intra-peripheral dynamic, not beside it. Writing to Abrams once more, O'Reilly gently rebuked his idea of including a researcher in the troupe so that Keskidee might be given the data to produce a performance of a 'New Zealand nature'. To O'Reilly, this suggestion had 'all the overtones of colonial anthropology'.[22] After all, the point of the tour was to be *with* a community rather than perform *for* one. For this purpose, the relationship that the national collective proposed was not so much a formally separate one between employee/employer, but more an intimate co-habitation along the lines of a *whānau* (extended family).

Jujuman's biblical injunction to walk out of Egypt was by no means alien to the sentiments expressed at the time by Māori and Pasifika activists. In the 1975 Land March to parliament, the impression that Māori activist Saana Murray received, upon catching sight of the white flag that led the way, was 'almost like … when Moses led the slaves out of bondage'.[23] The Land March itself had started in Murray's home area, Te Hāpua, where she had been part of an important legal battle that challenged the establishment by government agencies of a scientific reserve on tribal land.[24] The national collective planned to start the Keskidee tour at the same place, mapping a political history of *mana motuhake* (self determination) onto the artistic proceedings. For her part, Murray was keen for the Keskidee tour to begin at her home.[25] Indeed, her understanding of the land struggle had comfortably pre-empted the global vision of Keskidee Aroha. Writing to Tom Poata of the Māori Organization on Human Rights in 1972, Murray had hoped that 'perhaps your great endeavour will be supported by all the coloured races of the world against the minority white man's laws of defying the natural order of god's creation for the human race, with their superhuman legislations to change the Māori into a Pākehā race'.[26] So in May 1979, Ngāti Whatua, the people of the land whose *mana whenua* (authority of the land) covered Auckland airport, enthusiastically welcomed Keskidee upon their arrival.[27] The troupe was quickly driven up to Te Hāpua, and there the ancestors met.

The repertoire that Keskidee brought with them expressed the interconnected issues of racism, sexism and classism prevalent in the work, family and religious lives of the African Diaspora. Steve Carter's *Eden* was the most popularly received play in the tour, which focused on the internalized racism of two families living in 1920s New York, one Jamaican and ruled over by a firm patriarch (a Marcus Garvey supporter), the other an African-American aunt and nephew from the South. Steve Wilmer's *Scenes from Soweto* often raised the tension of the Keskidee performance to its peak. The play follows an apolitical academic's return from Oxford to his native Soweto where, during the student riots, he is finally forced to take a stand before being murdered by a white policeman. Excerpts performed from *Lament for RasTafari* included the final callings of Jujuman for liberation from Babylon, but also the provocative scene wherein a clergyman is questioned about his theological inability to believe in a Black spirit, as well as Hilda's Soliloquy on the thankless labour relation between Black help and white families. The later sketch was especially remembered by audiences.[28] Other performances included the beginning scene of Alex Baldwin's *If Beale Street Could Talk*, wherein a young woman describes breaking the news of her pregnancy to her incarcerated boyfriend, a scene that was particularly poignant when performed at the Arohata Women's Prison.[29] Furthermore, a sketch written by Wanjiku Kiarie of the raping of a black woman by a white prison guard had a notable impact upon young gang members in Whakatane, some of whom had taken part in "block" (group) rapes and for the first time were forced to intimately empathize with the woman's experience.[30]

These performances resonated deeply among audiences, and all the more so because the fiction of the stage gave permission to air themes of racism and sexism that were usually not presented so starkly in the different public spheres wherein they were performed, whether in local halls or in *marae*. Indeed, the performances tended to foster a conscientious awareness of these issues, especially in more geographically isolated communities that might not have been directly privy to the urban insurrections of Ngā Tamatoa et al.[31] Young and elder Māori listened side by side to the messages of the children of Legba, and somehow their performances did not produce quite the intergenerational 'talking past' that had been the complaint voiced in the recent Young Māori Leaders Conferences against elders of the Te Aute Old Boys tradition.

Merata Mita, participant and documenter of the tour, suggests two reasons as to why this was the case.[32] First, with respect to the 'cultural cringe', the Keskidee troupe was considered by their audiences, including Māori, to consist of professional performers from London, the imperial centre, and, along the lines of the *Graphic*'s imperial world map, were therefore considered to be authoritative cultural speakers and commentators. Second, even if these actors were performing in the confrontational register of Black Power as they addressed issues of racism and colonialism, *kaumātua* (the eldership) had to accord Keskidee the hospitality and respect traditionally due to *manuhiri* (visitors) that had been welcomed onto the *marae*.

For these reasons the Keskidee performances provided the public stage on which young, old, reformist and radical Māori could symbolically unite as the colonially oppressed against the oppressor. Hence, as Keskidee performed their repertoire, Māori shared the same fate as Black peoples: i.e. young Māori interlopers in the Pākehā world would have to radicalize themselves to the plight of their peoples; Māori would work for Pākehā for nothing (not even gratitude); Māori and Pasifika families would internalize a colonial mentality and fight among themselves; Māori couples would speak to each other through prison windows; Māori and Pasifika women would receive the brunt of patriarchal and racist barbarism; and indigenous spirituality, including its prophetic traditions, would be dismissed by the Pākehā as uncivilized.

Thus, unlike political activism, art affected a direct inhabitation of Blackness; through this medium Black Power required no comparative analysis or theological translation into *mana motuhake*.

For Pākehā society, to witness this catalysing of indigenous soul power at the hands of Black artists made for unpalatable theatre. Public complaints were forthcoming after mention of the tour on the evening news. One letter written to the Minister of Internal Affairs provides a snapshot of the felt need by the majority of Pākehā to protect their narrative of exceptionalist paternalism that justified their control of public spaces: 'viewers were shown scenes depicting the most evil of degenerate incitement to racial disharmony ... The violent hate-ridden, crime infested environment of the London West Indian ghetto has no place or parallel whatever to the New Zealand context, either in the European or Māori cultures.'[33]

Other examples of Pākehā 'backlash' abound. In the rural town of Masterton, a school group heard the South African consul general giving a pro-apartheid speech to a town function, and later the same day experienced Rufus Collins, artistic director of Keskidee and greeter of the ancestors at Te Hāpua, espousing Black liberation.[34] But reporting on the evening's performance, the local newspaper chose to pass judgement in a technical language that refused to engage with the political challenge that Keskidee had laid down to local race relations: 'it is possible people walked out because it was overacted and the actors' overstated performance detracted from the dialogue.'[35]

The groundings with Keskidee Aroha

Tigilau Ness's motif, pre-empting the groundings with Keskidee, was an intimate one: *kowhaiwhai* and dreadlocks rooting together. But how did the actual grounding compare to the image?

In many ways, the groundings were extremely positive. The Māori custom of *manaaki* (hospitality, support) greatly affected the Keskidee *manuhiri* (guests), especially, and in contrast to, their racist British experiences, when it came to the basic appreciation of their talents as a professional arts group.[36] Rufus Collins reflected on these experiences:

> I have not been to almost any *marae* ... where I did not feel that the entire energy of those group of people in their own particular style went towards making us welcome, comfortable and trying to find out what they could about our experience in life [and] at the same time trying to open up to us a kind of ritualistic living that the *marae* proposes.[37]

The RasTafari musicians remember similar experiences. Kirk Service found many resemblances between his Africentric cosmologies and those of Māori.[38] Glasford James Hunter remembers that, in acknowledgement to him and his ancestral point of departure, Māori elders would sometimes personally *whakapapa* back to Africa.[39] To the Ras, this must have been remarkable considering that many of the diasporic children of Legba would not dare to journey in that direction. At the time, Chauncey Huntley expressed his appreciation – and understanding – of the relating skills of his hosts thus: 'When you just go and shake a man's hand, it's over. But when you bring him to a place where all your fathers rest and sing him a song fe get on the same vibrations as him, and him sing you back a song, you know? Yes! That's what I call a greeting!'[40]

In effect, grounding with Māori had the same affect upon Keskidee and the Ras Messengers as it had had upon Spivey and the African-American churchmen. Nevertheless, O'Reilly suggests that these experiences also 'touched something in some of [the Keskidee troupe] that really became quite disturbing to them.'[41] After all, the tour immersed a group of people, heretofore living relatively individualistic urban lives, into a sometimes rural and always intensely communal form of living.[42] Furthermore, on tour in Aotearoa NZ the troupe usually had to mingle with the audience before performing, and afterwards they would eat and sometimes sleep collectively near to the same audience, some of whom were hosts.[43] Kiarie remembers that, with the

partial exception of Edgar White, none of her fellow Keskidee artists
had worked and lived so intimately with their putative audiences back
in London.[44]

How to make sense of this unease brought about by the groundings?
First and foremost, we must remember that different intensities and
modalities of relating to land exist between the diasporic children of
Legba and those of Tāne/Māui. Consider the *whakataukī* (proverb),
ka kotia te taitapu ki hawaiki – 'the sacred path to Hawaiki is cut off'.
The quotidian meaning of this proverb can be glossed as 'there's no
going back now'. The deeper meaning, though, expresses a process of
intentional and self-directed inhabitation of the new lands of Aotearoa
NZ whereby the previous land of the ancestors, Hawaiki, recedes into
Te Pō (the dark realms of potential). Now contrast this meaning with
that of the RasTafari chant inspired by Psalm 137:

> For the wicked dem carried us away in captivity,
> required from us a song.
> But how can we sing RasTafari song in a strange land?

Here lies testimony of an altogether more violent and non-consensual
uprooting from homelands: to be put to work on stolen lands turned
into plantations, to be dehumanized and de-sanctified via a legal status
of chattel commodity, and to be systematically denied land access and
meaningful inhabitation upon emancipation.[45]

The Keskidee Centre was initially set up to attend precisely to the
effects of these violent and unjust uprootings of peoples from their
homelands and from their kith and kin. And we should remember too
that from their new residences in the Caribbean many would, through
the dull compulsion of economic logic, have to take a further oceanic
voyage to the concrete jungles of Britain – the 'second Babylon', as
Cosmo from the Ras Messengers put it.[46] Certainly, the sacred thread
to 'Guinea' held tenaciously throughout all these sojourns, yet by the
1970s it had been thoroughly hacked. Gleaned through this context,
the possibilities of self-determining a postcolonial cultural space back
in such an unforgiving place as London must have seemed thin

indeed in comparison to the marginalized, oppressed, yet in relative terms, much more inhabited and directly transmitted Māori cultures. Witness, for example, Rufus Collins:

 There is a greater strength in the [Māori] people because they haven't gone under a kind of demoralization where you feel you have nothing and therefore the land has totally been robbed from you ... There is a possibility here that I have not recognized in any other country which has a colonial background as this one.[47]

Grounding is a skill of knowledge cultivation, a knowing of oneself again through knowing other selves in relation. We have witnessed previously how grounding can be a contentious affair. RasTafari would characterize the contentious nature of grounding experienced by some of the Keskidee troupe as 'dread', meaning, the awe of consciously inhabiting both the *agape* (sanctified communal love) of Blackness but also coming to terms with the deep wounds that Blackness bears. This is the meaning of 'dread love', and perhaps these groundings with the *tāngata whenua* intensified it. After all, it is a significant burden, carried inter-generationally, to have been excised from natal lands, placed on new lands solely for the extraction of the life energies of blood and earth, and subsequently to reside in hostile territories. And let us remember as well that inhabitation is an enaction of creation, so to be denied inhabitation is to be denied sanctity. In sum, when identification gives way to inhabitation, the stakes are raised on all sides.

But what of the Aotearoa collectives? In order to make sense of their experiences let us recall, once more, the *Graphic's* world map. Paradoxically, the same metropolitan status that facilitated the dissemination of radical modes of cultural self-determination on stage created difficulties off stage in terms of the felt hierarchy of metropolitan/periphery. Visiting poor communities and encountering gangs with names such as the Stormtroopers and Headhunters, Rufus Collins, as director, would often point out that Keskidee were not social workers but professional artists.[48] Such a tension between art and social justice had already manifested back in London, as I noted above. In fairness we should acknowledge that Collins had been a participant in the American civil rights struggles and was not afraid of political confrontation. On one occasion during the tour he severely chastised a white employee of a borstal for his demeaning treatment of the young, predominantly Māori children.[49] Nonetheless, a principled professionalism gradually combined with an under-developed capacity for communal life as well as sheer tiredness to re-create a distance, if not quite segregation, between the guests and the hosts. The unkindly quip of one regional organizer from Gisborne reflects this distance: 'I think the folksy brotherhood of Keskidee Aroha got the run-around from the Chelsea Blacks.'[50] All this came to a head when Keskidee visited Ōtara in South Auckland.

At this point Ōtara was still considered to be a 'raw community'.[51] Created as a dormitory town in the early 1960s, Ōtara not only possessed few urban facilities but was also surrounded by paddocks and creeks to the extent that many of the resident youth did not consider the district to be part of a city.[52] Initially, the children of Ōtara enjoyed a good sense of *tikanga* (custom, correct way), but at the same time, the community suffered from a lack of inherited leadership structures.[53] In fact, by 1976, 57 per cent of Ōtara residents were under the age of 20 (62 per cent of residents being Māori or Pasifika).[54] Some of the older children even considered themselves to be the first elders of Ōtara.[55] The local school, Hilary College, which we have briefly encountered before, became an especially important institution in this respect when the Ōtara youth used its Polynesian Club to develop their leadership skills.[56] However, by the second half of the 1970s the nearby factories had closed down and families in Ōtara were put under severe pressure. Meanwhile, encouraged by such policies as the dawn raids, police persecution of the youth had intensified. Discrimination based on colour and a homogenized categorization of 'Polynesian' made affiliation to the Stormtroopers gang or Polynesian Club a moot point in the eyes of the police.[57]

For all these reasons Ōtara was an unusual urban area in 1979. It had never been consolidated as Pākehā territory. Its youth were trying to meaningfully inhabit the town. Yet at the same time they were at the sharp end of the settler-colonial logic of segregation and discrimination. And perhaps it is this project of intentional inhabitation that encouraged in them a focus on cultural renewal more pronounced than many other contemporary activists.

After having formed a short-lived 'junior' Polynesian Panther group, some members of the Hilary College Polynesian Club determined to create a youth drop-in centre.[58] Key to their philosophy was the principle of retaining the positive aspects of their varied Māori and Pasifika heritages. For this reason they called their organization Whakahou (to make new).[59] Like many political activist groups, Whakahou refused to accept the fate of being 'brown skinned Pākehā'.[60] However, they addressed this challenge through a focus on art and music as a means to encourage *whanaungatanga* (family-like relationships).[61] Along these lines, Whakahou pursued a question: 'What is our culture, and how is it expressed?'[62] This, effectively, was the South Auckland version of Keskidee's motto: 'a community discovering itself creates its own future'. By 1979 Whakahou were busy contributing to the organization of a festival for 'multiculturalism and the youth' through the Manukau Arts Collective.[63] As part of this work Whakahou organized a week-long workshop at Ngāti Ōtara marae that would examine themes of racism and sexism and develop skills to express accompanying sentiments. Tigilau Ness and Ross France, both members of the Keskidee Aroha national collective, had also been contributing to these activities.[64] In the middle of the week Whakahou hosted Keskidee for a number of days.

In some respects, Keskidee's impact on Whakahou was straightforwardly positive: the troupe's professionalism, discipline and technical know-how were instructive, especially to Maranga Mai, the first agitprop Māori theatre group with whom Keskidee workshopped. And at least with the Ras Messengers a 'warm relationship' developed.[65] Crucially, Ōtara participants noted the centrality of an African-rooted aesthetic in the RasTafari musicians and their public and professional embrace of 'roots' instruments, especially drums. In a previous chapter I explained that drums are a crucial instrument of grounation in the RasTafari faith: 'when a skill man play 'pon de peta [repeater], de drums bring forth de spirits of all de Ancients ... de drum is de ancient Ethiopian form of communication.'[66] The use of drums by Ras Messengers therefore inspired a resolve in Whakahou to publicly promote art forms indigenous to Aotearoa NZ and Oceania through the Manukau Arts Collective.[67] Here, the children of Tāne/Māui and Legba were positively grounding, assisting each other to artistically bind their colonized presents back to their decolonial pasts in the pursuit of restitutive justice.

Nevertheless, many of the Whakahou participants became intimidated by the Keskidee actors. Zena Tamanui, for instance, felt that she was manipulated by Rufus Collins into cancelling important social activities on the weekend for the sake of providing (much needed) leisure and rest time for Keskidee.[68] Additionally, the majority of the theatre troupe did not stay on the *marae* and, no doubt mentally and physically exhausted, sought solace instead in non-communal personal spaces.[69] A distance fed by implications of 'professionalism' grew between the groups. But Whakahou refused to be mere subalterns, consuming the performance of metropolitan agents. In the space between, a question arose similar to that faced by the Programme to Combat Racism earlier in the decade: was soul power – theological or artistic – to be an exercise in grounding, or was it to be an exercise in uprooting indigenous *wairua* (soul)?

And yet this tension had perhaps the greatest galvanizing effect on Whakahou. In an evaluation of their encounter with Keskidee, previously shy and self-doubting teenagers confidently articulated their experiences of the week, their renewed interest in embracing Polynesian art forms, and their new commitment to the *marae* and its patterns of communal living and learning.[70] Most importantly, the Keskidee tour provided Whakahou with an epiphany: 'people from overseas are not gods, and ... what they have to offer may not be very relevant here'.[71] With this realization, the grounding, although bittersweet, had a positive outcome: '[Keskidee's] greatest contribution was to give us confidence in ourselves', and '[i]n terms of the vision that Keskidee Aroha had for the tour it was for us an unqualified success. For the first time the overseas budget of the Arts Council was spent on a tour that had meaning for our community'.[72] Warren Lindberg, who at the time was manager of Te Puke Ōtara Community Centre Community, recalls how the episode confirmed to Whakahou that, romantic identifications with Black Power and global liberation struggles aside, it was only they who could plot a path out of Egypt land through the creative cultivation of their inherited resources.[73] By grounding with Keskidee and Ras Messengers, Whakahou managed to dispense with their subaltern status at home and abroad.

Thirty years later, Tamanui argues that Keskidee and Ras Messengers provided tools for defeating 'cultural genocide' in two respects. First, their work validated the importance of politicizing art and culture on the *marae*. Second, the experience confirmed Whakahou's principled position that struggles over *mana motuhake* must be based on an articulation of the 'heart':[74] a 'dread love', RasTafari would say. These validations are shared more widely among the national collective. Taape O'Reilly reminisces that the Keskidee experience built within her the determination to support her *whānau* (extended family) back in Hawke's Bay.[75] The message of 'know your roots' was not lost on another contributor to Keskidee Aroha, Will 'Ilolahia, who had spent years struggling in Aotearoa NZ with the Polynesian Panthers with little thought for his own homeland, Tonga.[76] 'Ilolahia subsequently returned for some years, albeit not before the drama of the Springboks protest.[77] Indeed, back in 1979 the tour sometimes encouraged a broader process of binding the urban youth back to their *tūrangawaewae* (places of belonging). For example, at one *marae*, a cultural group was reformed for the visit after 25 years of inaction, and local Black Power gang members returned to their *marae* to help with preparing the *hāngī* (earth oven).[78]

I have noted in previous chapters that only after the Springboks tour was it common for Pākehā to seek atonement for consistent breaches to Te Tiriti (The Treaty). Nonetheless, it was still uncommon both

before and after the tour for Pākehā to invest in a decolonial and restitutive relationship to the *tāngata whenua* (peoples of the land). Chris
McBride, an Irish Pākehā member of the Keskidee national collective,
remembers that Pākehā organizations in the 1980s often approached
Te Tiriti issues through a liberal guilt that sought to safeguard a
comfortable distance between Māori and Pākehā rather than cultivate
a deep relation. After Keskidee Aroha, McBride and Denis O'Reilly
refused to join at least one such organization. They had no need or
time to feel guilty; they had already been pursuing their redemption
through the arts.[79]

Conclusion

Subalterns do not possess soul power, neither can they cultivate it.
They look towards Britannica to be animated by her judgements. In
the manifest domain, (post)colonial peoples have to navigate through
and around the hierarchical and segregational topographies carved
out by colonial science. In the process they sometimes (irreverently)
meet, find out how they are already related, and thereby find the
deeper meaning of their own names. There can be no Britannica in this
relationship – not even a Black Britannica. Jujuman, the child of Legba,
commands the sufferers, 'walk out of Egypt land; give them music fe
walk!' Tamatāne and Tamāhine, the children of Tāne/Māui, reply, 'Yes,
we hear you! So we must find our own path back to the Promised Land
with our own music. And our redemption songs will resonate along the
way.' In the 1970s vernacular, the national collective called this process
'sussing out the soul'.[80] We can call it grounding.

In the last couple of chapters we have worked through the various
arenas of the manifest domain, examining the cultivation of a soul
power that could act as a compass and energy store for a long-term
project of *mana motuhake*. We have engaged with Blackness through
theological and artistic registers. In this chapter we have witnessed

how contentious identifications with Blackness impelled a recovery of indigenous soul power. But we have also witnessed a subtle shift from identifying with Blackness to inhabiting Blackness on indigenous grounds, symbolized by the rooting of *kowhaiwhai* and dreadlocks in Ness's motif of Keskidee Aroha. Now we take a deeper step in this direction. In the next chapter we will examine how some sufferers in Aotearoa NZ have inhabited a faith of the diasporic children of Legba on indigenous grounds, by proclaiming RasTafari – Haile Selassie I – to be their Jah and king.

Dread Love: Reggae, RasTafari, Redemption

Introduction

Over the last 40 years roots reggae music has been the key medium for the dissemination of the RasTafari message from Jamaica to the world. Aotearoa NZ is no exception to this trend wherein the direct action message that Bob Marley preached to 'get up stand up' supported the radical engagements in the public sphere prompted by Black Power.[1] In many ways, Marley's message and demeanour vindicated the radical oppositional strategies that activists had deployed against the Babylon system in contradistinction to the Te Aute Old Boy tradition of tactful engagement. No surprise, then, that roots reggae was sometimes met with consternation by elders, although much of the issue revolved specifically around the smoking of Marijuana, the wisdom weed.[2] Yet some activists and gang members paid closer attention to the transmission, through the music, of a faith cultivated in the Caribbean, which professed Ethiopia as the root and Haile Selassie I as the agent of redemption. And they decided to make it their faith too.

In this chapter we will consider these groundings with RasTafari. We shall retrieve a whakapapa of mana motuhake (self-determination) between Ethiopia and Aotearoa. We shall examine the renewal of a maligned indigenous culture through the cultivation of a 'dread love'. And, recalling Tigilau Ness's motif of kowhaiwhai dreadlocks, we shall witness, through RasTafari, the inhabitation of spiritual Blackness on indigenous grounds.

Roots reggae and Te Kupu (the messenger)

Although roots reggae was known to some already, the release in
1975 of Bob Marley and the Wailers' *Natty Dread* album marked the
definitive arrival of the genre.[3] Subsequent re-releases of *Catch a Fire*
and *Burning*, followed by new material such as *Rastaman Vibration*
and *Babylon by Bus*, consolidated the far-reaching impact of Marley
among the youth. The reception of Burning Spear and other roots
bands such as Black Uhuru and Culture deepened this impact.[4] Island
Records releases dominated reggae sales in record shops. However, the
predominant dancehall format – the '45 single – entered Aotearoa NZ
in a subterranean fashion via the same routes travelled by Black Power
literature, i.e. through relatives living abroad (especially in Britain),
arriving African students, or returning Māori and Pasifika merchant
seamen, a few of whom had passed directly through Jamaica.[5] Some
of the sufferers could also appreciate the island aesthetic of rudebwoy/
RasTafari films such as *The Harder They Come* with its roots reggae
soundtrack.[6] Many more could relate to the look and feel of the
musicians and actors – Black, poor and on the margins of the law
especially with regards to the smoking of Marijuana.[7] At a time when
there was little social capital to be gained from being young, gifted and
Māori, Marley – an international artist and 'soul rebel' – looked like
one of the 'cousins down the road'.[8]

The medium of roots reggae was in many ways familiar to Māori.
Orality is a key component of Māori sociability, and music has always
been a powerful medium of communication.[9] In fact, there exists a
long Māori tradition of musical activism against land appropriation
by Pākehā.[10] By the mid-twentieth century, Māori songwriters such as
Tuini Ngawai were appropriating popular Western tunes and 'dubbing'
in their own, sometimes subversive, lyrics to produce *waiata haka*
(dance poems). Additionally, the folk/biblical bases for the proverbs that
Marley and others used to convey their messages also existed in Te Ao
Māori (the Māori world) wherein there exists a tradition of publically

narrating meaning through proverbs (*whakataukī*). Moreover, for well over 150 years, biblical verses had been recited and realigned to constitute the next iteration of the long *whakapapa* of Māori prophetic movements (to which we shall turn in the next chapter).[11] For instance, the Ringatū faith has a tradition of utilizing old Māori songs through which to sing certain Psalms.[12] So perhaps the RasTafari who, in the mid-1980s, emerged around Ruatoria on the East Cape, an area where the Ringatū Church is common, already recognized many of Marley's lyrics as Māori spiritual utterances.

Even the specific rhythms of roots reggae and its accompanying modes of vocal expression were familiar to many Māori. This was especially the case when it came to the practice of chanting, which, as a musical form, is highly respected in Te Ao Māori (the Māori world). Knowledge of the chant was placed in the third of Tāne's baskets (*kete*) as he reached the highest levels of the spiritual domain and brought back the baskets of knowledge to humankind.[13] Māui himself regularly used chants as part of his binding skills, for example, when forcing the sun to slow down its passage across the firmament.[14] Even the basic triplet rhythm of Māori chanting resonates with the pronounced triplet pattern found in much reggae music, for example, in Marley's *Exodus*.[15]

In all these ways, then, roots reggae could resonate with Māori sensibilities across political, aesthetic and spiritual dimensions. Listening to this music, Aotearoa sufferers would pick up on the message because '*te kupu te mea nui*' (the words are the main thing), while the rhythm 'showed ourselves again in another form'.[16] Above all, by playing the 'music of the afflicted people', Marley manifested, in the estimation of Te Hoko Whitu, a RasTafari from the 'Ruatoria Dread', as *te kupu* (the messenger).[17] Many listeners of the 1970s and 80s will testify that Marley convinced them to emancipate themselves from 'mental slavery'.[18] Although not all young sufferers were Māori or Pasifika, here too, the 'words got through'.[19] For instance, Denis O'Reilly, Pākehā member of the Black Power gang and instigator of Keskidee Aroha, listened to the album *Catch a Fire* after 'getting the bash' from the police one day, and felt a growing sense of outrage.[20]

In April 1979, one month before the Keskidee Aroha tour, Marley arrived to play a legendary concert at Western Springs, Auckland. The event was attended by 21,790 people including university students, musicians, activists and gangs who, rather than fighting each other, threw ounces of Marijuana on stage.[21] David Grace, a popular and politically astute Māori reggae artist, saw Bob Marley the same year in Sydney, Australia, but the effect was the same: 'Jesus Christ walked on stage!'[22] Some activists managed to meet Marley at White Heron Lodge in Auckland where the Jamaican entourage was staying. Miriama Rauhihi-Ness – Panther, Black Womans Movement and Keskidee Aroha member – hosted the I Threes (Rita Marley, Judy Mowatt and Sister Hines) at her house and subsequently held grounding sessions with Mowatt concerning the Twelve Tribes of Israel – the RasTafari organization of which Marley had become a member.[23]

Upon arrival to the country Marley was greeted at Auckland airport with a *pōwhiri* (welcome ceremony) by Ngāti Whātua, the local people of the land. And just as had been the case with Spivey and would be with Keskidee and Ras Messengers one month later, Marley was greatly affected by the warmth of the greeting and the way in which it grounded him in the people and the place.[24] That the greeting was offered by Ngāti Whātua was especially poignant. One year prior, they had lost a struggle against the selling of Takaparawha by Auckland council to corporate interests. Also known as Bastion Point, this land had previously been gifted by the tribe to the council as a reserve. Many of the key Māori, Pasifika as well as Pākehā activists came to stand in solidarity with Ngāti Whātua at Bastion Point. But after 507 days, they were all forcibly removed by over 500 police who subsequently tore down the marae complex called *Arohanui* (deep love) that had been erected.[25] The land was returned, much later, under the Waitangi Tribunal process; Ngāti Whātua re-gifted it to the people of Auckland as a recreational space. During the 1977/8 resistance at Bastion Point, Marley's *No Woman No Cry* was played 'time and again' along with *Redemption Song*.[26]

The most famous Oceania reggae group to date emerged out of this politically charged context. Herbs had begun as a social band.

However, with helpful direction from Ross France (founder of the Ponsonby Workers Cooperative and member of Keskidee Aroha), and Polynesian Panther Will 'Ilolahia (who became their manager), the group's first songs inflected contemporary political issues and spoke intentionally to 'street Ponsonby'.[27] One group member, Dilworth Karaka, had 'come through Bastion Point' and had also been involved in Keskidee Aroha.[28] The front cover of Herbs' first album featured a picture of Bastion Point with the title, 'Whats' Be Happenin'?' Released in 1981 on the eve of the Springbok tour, the album contained an anti-Apartheid anthem, *Azania* (penned by Ross France), which was not played on some radio stations due to its message.[29] Also included was a tribute to Marley entitled *Reggae's Doing Fine*, which was recorded the morning after Te Kupu had joined the ancestors in the realms of Te Pō (the realm of dark potential).[30]

Herbs, though, was not the first Māori or Pasifika reggae band. Polynesian Panther Tigilau Ness had set up Unity in the Ponsonby area as a response to Alma Rei's band Chaos that had already emerged out of Takapūwāhia Pā in Porirua. Chaos toured with Keskidee Aroha, and the Porirua Pā also hosted the troupe; Ras Tafari from the Pā still remember this visit as a formative moment.[31] By 1982, according to David Grace, the Pā was 'full of dreads'.[32] Indeed, it is no exaggeration to say that Porirua Pā had a fundamental part to play in the opening up of Te Ao Māori (the Māori world) to roots reggae and the Ras Tafari message. This drawing together of energies is understandable if we consider that urban Porirua developed around the Pā, which remains one of the markers of the *tūrangawaewae* (place of belonging) of Ngāti Toa. In this sense, the youth at the Pā could, as Ras Tafari say, 'sight up' the message because they already inhabited the ground they stood upon. There are some parallels here to the peculiar nature of Ōtara as an urban space, and the early focus put by the youth there on cultural rejuvenation as we witnessed in the last chapter.[33]

Emerging from Porirua's eastern suburbs, where many migrant Māori families resided, was another roots reggae band called Sticks and Shanty. Thai Sticks are a form of Marijuana that at the time were readily available in Aotearoa NZ. Shanty Town was the name of a hut in the Porirua suburb of Titahi Bay; influenced by the anti-apartheid/honour the Treaty movement of the 1970s, the word Shanty was intended to connect the poor people of Porirua to the shacks of Soweto.[34] With music equipment borrowed from the Mighty Mongrel Mob gang, Sticks and Shanty also struggled for airplay of their messages within a Pākehā-controlled broadcast industry.

In retrospect Reihana Ngatoro, a member of Sticks and Shanty, is convinced that reggae was – and perhaps remains – a 'stepping stone to *tikanga*', a term that connotes the culturally correct way to do things for the sake of wellbeing.[35] Ngatoro had moved to east Porirua as a teenager. Living in a viscerally racist urban context with separated parents who spent the majority of the time working for a living under great stress, and with no grandparents immediately available to fortify him with a sense of integrity, Ngatoro was confronted with a stark choice. The 'fatal impact' thesis of settler colonialism posited that the indigenous can either survive by dispensing with their culture or die practising it. However, Marley's message taught Ngatoro another thesis, a decolonial one: survival was itself a culture; and in order to survive one had to have a culture. This was the compass and energy store provided by Marley. In this sense, the RasTafari message was not only a stepping stone to *tikanga* (the correct way) but a revitalization of the very notion of *tikanga* itself.

For all these reasons a number of reggae bands in the 1980s would align themselves closely with the Māori reparations movement concerning breaches to Te Tiriti o Waitangi (The Treaty of Waitangi). Dread, Beat and Blood – featuring David Grace – was one such band that hailed from Porirua Pā. Aotearoa was another band whose members were influenced by Marley and the Wailers and Herbs yet purposefully wrote songs in Te Reo (the Māori language). Many of Aotearoa's songs were influenced by the band's attendance of political *hui* (meetings), with their gigs feeling more like 'political rallies'.[36] Thus, within a short period of time, roots reggae had quite literally become the soundtrack to the Māori renaissance.[37]

The medium of roots reggae facilitated the most intimate grounding between the children of Tāne/Māui and Legba of the time. In fact, 'Uncle Bob' was such a household name that it was not unusual for youngsters to assume that he really was a familial relation.[38] Marley has, on occasion, even featured in family shrines.[39] Ruia Aperahama, a member of the Rātana faith and Māori musician who translated the Wailers' songs into Te Reo (the Māori language), provides a potent example of this intimate grounding with RasTafari. In 2008, he undertook a pilgrimage to Jamaica and brought with him a very special gift (*taonga*) for Marley's *whānau* (family) that signified a covenant between the Māori and Jamaican peoples. The gift was carried in a *waka huia*, a sacred container – sacred because the gift it carries is imbued with the personal spirit of the giver. The inscription on the container translates as: 'it was Māui who changed our world forever, little by little'.[40] (We might remember that through chanting, Māui harnessed the power of the sun for the good of humanity.) Woven into personal and spiritual *whakapapa*, binding back the children of Tāne/Māui to their decolonial pasts and selves, Marley is *te kupu o Āwherika* (the African messenger), child of Legba, relative of Māui.

Nonetheless, we need to make a distinction between reggae music and the RasTafari faith. The latter is sometimes communicated through the former medium as roots music. However, reggae is not foundationally a RasTafari medium. And Marley was first and foremost a messenger of RasTafari, the Black liberation faith that spoke so acutely and poetically of injustice, resistance, emancipation and redemption. RasTafari proposes that sanctification lies in inhabiting Blackness as a righteous condition. With this 'dread love', RasTafari venerate a particular personality, the African-Ethiopian emperor Haile Selassie I alongside Empress Menen Asfaw. In both rural and urban Aotearoa NZ I can testify that many houses have posters of Marley adorning their walls in prominent positions. However, portraits of Selassie I are few and far between.[41]

But some sufferers did look to where Marley directed them and 'sighted up' the Conquering Lion of Judah as their King too. They began to inhabit RasTafari on indigenous grounds in order to practise a dread love among their people. Small in number, they were big in effect. Although far from Jamaica, they were closer to Ethiopia. For, while South Africa and Aotearoa are bound together in a *whakapapa* of colonial injustice, Ethiopia and Aotearoa are bound together in a *whakapapa* of *mana motuhake* (self-determination).

Aotearoa/Ethiopia

From 1855 Emperor Tewodros II began in earnest the centralization of a loose patchwork of principalities that at the time formed Ethiopia. Without embarking on such a process, Ethiopia would have soon been carved up between Italy, France and Britain – the key encroaching imperial powers in the region. The defensive project to consolidate and express Ethiopian sovereignty on the world stage reached its apogee when Haile Selassie I, as crown prince Ras Tafari, entered Ethiopia into the League of Nations in 1923. However, in the intervening time period, European powers regularly sought to militarily and diplomatically neuter Ethiopia. In many ways, this history is contemporaneous and cognate to the Māori pursuit of *mana motuhake*, with the Kīngitanga (Māori King Movement) emerging around 1854, a series of other *kotahitanga* (unity) movements following alongside and in its wake, and the last Māori prophetic movement of this era beginning in the early 1920s under the ministry of T. W. Rātana.

Charles Speedy – known euphemistically as Captain Speedy – is a useful character through which to start to draw out the constitutive linkages between these two defensive projects.[42] The Captain's father, Major James Speedy, was an imperial army veteran who retired to Aotearoa NZ in 1856. After 1861 Captain Speedy travelled extensively in Ethiopia before joining his family at Mauku in 1864. He arrived in the most pivotal episode of the wars over land when imperial troops invaded the Waikato, the home of the Kīngitanga. At this point, Captain Speedy served as a captain and adjutant of the Auckland militia, later receiving a Māori Wars medal. In 1867, Captain Speedy joined Lord Napier's staff as advisor on the expedition to Ethiopia wherein British forces stormed Magdala, inflicted a decisive defeat on Tewodros II's forces, and robbed churches and other houses of many artefacts. On Queen Victoria's suggestion, Captain Speedy was appointed guardian to Prince Alamayu Simeon, the son of Tewedros II, who had committed suicide at Magdala. The son died in Britain. However, a young boy called Emir Ali, a cousin of Emperor Menelik II, was also 'saved' by the British army, and entrusted to Captain Speedy, who delivered him to the coast, and ultimately, Britain. Ali left Britain within one year as a ward of the ship's captain of the *Star of India* and, perhaps after hearing of the land of the long white cloud from Speedy, eventually arrived in Auckland in 1874 where he was to remain for the rest of his life.[43]

On two occasions – 1868 and 1886 – Captain Speedy lectured on Ethiopia to mainly Pākehā audiences in Aotearoa NZ.[44] But Māori were also paying attention to the struggle over Ethiopian self-determination. A key moment in the imperial showdown between Ethiopia and Europe came with the Battle of Adwa in 1896 wherein Italy was roundly defeated by the armies of Menelik II. Four years later a newspaper representing the *Paremata Māori o te Kotahitanga* (the Māori Parliament) ran an article in Te Reo entitled 'Te Kīngi o Etiopia', which relayed the biblical encounter of Makeda, Queen of Sheba, with King Solomon, siring the Solomonic lineage (to which Selassie I claimed 225th direct descent). The article ended with a brief report on the recent Battle of Adwa.[45] The message was clear: learn from those biblical African polities that have been able to retain and defend their *mana motuhake* in the face of European slavery and imperial expansion.

From 1923 onwards New Zealand civil servants followed the discussions in the League concerning Ethiopia's putatively uncivilized status by virtue of the slave-raiding and slave-holding that still occurred within and across its borders despite Selassie I's attempts at reform. Regular calls were made by European observers for what would nowadays be termed humanitarian intervention.[46] In September of 1935, with the Italian army massing on the border of Ethiopia ready for invasion, the New Zealand delegate to the League announced that his country was prepared to hold to the principle of collective security and support sanctions against Italy.[47] New Zealand was one of only a handful of League members who consistently supported Ethiopia's sovereignty during the Italian occupation. When he re-entered Addis Ababa on 7 May 1941, five years to the day from his departure into exile due to the Italian invasion, Selassie I sent a personal telegram of good wishes to the New Zealand Prime Minister.[48]

Defending his country's principled position (which soon became contrary to that held by Britain) Walter Nash, minister of finance, argued that the peoples of Aotearoa NZ most certainly cared about what would happen to Ethiopians under Italian occupation. Nash reckoned that 'we [have] such a regard to our own coloured race that it [seems] natural that regard would be extended to other coloured races'.[49] Certainly, Nash was wearing the rose-tinted glasses of settler exceptionalism. But he was not wrong in his assessment of the support held by many of the working class for the Ethiopian cause, which is demonstrated by a set of stop-work meetings held by the New Zealand Seamen's Union in Wellington, Lyttelton and Auckland on 5 October 1935.[50] One newspaper commentary in the lead-up to the war was given by an elderly Emir Ali himself.[51] And positive assessments of Selassie I's post-exile governance appeared in newspapers during the rest of the war.[52] Were these assessments garnered from Captain Speedy's famous lectures decades earlier, wherein he had informed the Pākehā chattering classes that Ethiopia was none other than the fabled Christian land of Prester John?[53] And had some Māori perhaps remembered the reports of Adwa from the *Kotahitanga* newspaper?

Let us return to the first half of the 1980s. Rauhihi-Ness recalls that shortly after her return from Jamaica, where she had committed herself to the RasTafari faith, a *tangi* (funeral) required her to return to her family home in Levin. Already somewhat chastised by some of her Māori *whānau* (family) for supporting the struggles of Pasifika peoples as a member of the Polynesian Panthers, Rauhihi-Ness had apprehensions about now greeting her family in the divine and precious name of an African emperor, Haile Selassie I. And yet when she did so, some of her elders recognized the name approvingly. They had served in the North Africa and Italian campaigns of the Second World War as part of the 28th Māori Battalion and during these sojourns they had met and talked with Selassie I, who expressed his admiration for the Māori people.[54]

There is one more chapter to this story. On 13 October 1941, in gratitude for New Zealand's refusal to recognize Italy's claims to sovereignty over Ethiopia, Ethiopian Minister Blatta Ayela Gabre gifted to W. J. Jordon, New Zealand High Commissioner to London, a signed portrait of Selassie I in a gold and silver frame.[55] This portrait subsequently disappeared only to emerge again in 2010 as part of an auction of UNESCO items. A private interest successfully bid against the National Museum for the item. At the first national grounation of RasTafari in January 2011 at Wainuiomata, a Twelve Tribes of Israel member, Ras Mark Solomon, along with his *whānau* (family) from Porirua Pā, presented the portrait and affirmed that RasTafari would henceforth be its guardians.

A dread love

Ras Solomon was one of the sufferers of Aotearoa who in the 1980s were to build a relationship with Selassie I on domestic battlefields, especially, the streets and prisons populated by gangs and activists. There, they would rejuvenate past anti-colonial connections between Aotearoa NZ and Ethiopia in order to cultivate a 'dread love' for their peoples as they pursued *mana motuhake*.

By the late 1970s many members of Māori and Pasifika gangs – from the Mongrel Mob to Black Power to King Cobras – were enthusiastically listening to roots reggae. For some members, RasTafari even provided a non-aligned pathway – a way out and a chance to retain a non-conformist position towards society but not by committing apostasy to one gang by joining another.[56] The 'soul rebel' stance of RasTafari was largely respected by gangs. Sometimes, those who proclaimed themselves RasTafari in prison, whether gang member or not, were left alone by inmates and not required to affiliate one way or the other.[57] As I have already noted, prison in the United States and in Aotearoa NZ acted as an incubator of Black Power. So too for the RasTafari message, usually transmitted through reggae. In the early 1980s reggae radio shows received many letters from inmates.[58] At this point some prisoners were serving sentences related to political activism. Here are the written sentiments of another activist and political prisoner, a member of the Patu Squad (the military wing of the Springbok protest movement): 'That Musical Youth song [*The Youth of Today*] is on and fuck man, everytime I hear it, I can feel the vibes, man, da fucken power the youth represent. If you listen to the lyrics carefully you can comprehend.'[59]

Tigilau Ness, a Polynesian Panther and member of the Keskidee Aroha national collective, had also been given a significant prison sentence in 1982 for his part in the anti-apartheid protests. Noticing that Ness had started to grow dreadlocks, the Warden asked him what religion he was and replied on his behalf, 'Rastafarian'. Ness accepted the naming; he had been travelling in that direction anyway.[60] As a dreadlocked RasTafari, fellow inmates including gang members held him in 'a kind of reverence'. But one Māori youth from the East Cape, Chris Campbell, was curious as to why a dreadlocks was reading the white man's Bible.[61] The two would proceed to have regular grounding sessions in prison regarding the RasTafari faith. Ness shared with Campbell that according to the Twelve Tribes of Israel order, the East Cape youth was of the tribe of Gad. Campbell provided Ness with a gift of sand shoes, a precious commodity in prison. After leaving prison the two visited each other and met up on the 1984 *hikoi* (march) to Waitangi to protest against continual breaches to Te Tiriti (The Treaty).[62] Returning to the East Cape, Campbell led the

Ruatoria Dreads, a number of whom had previously been members of the Mongrel Mob.[63] Campbell brought back from prison the 'face of the King of Kings', that is, Haile Selassie I, as prophesied in Psalm 24.6: 'This is the generation of them that seek him, that seek thy face, O Jacob. Selah.'[64] The Ruatoria Dreads would become (in)famous for confronting the local government, state and even some of their own relations over the return of tribal lands taken on long-term leases (mainly by members of the Church Missionary Society), and especially the return of the sacred mountain Hikurangi to the *tangata whenua* (people of the land), Ngāti Porou.

A few years later, some members of the Ruatoria Dread were serving prison terms in Mangaroa prison. There they grounded with Api Mahuika, the Ngāti Porou Rūnanga (council) chairperson, who explained to them the tribal contexts of their struggles.[65] In prison they also encountered Harold Turner, a world-famous theologian of new religious movements. Turner, in his retirement, had become curious about the burgeoning RasTafari faith in Aotearoa NZ and had lectured on the topic to the Secretary for Justice and superintendents of prisons.[66] Turner then facilitated the Dread's engagement with Norman Perry's Mana Trust.[67] Perry, a respected Pākehā, had served in the Māori Battalion during the Second World War and had been a secretary to Sir Apirana Ngata, the original Te Aute Old Boy. Perry had also cultivated a relationship with the Ringatū faith. Perry's Mana Trust worked with Māori prisoners so as to rehabilitate them through the teaching of their tribal traditions and associated *tikanga* (correct ways). Ringatū ran through many of the Dread's families, and they themselves had been reintroduced to the faith by Tame Te Maro, an elder of Ngāti Porou.[68] Te Maro was a staunch activist for indigenous rights and an early influence upon Ngā Tamatoa in terms of reviving the principles of Te Tiriti. Te Maro himself had studied with a famous Ringatū *tohunga* (learned one) called Hori Keti, who maintained that Te Tiriti was no less binding than the covenants of the Old Testament.[69] Perry facilitated further study by key members of the imprisoned Dread, leading to a deeper grounding of RasTafari and Ringatū.

After these prison groundings the Ruatoria Dreads then began to hold regular gatherings along the lines laid out by Ringatū. On holy days (called Rā) the Dread would come together – elders, women, men and children – in a supportive environment. Young men would be treated with respect and would treat women with respect. We should note that some of the Dread, although themselves now having children, had rarely in their personal lives experienced a caring environment.[70] So, just as the RasTafari message had reintroduced some of the youth to the very principle of *tikanga*, i.e. living according to a correct way, so did the faith reintroduce some of the youth to the very principles of *manaaki* (care) and *aroha* (sympathy, love). For the Ruatoria Dread, RasTafari thus provided a compass and energy store with which to retrieve a dread love of one's people.

Let us now turn to examine the retrieval of a dread love by activists. Central, in this regard, is the forming of the Aotearoa NZ chapter of the Twelve Tribes of Israel. By the late 1970s visceral street politics had started to exhaust activists who had little substantive to show for a decade's worth of confrontation except increasing right-wing turns by the government of the day. As the Keskidee Aroha project testifies to, strategies had to change so that the protesting body could be nurtured in the long run by a liberated soul.[71] At the time, Miriama Rauhihi-Ness, who, it will be remembered, had grounded with the I Threes during Marley's visit, explained the shift as follows: 'Back then we were angry, angry, angry, hitting out at anything. Now, we know what we're angry about. That's what Rasta and reggae have given … Back then, black Americans put us in contact, and gave us a blackness, a political vehicle we could use. Rasta is another vehicle.'[72] Ness expressed similar sentiments: We haven't time to fight this black/white thing. It wearies you. Rasta is an alternative way. A way to teach your children the truth, and to practice a dread love among your people.'[73] These testimonies indicate that activists felt a need to at the very least complement opposition to the system with a positive love (*agape*) for their communities. For some, as I mentioned in Chapter four, this meant returning to various *tūrangawaewae* (places of belonging) that assimilation through urbanization had sought to segregate them from. (In fact, the cartoon magazine that Keskidee Aroha members sold in order to raise funds for the tour dramatized the story of just such a return.) But for a few activists this process (also) led to a grounding with RasTafari.

At a Black Women's *hui* in June 1982 arguments flared over Māori and Pasifika relationships and the use of the identifier Black instead of Māori. Rauhihi-Ness and a number of her close activist acquaintances, tired of the arguing, left the meeting. From identifying with political Blackness Rauhihi-Ness and others sought to inhabit a more expansive spiritual Blackness through the RasTafari faith. With the help of Hensley Dyer, a Jamaican Twelve Tribes member resident in Auckland, Rauhihi-Ness, also accompanied by Herbs musician Toni Fonoti, journeyed to Jamaica to meet with Gadman, the prophet of the Twelve Tribes of Israel. The RasTafari 'mansion' to which Marley had belonged. Having decided that she could no longer function as a 'political animal', Rauhihi-Ness returned and in November 1982 the first meeting to 'praise Jah' was convened in Auckland.[74] In 1985 the New Zealand chapter was incorporated within the international structure of the Twelve Tribes; in 1986 the prophet Gad visited New Zealand to 'seal' the house, returning once more in 1989. In the intervening period, many of the Aotearoa NZ executive visited both Jamaica and Ethiopia.[75]

The Twelve Tribes in Aotearoa NZ operate along the lines set out by HQ in Jamaica in terms of liturgy, administration and mission. A central practice among the Twelve Tribes is the reading of one chapter of the Bible every day, so that the reader might find the truth for her/himself. However, a central aim for each Twelve Tribes house is to ensure that its membership can feed, clothe and shelter themselves. In this respect, the spiritual mission of the Twelve Tribes can be said to be underpinned by a Black Power ethos of economic self-sufficiency arising out of Marcus and Amy Ashwood Garvey's Universal Negro Improvement Association (UNIA).[76] In the Auckland house, Garveyism mapped onto the same ethos of self-determination that had already been put into practice by Māori and Pasifika activists. Indeed, the majority of the foundation members of the Twelve Tribes house in Aotearoa NZ were activists associated with the Polynesian Panthers from the Ponsonby area of Auckland.[77] And the house also attracted other politicized youth; one group from Porirua were planning to join the Ruatoria Dread in the East Cape but upon hearing about the Twelve Tribes diverted instead to Auckland.[78]

For these spiritual and economic purposes the Twelve Tribes set up a physical headquarters in Auckland where revenue-raising and conscious-building dance parties were held. (Many more came to the Twelve Tribes through this route.[79]) In preparation for these events, sewing, cooking and musical bodies were formed.[80] With regards to the latter, the Twelve Tribes leaned on its activist connections and sent some of the children of members to a music school run by Taura Eruera (the old chairperson of Ngā Tamatoa).[81] The Dread Lion band was subsequently formed, which then morphed into the Twelve Tribes of Israel Band. Yet although music was an economic base of the House, the executives had bigger plans. Hensley Dyer, who was for a while the de facto leader of the House, aimed to eliminate unemployment among its members within five years.[82] This was an urgent task because in the years immediately following its inauguration the unemployed composed 80 per cent of the Twelve Tribes membership.[83] Towards this aim the Nu Vision Work Trust was formed, which cooperatively sought and provided employment for members, alongside the teaching of trades, crafts, budgeting and pre-school education.[84] This was the economic manifestation of a dread love.

And so, by retrieving a dread love for their peoples, the Aotearoa followers of Haile Selassie I renewed the *whakapapa* of Aotearoa/Ethiopia. But just as in all groundings between the children of Tāne/Māui and Legba, this retrieval was not without its contentions. Let us now examine some of the challenges specific to inhabiting RasTafari on indigenous grounds.

Inhabiting RasTafari

As we have witnessed with Keskidee Aroha, even the peripheries on the imperial world map can be ranked hierarchically against each other. In the 1970s the Caribbean 'soul rebel' enjoyed a cultural cache that Te Ao Māori (the Māori world) had yet to really instil among its youth (Ngā Tamatoa and other vocal activists notwithstanding).[85] Many in Aotearoa NZ were attracted to wearing another self and story, despite the fact that the RasTafari faith sought to emancipate the sufferers from mental slavery and to know themselves in the world on their own grounds.[86] This was the clear message that Marley himself gave during his stay in Auckland: Aotearoa sufferers could not be RasTafari and Jamaican; they would have to be RasTafari *and* Māori, Samoan, etc.[87] It was a straightforward commandment, but a complex practice.

Hensley Dyer, de facto head of the Twelve Tribes in Auckland, possessed significant prestige when it came to setting the terms of debate regarding the place of RasTafari in Te Ao Māori (the Māori world). As the only 'bona-fide' African-Caribbean resident in Auckland representing the only RasTafari organization imported directly from Jamaica, Dyer exuded authenticity whether he wanted to or not.[88] A major incident took place when Hensley and other members of the Twelve Tribes travelled to the East Cape to meet the Ruatoria Dread. Hensley later recollected his message to the Dreads, which was, in fact, at odds to that given by Marley: 'You can't serve two masters. You can't be half Māori and half Rasta. If you're going to be a Māori, be a full Māori, because that is beautiful.'[89] While Hensley certainly did not demean or disavow the Māori world, his statement inferred that to inhabit RasTafari one would have to vacate indigenous personhood. The Ruatoria Dread did not take kindly to the advice; and when asked how one can be Māori and Rasta, the sardonic reply was – and remains – 'How can you be Māori and a bus driver?'[90]

Dyer's logic seems to have encouraged some Māori members of the Twelve Tribes to even associate Te Ao Māori (the Māori world) with Babylon – a force of disunity and division. And at least some members of the Twelve Tribes identified this feature in the tribal nature of Māori social and political organization; or, as one member once memorably put it: 'up with Rasta, out with the schisms of Māori'. Some members even chastised Ness for keeping an association with activist groups such as the Waitangi Action Committee, which were, in the early 1980s, contesting the dysfunctional Treaty relationship.[91] In this sense, even *mana motuhake* – the struggle to redeem guardianship and governance over ancestral land – could be interpreted as 'giving a strength' to Babylon.

While attending a Twelve Tribes monthly meeting in March 2010 I was witness to a revealing *kōrero* (discussion) that spoke to these contentions. Twelve Tribes organizations have an executive membership wherein each tribe is represented as well as a Sister Dinah who often provides key directions to the house. At meetings, the executive sit in front, on the 'bench'. The current representative of Dan at this time, a Māori man, equated Aotearoa NZ with Babylon claiming that this was not his land even if it was the place of his birth. Furthermore, Dan would be involved in no *mana whenua* (land) politics, nor would he use Te Reo as these would tie him further to Babylon. Sometime afterwards, Sister Dinah spoke and provided a *mihi* (greeting). Although not directly addressing Dan, her *kōrero* (speech) addressed the issues that he had raised. Sister Dinah recounted a visit to Ethiopia wherein an Ethiopian had asked her of her mother tongue. She had replied, 'English', whereupon the Ethiopian interjected, 'No, what's your mother tongue?' And at that moment Sister Dinah realized that, as a Māori woman, it was Te Reo. She further noted that the Twelve Tribes' prophet, Gadman, had revealed that spiritual Israel would be composed of many nationalities, not just one.

This *kōrero* (discussion) demonstrates that, within the Twelve Tribes, the practice of inhabiting RasTafari on indigenous grounds has been critically worked through in sustained fashion over a long period of time. And a number of long-term members have variously reassessed Hensley's original precept (while some never accepted it in the first place). Jules

Issa, for example, nowadays positively identifies with Ngāti Porou, 'my culture', and states that, as Māori, she was born with the *wairua* (spirit). She wishes to immerse her children in both the Māori and RasTafari worlds: 'Te Reo is a *taonga* [gift] that I'm going to take with me back to Africa.'[92] Indeed, the project to return to Ethiopia remains a fundamental aim of the Twelve Tribes house in Aotearoa NZ. But I would suggest that here, too, there have been subtle shifts, if not in the basic imperative then perhaps in the tactics, strategies and purposes of the movement of Jah people. For example, among long-term followers of the prophet Gadman there is now an inter-generational dimension to the journey: 'maybe not in our lifetime, but our children's or grand-children's'; and for many, the timeline now includes the pursuit of reparations for colonial wrongs in Aotearoa NZ and Oceania in general where there is 'work to do first'.[93]

This brings us, finally, to a fundamental pillar of the RasTafari faith – restitution for the children of Legba kidnapped and trafficked across the oceans. Marcus Garvey's call for 'Africa for the Africans at home and abroad' is given biblical authority in Micah 4.4, and it has been manifested in Haile Selassie I's granting of five hundred hectares in Shashemene in 1948 to the peoples of the African Diaspora for their support in the Italian/Ethiopian war. Some people see Garvey's espousal as aligning perfectly with the key principle of the second article of Te Tiriti o Waitangi (The Treaty), articulated by Saana Murray as 'Māori control over things Māori'.[94] For instance, reflecting on his relationship to the message of RasTafari, roots reggae musician David Grace argues that as *tangata whenua* (people of the land) he cannot culturally identify as African or Jamaican. Yet Garvey's calling – transmitted through RasTafari – resonates intimately with him as Māori: 'a people without the knowledge of their past history, origin and culture is like a tree without roots'. When Grace heard this statement from Garvey in a roots reggae song, he came to the conclusion that 'Yep, you're talking about us too.'[95] Back in the late 1980s, Grace had confrontations with the Twelve Tribes in Auckland over the significance of the Garveyite dimension of RasTafari philosophy and its logical and principled affirmation of *mana motuhake*.

Te Hoko Whitu, a Ruatoria Dread, inhabits the RasTafari faith through a similar disposition towards Garvey: 'soldiers chased Te Kooti as they chased Garvey out ... the message is the same'.[96] Te Kooti was a guerrilla fighter who partook in the land wars of the 1860s, and was also a prophet and founder of the Ringatū faith to which the Ruatoria Dread are strongly connected. For Te Hoko Whitu, the binding skills of Te Kooti and Garvey were the same: 'to tie the land and people together' against colonial forces. Here, Ringatū, Garveyism and RasTafari inhabit the same indigenous ground. Hone Heeney, another Ruatoria Dread, refigures the Genesis narrative to reflect this inhabitation. The Dread are the cherub who, with a flaming sword, guards the Garden of Eden. The task of the cherub is not to guard Eden from entrance by the sons of men; rather, it is to protect the people of the land of Eden from incursion by Babylonian forces.[97] This indigenous RasTafari has never left Zion, but has trod (spiritually journeyed) in it from creation; and he will stay to protect it.

Conclusion

When roots reggae played on the airwaves it transmitted a subversive message on a deeper frequency. Encoded in this message was a decolonial science designed to repair the wounds of near-fatal impacts. This science facilitated a renewal of soul power and of some of the cardinal values of Te Ao Māori (the Māori world): *tikanga* (the correct way), *manaaki* (hospitality) and *aroha* (sympathy). RasTafari redeemed for the Aotearoa sufferers a dread love for themselves. But the ground for inhabiting RasTafari had long been prepared through a *whakapapa* of *mana motuhake* between Ethiopia and Aotearoa NZ. In these ways RasTafari is inhabited on indigenous grounds; *kowhaiwhai* and dreadlocks have taken root together; and Aotearoa and Ethiopia are bound through a dread love.

Unlike knowledge production/consumption (a subaltern under-taking), knowledge cultivation turns matter around and folds it back on itself so as to rebind and encourage growth. This circulatory process of oxygenation necessarily interacts with a wider biotope, enfolding matter from diverse cultivations. So far in this book we have followed the children of Tāne/Māui as they ground with the children of Legba and retrieve anti-colonial designs for *mana motuhake*. We have moved from the political to the theological, to art and to faith, and from comparison to identification to inhabitation. But we are now moving towards an enfolding of RasTafari within prophetic traditions indigenous and endogenous to Aotearoa NZ. We are in the presence of the Dread cherub who guards the Garden of Eden and is adorned with dreadlocked *kowhaiwhai*. We have arrived on the threshold of the spiritual domain. Here we must respectfully ask for intercession so we might cross over and visit the uncolonized spiritual hinterlands. The prophets will channel us in the right direction.

Ham, Shem and the Māori Prophets

Introduction

John 5.23 commands: '[A]ll men should honour the Son, even as they honour the Father. He that honoureth not the Son honoureth not the Father which hath sent him.' Originally part of a forensic defence by early Christians designed to address criticisms of linking Jesus to God, missionary authorities appropriated this defence in order to buttress colonial hierarchies: no native could come to God – that is, be sanctified – except through the European avatars who alone were worthy to spread the message of his Son.[1]

There is no doubt that missionary Christianity has been used as a tool to uproot peoples in the expansion of the colonial frontier. It is, however, another thing entirely to presume that those among the colonized who embraced the Bible – and even Christ – were simply sacrificing themselves on the altar of cultural imperialism.[2] In fact colonized peoples often ignored the missionary interpretation of John 5.23. Instead, they were able and willing to acculturate the Bible into their own extant cosmologies, philosophies and cardinal values rather than be enculturated into a missionary Christianity.[3] Specifically, the theological and philosophical changes that accompanied the acceptance of the Bible as the word of God tended to follow the logics of existing worldviews and not the logics of colonial science.[4] Such was the case with the Māori tradition of prophecy.

In order for us to walk with the prophets it will be necessary to first return to some of the cosmological frameworks of Tāne/Māui and Legba that I discussed earlier in the book. In these frameworks the prophet appears as the channeller of biblical intercession between the manifest and spiritual domains. We shall then witness one prophet, Te Ua, finding Tāne/Māui and Legba walking the spiritual hinterlands together in their biblical manifestation as Shem and Ham. In Te Ua's context, the solidarity between Ham and Shem manifests as a binding together of struggles against (African) enslavement and (indigenous) dispossession. Te Ua addresses this shared fate by binding the kingly pursuit of *mana motuhake* (self-determination) to the redemption of the suffering Māori multitudes in one anti-colonial project.

Cosmology, prophecy and the Bible

To walk with the prophets we must first of all dispatch the colonial distinction between monotheistic and polytheistic religions. This distinction is part of the theological architecture that supports the missionary reading of John 5.23 in so far as monotheism is considered to be the seedbed of civilization and metaphysics (European Christianity) while polytheism is considered capable only of cultivating particular and provincial thought (native totems, fetishism, ancestor worship etc.).[5] However, neither the cosmologies of Legba nor those of Tāne/Māui display such crude binaries. For the fact that a cosmology incorporates a range of spiritual agencies (so-called 'polytheism') does not rule out the precept that a seminal force assures unity in diversity (so called 'monotheism'). This is certainly the case in much African ancestor worship.[6] So too in Oceania cosmologies, many of which exhibit an abiding theme of a creative epoch wherein extant matter differentiates itself without losing its seminal characteristics; hence, key differentiations – for example male and female – do not become binary opposites but retain a recursive relationship.[7]

This notion is important when it comes to understanding the deeper and ancient Oceanic meaning of the common word for god in Māori. *Atua* does not refer to a separate One who is invoked but, rather, denotes being from or of the 'other side'.[8] Hence, multiple entities that exist in the spiritual domain are *atua*. But *atua*, as demonstrated by Māori Marsden, all variously articulate the seminal force of creation. Crucially, these relational apprehensions of a seminal force are not the same as the European and missionary Christian notion of a begotten personality/entity that is distinct and separated from the manifest domain. Many decolonial apprehensions of Christianity question precisely this separation. For instance, within RasTafari (as in the Ethiopian Orthodox Church) there exists the notion of *theosis*, meaning that the flesh and the spirit are not categorically separate; rather, one can with thought and practice manifest divine nature.[9]

Having dispensed with the artificial distinction between monotheism and polytheism we can now consider the 'authenticity' of Io in Māori cosmology. Io is the suspiciously 'monotheistic' begotten force who has various names such as Io-matua (parent of all things), Io-mata-ngaro (the hidden face) or Io-matua-aho (seen in a flash, i.e. lightning).[10] By the mid-twentieth century some scholars claimed that Io was created as an approximation of the biblical Jehovah due to the fact that the deity entered into the public record only after the arrival in force of missionaries.[11] Alternatively, Manuka Henare argues that, being the highest of esoteric knowledge, i.e. the most sublime articulation of the concept of *atua*, Io was known only to a relatively few seers and so would certainly not be casually mentioned to newcomers.[12] As we shall see, Jehovah was subsequently acculturated into the Io concept.

Even the practice of baptism – the quintessential act of accepting the missionary interpretation of John 5.23 and being reborn into a new family of Christ – was acculturated by the children of Tāne/Māui and Legba into their existing cosmological frameworks. Water often holds significance as a medium of transmission between the manifest and spiritual domains. It is common across African cosmologies for water sites to function as 'aquatic temples', residencies of ancestral deities and spiritual agencies including the famous 'water mamma' known also in the Caribbean.[13] In Māori cosmology, Wainui is the female personification of water.[14] An early European visitor to Aotearoa NZ was so astonished at witnessing the Māori 'custom of sprinkling their children with water at the time they name them' that he believed that they must have been 'familiar with the Mosaic account of the creation'.[15] In truth this sojourner was probably witnessing the Tohi rite wherein the child is prepared for dedication to a spiritual agency.[16]

As with Io, Jehovah, Tohi and baptism, so too with the Bible itself, which was acculturated by Māori as a story of ancestral redemption. It might be remembered that in Bob Scott's anti-racism workshops Hone Kaa challenged the missionary fantasies of John 5.23 by narrating his own *whakapapa* back to creation. It was precisely this acculturation that allowed Kaa to do so.

The Māori concept of *mana* denotes 'lawful permission delegated by the gods to their human agents and accompanied by the endowment of spiritual power to act on their behalf and in accordance with their revealed will'.[17] In the manifest domain, *mana* is pursued by reciprocating and balancing relations with others over the long run (*utu*), whether peacefully or forcefully.[18] In this way *mana* is heavily implicated in the moral legacies of the actions of ancestors. Similarly, in many West African cosmologies, while the Most High is omnipotent, sin, forgiveness, love and punishment emanate from the human experience, which is why ancestors take on unique importance as channels to the higher realms.[19] In short, the ancestors act as – and affect – the moral compass. And this is why enslaved Africans and early nineteenth-century Māori seers often qualified the central significance of Jesus Christ the Son via retrieval of his Old Testament ancestors and, indeed, his father – Jehovah.[20] These ancestral stories were morally instructive, detailing a people's captivity, their exodus and liberation, while the New Testament revealed the means of spiritual redemption in a world of incarnate suffering.[21]

It is the prophet who interprets and envisages the material as material-and-spiritual. In so doing, the prophet channels the *atua* (the spiritual agencies) of intercession on behalf of suffering communities in the manifest domain. In this respect, the prophet is less a charismatic agent and more an elected agent of a 'history-shaping power'.[22] While certain prophets can be co-opted by the political and hierocratic power bases, I am concerned with those who stand apart to pursue a Jeremiad vocation – i.e. the witnessing of injustice and testifying to the consequences.[23] To undertake such a vocation, the prophet stands at the crossroads of the manifest and spiritual domains. There, she/he channels the agents of intercession (Legba, Tāne/Māui and Arcadian Hermes too) in order to redeem a beloved community. In this respect, the prophet facilitates binding activities and can therefore be an important practitioner of decolonial science.

As a channeller of intercession the prophet exists in many African cosmologies. For instance, among the Zande there are diviners who deliver messages from the spiritual domain and diviners who 'judge and appreciate the conjunction of signifiers and signified in a divinatory theme'.[24] This agent also appears in Te Ao Māori (the Māori world). Before any engagement with the biblical prophets, Māori relied upon *tohunga*, imperfectly translated as 'priest' but more accurately denoting those with expertise in a multiplicity of pursuits, skills or social organizations.[25] *Tohu* can be glossed as 'sign', hence, the expertise of *tohunga* emanated from their ability to interpret signs, including signs of change related to sustaining life or avoiding illness.[26]

Prophetic interpretations of signs implicate particular notions of temporality. In Chapter two I demonstrated that for Tāne/Māui and Legba the past is not dead but rather the prime site of agency composed of ancestors and attendant relationships that are contentiously bound up in issues of reciprocity, balance and justice, which resonate in the present. The prophet inhabits this temporality. Standing at the crossroads, the prophet senses the motile energies of the past through manifest signs that demand intervention in the present. The prophet therefore channels the binding skills of Tāne/Māui and Legba so that colonized History can give way to decolonial pasts. And key among these skills is the use of voice.

The words that the prophet enunciates are a passionate summons, an 'act formed with intention, depending on free will, the result of decision and determination'.[27] Unlike vision, sound is a sensibility that is constantly in movement; always fading from the moment of its reception, sound has to be consistently re-created and thus cannot exist without the use of power.[28] In Te Ao Māori this power is represented in the skill of chanting that Tāne recovered from the realm of *atua* in the third of his baskets of knowledge and that Māui utilizes to manipulate manifest arrangements into a more restitutive configuration. In a cognate register, some African cosmologies posit that the begotten force manifests order out of chaos by uttering the name of all things.[29] Humanity is then gifted this creative propensity. Furthermore, it is a commonplace assumption in many African cosmologies – including Diaspora variants – that to know the name of an entity is to have some degree of control over it. And as John 1.1 declares, 'In the beginning was the Word'.

The notion of 'wordsoundpower' in RasTafari encapsulates these cosmological propositions. In the RasTafari language certain words have to be changed either to expunge their negative vibration or because their sound masquerades their deeper meaning.[30] This language is also called I-yaric, which has the same relationship to Jamaican ('patois') as Ge'ez – the liturgical language of the Ethiopian Orthodox Church – has to the dominant Ethiopian vernacular, Amharic.[31] I-yaric seeks to heal the racial dehumanization that accompanied enslavement. To this end RasTafari use 'I' as an expansive pronoun that signifies a sanctified connectedness, i.e. 'I and I' (*tātou tātou*).[32] Therefore wordsounds do not just represent or signify power; their enactment and vibration *is* power.[33] Māori cosmologies share the concept of wordsoundpower. Indeed, *tohu* are not only nonverbal signs but must be enunciated as *kupu tohutohu* (words of import). Traditionally, these words are connected to discussion of *whakapapa* within *whare wānanga* (houses of learning).[34] Hone Kaa explains why wordsoundpower is crucial for the political vocation of the prophet: 'I believe that the reign of God is here now. The prophetic voice must be heard now. And the only way these things are realised is when you see justice being meted out.'[35]

And so the missionaries arrived in Oceania and the Caribbean. At the shores and borders of homelands, at the gates of plantations, or in the Baptist- and Quaker-sponsored free-villages that spotted the countryside post-emancipation, the recipients of this new knowledge acculturated biblical narratives and cosmology into their prophetic traditions. The diasporic children of Legba mapped the Christian cross of suffering onto the crossroads of healing that had travelled the Atlantic;[36] while in Aotearoa NZ, certain *tohunga* became *poropiti* (prophets), i.e. those who channelled the most sublime articulation of the concept of *atua*, Jehovah.[37]

As seers became prophets, their wordsoundpower was now required to proactively address the living consequences of enslavement, dehumanization, and/or war and dispossession of land. In this respect, anti-colonial prophets had to be redemptive agents of the Most High, invoking injustice, reparation, compassion, dread but also hope.[38] Redemption refers to both deliverance from (evil) and the recovery of what has been lost.[39] The voice of the prophet must open pathways to the uncolonized spiritual hinterlands that facilitate restitutive relationships between past and present, *tātou tātou* (I and I). Let us now witness these openings.

Israel and the Māori prophets

In 1807 Samuel Marsden persuaded the Church Missionary Society (CMS) to spread the word of God to Māori, and in 1814 he performed the first Christian service in Aotearoa NZ at the Bay of Islands. The CMS made clear to its missionaries that they were only to administer to Māori. Thus, for the first 40 years, Te Hāhi Mihinare (the Missionary Church) was effectively a Māori church.[40] In the early 1820s the CMS increased its promulgation activities; yet at the same time the number of Māori communities requesting a missionary in residence also grew.[41] In fact, the spread of Christianity outpaced the supply of missionaries.[42]

It is fair to say, then, that Māori – at least initially – proselytized themselves.

Māori became increasingly interested in the Christian faith, in part due to the debilitating effects of the Musket Wars, a multitude of battles spanning the first part of the nineteenth century fought largely between Māori tribes over existing fault-lines but with Pākehā weapons. But while war raged among Māori, the healing powers of *tohunga* could not seem to address the several diseases that accompanied the arrival of Pākehā. How could it be, then, that Māori were dying through war and disease, yet Pākehā remained relatively healthy and alive? (One influential explanation contended that the Pākehā god had sent the *ngārara* (lizard) to eat the entrails of its opponents.[43]) For all these reasons, the Pākehā god could not be ignored by Māori, but had to be interceded with.

Meanwhile, European missionaries claimed that providence had directed them to discover the peoples of Oceania through a colonial reading of Isaiah 11.11:[44]

> And it shall come to pass in that day, that the Lord shall set his hand again the second time to recover the remnant of his people, which shall be left, from Assyria, and from Egypt, and from Pathros, and from Cush, and from Elam, and from Shinar, and from Hamath, and from the islands of the sea.

But this verse can also be attributed an anti-colonial gloss because any interpretation hinges upon which people providence is said to be working for and through. Therefore, in order to properly acculturate the Bible, Māori would have to re-identify themselves as the elect of the apparently Pākehā god. Such a spiritual realignment required binding the children of the 'islands of the sea' into a redemptive *whakapapa* that preceded Christ and hence could be more venerable than the established European church in Christ's name. In this re-creation, Māori would become the true Israel.

One of the first Māori prophets to undertake this task was Papahurihia, who emerged into prominence around 1833, a time of

large-scale baptisms of Māori converts.[45] (In fact, there might have
been more than one figure who took on the titles associated with
Papahurihia.[46]) Taught to read at mission school, Papahurihia sought
to appropriate the power of the Bible by acculturating its narrative into
extant Māori cosmologies.[47] To this end he wove a spiritual universe
out of stories of Te Rēinga (the departure place for souls), Tāwhaki
(he who climbed to the highest heavens) and the Christian heaven
and hell.[48] Visiting Papahurihia on behalf of the CMS, Charles Baker
reported that his followers believed that 'the Bible was true, but that we
gave a wrong interpretation to it'.[49]

Similarly, for enslaved Africans and their descendants, the Bible was
often interpreted as their own story – the story of the Black Israelites.[50]
Even today it is not uncommon for biblical faith systems of the African
Diaspora to invoke spiritual Israel,[51] as is the case with the RasTafari
organization, the Twelve Tribes of Israel. Likewise, Papahurihia's
followers called themselves Hūrai (Jewish) and practised the Sabbath
on the Saturday and not Sunday.[52] By the late 1830s, Henry Williams
of the CMS found that half of the Māori he engaged with professed
Christianity, but the other half considered themselves Jews.[53] Two
years later, William Williams found that some of those who formerly
professed Christianity had now decided to also call themselves Jews.
By 1846 another CMS missionary, Richard Taylor, reported that Māori
had taken on the idea that they were the lost tribe of Israel.[54]

As was the case with enslaved Africans, Papahurihia's intimate
identification with Israel was also tied to the notion of redemption
and a return to ancestral land. Indeed, Papahurihia seems to have
imbibed the notion of Māori nationhood grounded in authority of
the land (*mana whenua*), a notion communicated to the world by the
1835 Declaration of Independence of Nu Tireni (He Wakaputanga o
te Rangatiratanga) and entered into by many of the chiefs who would
sign Te Tiriti five years later. Papahurihia hoisted a flag on a pole at
his encampment: a claim to national independence.[55] What is more,
the anti-colonial nationhood that he envisioned had its seedbed in
the spiritual hinterlands and evangelical missionaries were specifically

excluded entrance to heaven.[56] In the manifest domain, Papahurihia
was intimately involved in armed struggle over land. In fact, he acted
as a seer and spiritual influence for Hone Heke, a lay preacher as well as
celebrated warrior who began the Flagstaff War over the first colonial
settlement at Kororāreka. Writing in 1845, during the battles between
Heke and British soldiers, Rev. Robert Burrows reported in his diary
that '[o]ur native teacher was out holding service with Heke's people.
On his return he reported to me that Heke had been addressing the
people, comparing themselves to the persecuted children of Israel.'[57]

We should, therefore, approach Papahurihia less as an isolated
individual and more as the concentrated expression of a broad
movement that politicized the biblical hermeneutic as part of the defence
and pursuit of *mana motuhake*. Indeed, the construction of Māori
nationhood pronounced in the 1835 Declaration of Independence had,
to some extent, a biblical provenance itself. James Busby, the original
CMS missionary who at the time supported the preservation of Māori
authority against sinfully living settlers, suggested the idea of invoking
a new law. In and of itself, this is not an alien concept to Māori understandings of social order. For example, *tikanga* (the correct way) can
refer to not just what is right to do, but what is right *for the time*.[58]
Busby spoke of the new laws of Moses in this way – as precedents for
the formation of a redeemed nation. Hence, the Old Testament law
(Torah) was transliterated as *ture*, and manifested in the Declaration.[59]
The Māori text of Te Tiriti o Waitangi (The Treaty) that followed in
1840 deployed a word also transliterated from the Bible to express
the form of political authority that the British Crown would exercise
over Māori. *Kawanatanga*, as many Māori *rangatira* (chiefs) would
have been aware, referred to a specific kind of 'governorship' exercised
by Pontius Pilate over Israel – one that was not based on sovereign
ownership.[60]

If we envisage the 1835 Declaration and 1840 Treaty as one coherent
project to announce and defend Pan-Māori *mana motuhake*, then it
could be said that the construction by Māori of a mode of politically
relating to Pākehā at least partly rested upon the Māori assertion that

they were the Jews of the Bible. And so too did the response to the Treaty's abrogation.

One of the most influential responses was a movement that sought to put in place a Māori king who could bring *hāpu* and *iwi* (familial and political groupings) together in a way that would match the unity of the British imperial state under Queen Victoria. Wiremu Tamihana Tarapipi Te Waharoa, known as the 'king maker', played a key role in adjudicating genealogical lines of *rangatira* (chiefs) in order to find such a personality who might bind the peoples together in unity (*kotahitanga*). The king maker was himself baptized, heavily versed in the Bible, and took 1 Samuel 8.5 as his instruction: 'give us a king to judge us.'[61] Tamihana found his king in the person of Pōtatau Te Wherowhero, who had signed the Declaration of Independence sometime between 1835 and 1839.[62]

The Kīngitanga (Māori King Movement) also affirmed a shift in the meaning and practice of *mana* ('lawful authority delegated by the gods'). After the constant warfare of the past decades, a new spiritual law was required to bind Māori together in unity and the Christian focus on forgiveness and *agape* (beloved community) was mobilized for this purpose.[63] However, once more, *mana* pursued through *aroha* (love, sympathy) was no alien idea. In some Māori cosmologies the valedictory address given to those who were departing mythical Hawaiki for islands anew was to 'go, then, and live in peace with all men, and leave war and strife behind you.'[64] In the service that conferred kingship on Pōtatau, Tamihana the king maker, after invoking the name Aotearoa, rehearsed a hymn sung at that time in the Māori churches, *Ka Mahue a Īhipa*, which testified that 'forsaken now is Egypt, the land of sin and shame. A new home (we) now seek.'[65] But Pōtatau was at pains to embed the new *atuatanga* (practice of worship) within a *whakapapa* of Māori indigenization: 'in the time when our ancestors travelled from Hawaiki to Aotearoa, it was Uenuku – the consumer of mankind. Today, and forever more, it shall be Jehovah of the multitudes.'[66] Here, then, was a dread love, a redemptive love of community that sought to manifest Zion on earth.

In all these ways the God of the Bible was acculturated as the Māori God who would usher in a new dispensation of *mana motuhake* for the Israelites of the 'islands of the sea'. Announced in 1835, this dispensation was to be pursued subsequently by the Kīngitanga with the help of the prophets.

Ham and Shem's redemption

As a site of anti-colonial struggle the Bible became implicated in two distinct but intimately related projects of reparation. The first focused upon the defence and reconsolidation of claims to political autonomy among *rangatira* (chiefs), as enunciated in the 1835 Declaration and 1840 Treaty. The second focused upon the multitudes that were suffering from the wider effects of war, enslavement and dispossession. Prophets mobilized the authority of the Bible to conjointly redeem chiefly autonomy *and* the suffering multitude. This pursuit led one prophet to cultivate an anti-colonial relationship between the biblical Tāne/Māui and Legba – Shem and Ham.

The scene had been set by the Musket Wars of the 1820s, which resulted in significant numbers of Māori being captured by various northern tribes and taken away to become *mōkai* – slaves. Enslaved, the captives would usually be taught the Christian *rongopai* (Good News) at missionary schools, especially around the Bay of Islands.[67] However, when *rangatira* (chiefs) accepted the new faith, they would often free *ngā mōkai* (the slaves) because Christians could not own other Christians as slaves. The freed would then return to their homelands taking their teachings of Christian deliverance with them.[68]

These teachings were of great value to the Māori sufferers affirming as they did the radical equality of all souls in the presence of Jehovah, thus redeeming their own standing that had been stripped when they had become *mōkai*.[69] A subsidiary effect of this movement was to democratize knowledge of Io – the begotten – as Jehovah, who then began to appear in historical records.[70] In this respect, and similar, we might remember, to the cosmologies of enslaved Africans in the Americas, emergency conditions impelled a more direct intercession with the Most High. Yet this did not mean that other spiritual agents and agencies were to be ignored. As we shall now see, Tāne/Māui and Legba would still be engaged with by the Māori prophetic tradition, but in their biblical personalities of Shem and Ham.

One prophet emerged who bound the redemption of the multitude of sufferers to the kingly pursuit of self-determination. Te Ua Haumene was born in Taranaki and raised as a slave of the Waikato in Kawhia. Baptized, Te Ua returned to his birthplace and worked in the local Wesleyan mission school.[71] Te Ua's first recorded political act occurred fairly late in his life: in 1861, he refused Bishop Selwyn passage through the boundaries that delineated the authority of the Kīngitanga (King Movement). Following the missionary reading of John 5.23, Selwyn had sought to convince Māori that their new faith was born 'half-caste' (he transliterated the English racial term as *hawhekaihe*) with English 'fathers in God'.[72] Te Ua begged to differ. One year later, he had formed his own church; he had no need of a European avatar in order to find intercession with Jahovah.

Te Ua's church continued many of the practices instigated by the prophet Papahurihia. Communion and prophecy took place around flagpoles, called *niu*, a term that denotes the traditional divination sticks used by *tohunga*, and which is also a transliteration of 'news'.[73] Additionally, Te Ua continued the prophetic identification of Māori as Jews. He considered Aotearoa NZ to be the 'new Canaan', the books of Moses to be the law (*ture*), and Saturday the Sabbath.[74] Furthermore, Te Ua's mission was closely related to the Kīngitanga and the political struggle for *mana motuhake*.[75] Te Ua himself baptized the second Māori king as Tāwhiao, after the movement's military defeat in the Waikato wars of the early 1860s. Following Te Ua, Tāwhiao subsequently rejected the European Christian missions.[76]

Wordsoundpower was an important weapon for Paimārire, the name that Te Ua gave his mission and which meant ineffable or perfect goodness. But the settlers called it *hauhau*. And in their minds, this term marked Te Ua's liberation theology as savage fanaticism, far from God. However, *hau* can be glossed as 'breath' and is a term that is fundamental to Māori cosmology. Hauora, along with Tāne, a child of Ranginui (sky father) and Papatūānuku (earth mother), personifies the spiritual impulse of *hau* that 'urges reciprocity in human relations with nature and in relations with other people'.[77] Te Ua's followers practised the rapid uttering of this word so as to channel such divine force.[78] Thus, far from barbaric fanaticism, *hauhau* was the wordsound of divine restitution on earth.

In a cognate strategy to the I-yaric tongue of RasTafari, Te Ua transliterated English words and combined them with original Te Reo (Māori language). Some of these words would even be taken from the sounds made by European soldiers marching. With these wordsounds Paimārire members could gain access to the power held by these soldiers. The wordsound itself was provided by *hau* (the sacred breath), not by Europeans, and none but members of Paimārire could speak it.[79] Such practices were, of course, in line with Pentecost and the practice of 'speaking in tongues' that also regularly accompanied prophesying around the *niu* (flagpole).[80] In fact, one Pākehā reverend reported that Paimārire members called this practice 'talking English'.[81] So Te Ua's Israelites were not mute subalterns; but they did choose to be unintelligible to Britannica.

Te Ua wrote a gospel. It begins by bringing together God's covenant with Abraham and the eschatological revelations of John.[82] With these elements, Te Ua addresses the fundamentals of liberation theology by claiming the genealogical authority for Māori as the elect of God, as well as prophesying the redemption of righteous Māori. Identifying Māori as God's people, Te Ua affirms that they 'will be restored, even to that which was given unto Abraham, for this is Israel'.[83] But then Te Ua makes a moral argument for the restitution of indigenous *mana whenua* (authority of the land) by binding the fate of Māori with that of the Africans under European colonialism. Te Ua claims that it was wrong that Esau as well as 'the black race of old were excluded, because he [God] made both black and white. Thus are they one body in the god of peace.'[84] Esau was firstborn of Isaac whose birthright was robbed by Jacob. And the Black race that Te Ua refers to are, of course, the descendants of Ham, whose son Canaan was bound by Noah to be a servant to his uncles Shem (ancestor of the Jewish peoples) and Japheth (commonly considered as ancestor to European peoples).

Te Ua's gospel is remarkably decolonial if we compare it to the interpretations of Ham's fate prevalent in contemporaneous missionary theologies. At this point, existing colour descriptors in Te Reo had started to articulate with the categories and valuations of racial and racist settler-colonial discourse. *Kiri mā / kiri mangu* now marked the archetypal Manichean distinction between 'white skin' and 'black skin' that formed the fundamental grammar of Atlantic slavery.[85] And the missionaries in Aotearoa NZ by and large perpetuated the messages formed by this grammar, even after the proclamation of formal emancipation in the British Caribbean colonies. For instance, in 1847 the CMS wrote in Te Reo (the Māori language) that 'this passage about all the descendants of Ham, the people of Africa, is true: they are the people who are enslaved and degraded by each other and by other nations of Europe and Africa'.[86] A conversation in 1828 between Henry Williams and a Māori, who confirmed to Williams that the tempter of Adam and Eve had been a black man, demonstrates that the dissemination of CMS ideology was at least partially successful.[87]

Yet Te Ua's gospel marks a radical departure from the colonial segregation of Ham's children from humanity at large. In his gospel, Africans and Māori, enslavement and dispossession, all bind together as elements in the same global colonial injustice. It is a distinct moment. In Te Ua's early life, land dispossession and enslavement have, for a time, conjoined as part of the same Babylon forces that conspire to destroy Te Ao Māori (the Māori world). He himself has grown up as a *mōkai* (slave) – those sufferers whom missionaries have already coloured black and African. Using the Bible as a compass Te Ua opens himself to the intercessionary energies of Ham and Shem who he witnesses walking together in the spiritual hinterlands, facing the colonial frontier in solidarity.

The relationship between Africa and Oceania that Te Ua channels from the spiritual hinterlands into the manifest domain is a very different one from that proseltyized by the Pākehā avatars of Christ. Te Ua's gospel expunges the racist missionary ideology that offers salvation for Shem on the condition that he affirms damnation for Ham. Rather, Te Ua channels the decolonial solidarity between Ham and Shem into a project that seeks to bind the kingly pursuit of *mana motuhake* to the redemption of the suffering multitudes. For Ham is the agent of the enslaved, those stripped of rank and status – the sufferers; and Shem is the agent of rightful rulers who have been dispossessed of their *mana* (authority delegated by the gods). Te Ua announces that the restitution of *mana motuhake* requires the redemption of both the sufferers *and* the kingly. He has found a balm to the categorical segregations that colonial science seeks to visit upon black and brown, the enslaved and dispossessed, the kingly and the sufferers.

Might this specific conjuncture, wherein Ham and Shem intercede in the same struggle against colonial injustice, have also influenced the Kīngitanga to think along the same lines? There is, indeed, evidence that some who associated with the Kīngitanga identified with the Blackness of Ham. Hora Ngātai-rākaunui, for example, implored Māori to separate from Pākehā, reasoning that 'my skin is black skin, my canoe is a Māori canoe'.[88] Tāwhiao, the second Māori King, baptized by Te Ua, proclaimed: 'in the past we were noble people. Now, although the skin is black, let the business of those who organize things be clear, to cleave to the law, love and faith …'[89] Against the imperial army, Tāwhiao also called for Māori support by invoking the unity of race: 'all black skinned people, whether on the side of the Queen [Victoria] or [Māori] King'.[90]

Ngā Tamatoa were therefore right to claim that Black Power was not a foreign invention and had an indigenous provenance. Yet they were wrong to think that this provenance was not already bound up with the fate of the diasporic children of Legba. In fact, there is evidence that the identification with Blackness at this point was cultivated by explicit reference to the struggles of the African Diaspora against enslavement and colonial rule. For instance, Tamihana the king maker looked to the Black empire of Haiti as an instructive example of *kotahitanga* (unity) and *mana motuhake*,[91] that is, as a successful post-slave-holding, postcolonial independent polity. And Lachlan Paterson has drawn attention to the publication in the Kīngitanga propaganda newspaper of a series of reports on the Haitian Revolution wherein Wiremu Pātara Te Tuhi draws favourable comparisons between the contemporaneous Māori resistance of 1863 and the Black resistance of 1791–1804. Utilizing information probably provided by a French Catholic priest, the Haitian revolutionaries are described in the text as both *taua iwi Māori* – 'that native race' – and *tau[a] iwi kiri mangu* – 'that black skinned race', while the Spanish are described as *te iwi kiri ma* – 'the white skinned race'.[92] Taking Haitians rather than French or Americans to be the revolutionary people to emulate, the newspaper suggests: 'Wait a little and perhaps the Rangatiratanga [chieftainship] of this island will be like that of Haiti; possessing goods, authority, law … Perhaps God will protect his black skinned children who are living in Aotearoa'.[93]

Conclusion

On behalf of Israel, Te Ua stands at the crossroads and there channels an intercession between the manifest and spiritual domains. In the spiritual hinterlands he witnesses Ham and Shem facing in solidarity the manifest struggle against enslavement and dispossession. One of the chants of Paimārire members, which sought to disarm colonial soldiers, finishes with 'Shem, Ham, Father Glory, verily, Hau'.[94] This wordsound manifests the anti-colonial connectivity that has been retrieved from the spiritual hinterlands. Hauora, it will be remembered, is the spiritual agent of reciprocity. Hence the chant can be apprehended as a divine mandate: Shem and Ham will together redeem the sufferers from the segregations and de-sanctifications of colonial science. Let us at this point also recall Tigilau Ness's visual depiction of the grounding sought by Keskidee Aroha between the children of Tāne/Māui and Legba: *kowhaiwhai* rooting with/as dreadlocks. This is art as prescience, reaching deep to retrieve a relation across time and space already sighted by a Māori prophet of the nineteenth century.

Te Ua's gospel is concluded with a fragment added later at the hand of an unknown scribe of the Kīngitanga. It commands: 'Do not return to the house of Japheth, but return to the house of Shem ... The heavy yoke has been cast off ... I have returned to my birthright.'[95] In this text dispossessed Shem no longer stands with enslaved Ham. The topography of the spiritual hinterlands which Te Ua gleaned has shifted, and Ham has receded from prophetic sight. Perhaps the context that marked Te Ua's life, wherein enslavement coexisted with dispossession, had drawn to a close. Indeed, while the idea of an enslaved people was to be deployed a number of times subsequently, especially by the prophet Te Kooti,[96] most movements that followed Te Ua tended to focus solely upon the redemption of the house of Shem – the Māori Israelites, elect of God. By the turn of the twentieth century, Walter Edward Gudgeon, land court judge, colonial administrator and soldier, would write that *atua* was also called *Hema*, 'who the Māori delight to identify with Shem, the son of Noah.'[97]

But regardless, Shem and Ham still walk together in the uncolonized spiritual hinterlands. They are busy giving energy and direction to the *whakapapa of mana motuhake* that is binding Aotearoa NZ to South Africa and Ethiopia. Approximately 70 years after the end of Te Ua's mission, the invasion in 1935 of Ethiopia by Italy gives rise to mass movements of the African Diaspora whose Ethiopianism, similar to Paimārire, seeks both the liberation of the destitute sufferers and the preservation of kingly *mana motuhake* in the person of Haile Selassie I.[98] Both the RasTafari faith and the Māori prophetic tradition bind kingship and the suffering multitudes together in the pursuit of anti-colonial self-determination and restitutive justice. Forty years after Italy's invasion, no time at all really, a new generation of sufferers start to slowly enfold RasTafari into the living prophetic traditions of Aotearoa NZ. Shem and Ham will be reunited in prophetic wordsound.[99]

Rātana, Baxter, RasTafari

Introduction

At the start of this book I presented the key task of decolonial science as the repair of relations hacked by colonial practices of segregation. For this task, binding skills are required that can reach deep into the spiritual domain, all the way to its uncolonized hinterlands. Grounding seeks to recover this depth of relation. It is contentious and comprised of many moments – comparison, identification, inhabitation and enfolding – that are not organized along sequential lines but along degrees of intensity. The moment of enfolding requires a journey into the hinterlands to be made, there to retrieve seminal relations, in our case between the children of Tāne/Māui and Legba in their biblical manifestations as Shem and Ham. Relationality in the spiritual hinterlands is governed neither by existential (colonial) 'encounters' between discretely and pre-defined self and other, nor by an imperial desire to destroy relation for the sake of homogeneity (genocide). What we recover is rather a relation that is seminal, i.e. already part of oneself – *tātou tātou*, I and I. This has been the latent relation present in all the groundings that we have witnessed, but it is now manifest.

Before we walked with the prophets we examined how the RasTafari faith has been inhabited on indigenous grounds. We shall now consider how RasTafari has been enfolded into the prophetic traditions of Aotearoa NZ. To this end we shall walk with two prophets and prophetic traditions: one, an indigenous Māori faith – Rātana

– and the other an endogenous Pākehā poet – Baxter. (I have already suggested that between theology and the liberated spirit there stands art, the quotidian theology of the sufferers. Hence, it is not impossible to consider that some poets might also be prophets.) We shall witness how, in different ways, the Rātana faith and Baxter poetic enfold RasTafari into their prophetic matter, so as to redeem the *mana motuhake* (self-determination) of contemporary sufferers, and to provide restitution for the crimes of Cook and Columbus.

Te Māngai, Te Mōrehu and RasTafari

The coming of Tahupōtiki Wiremu Rātana was spoken of as far back as the 1820s.[1] Rātana's personal *whakapapa* connected him to the Kīngitanga (King Movement) as well as to other prophet movements. Tāwhiao, the second Māori king, baptized by Te Ua, even prophesied the day of Rātana's passing, 18 September 1939, as 'a time of godly presence and he it is, who will be a sacrificial lamb to the lord Jehovah'.[2] Rātana's aunt, Atareta Kāwana Roiha Mere Rikiriki, was well thought of by King Tāwhiao, who gifted to her a flag with the words *E te iwi kia ora* (blessings to the people).[3] Rikiriki emphasized the New Testament dispensation of the *Wairua Tapu* (Holy Spirit) but was also well versed in faith-healing techniques and traditional herbal healing.[4] Rikiriki prophesied that her nephew would become a redeemer of Māori, and counselled Rātana to follow 'the god of his ancestors' – the god of Abraham, Isaac and Jacob.[5]

When two whales beached themselves near his home, Rātana took this as a sign that he was called to be a fisher of men. In 1918 Rātana was visited by the *Wairua Tapu* (Holy Spirit) who, he recalls, revealed the following: 'I have visited the scene of the war which has recently waged in Europe. In my travels I have found that the whole world has forgotten me. I have looked all over for some place to establish myself.'[6] Rātana's wife, Te Urumanao, was also visited by the Spirit, who declared to her, 'you shall be known as Te Whaea o te katoa' (the mother of all).[7] The Holy Spirit had therefore decided to abide with Māori, in a context marked by the end of the First World War and the onset of the depression that deeply affected the Western world. Rātana's mission appealed to many Māori whose families and communities were still recovering from the effects of war and the influenza epidemic, and were then hit by significant job losses in the freezing works and forestry industry.[8] A certain militancy grew with this suffering, and Rātana catalysed these feelings as he travelled widely across the country collecting stories of hardship and dispossession.[9] His congregation flocked to Rātana Pa, also called Hiruhārama Hou – New Jerusalem.

I wish to situate Rātana as a prophet of the Te Ua tradition, that is, one who sought to bind the kingly pursuit of *mana motuhake* to the redemption of the dispossessed multitudes. 'In one of my hands is the Bible; in the other is the Treaty of Waitangi':[10] with this utterance Rātana followed the prophetic vocation of channelling the forces of biblical intercession, just as Te Ua had done. Furthermore, just like Te Ua, Rātana intentionally associated himself with the Kīngitanga, modelling his relationship along Old Testament lines: 'leave me as I am, a prophet. The work of the prophet is to show the way the king should go.'[11] Rātana also possessed a sense of historical Māori nationhood and announced, on more than one occasion, the name of the Māori nation set out in the 1835 Declaration of Independence – Niu Tireni. For example, in a cablegram to the British Prime Minister in 1924 Rātana identified his mission as *te iwi Māori o Niu Tireni* (the Māori tribe of Niu Tireni).[12]

Rātana had to contend with a hostile political climate wherein the prophetic tradition itself had become associated with quackery. Apirana Ngata, the founder of Te Aute Old Boys, had contributed to this interpretation when he, alongside Western-trained health professionals (both Māori and Pākehā), led the move to enact a Suppression of Tohunga act in 1907.[13] It is no doubt true that many charlatans existed who 'practised' under the label of *tohunga* (learned ones). However, there was a deeper political current that carried the act. For we should not forget that prophets such as Te Ua, Te Kooti and their followers had been actively involved in anti-colonial struggles. It is telling, for example, that in the debate over the act, Ngata described as 'bastard tohungaism'[14] the mission of Rua Kenana, a successor to Te Kooti who had set up a self-determining community at Maungapohatu, soon to proclaim himself the Māori brother of Christ.[15] In effect, the Act sought to disarm the prophetic tradition, to 'Christianize Māori',[16] and finally close the colonial frontier on the spiritual hinterlands once and for all.

Rātana himself was adamant that 'tohungaism' had to be 'annihilated'. However, being a child of Māui, he did not seek to destroy the Māori foundations of faith, but rather, wished to rearrange them in a manner useful for the present day. Specifically, Rātana sought to end the spiritual practices associated with some *tohunga* that caused illness and death.[17] In this respect, he was in the company of Te Ua who had also sought to eradicate 'witchcraft' but keep the 'worthwhile things' of Māori customs,[18] a platform that Rātana inherited through his aunt Rikiriki.

Increased government surveillance followed the Tohunga Suppression Act, focusing mainly on sanitation at the Rātana Pa. At the same time the established church, watchful of Rātana's popularity, began to question the prophet's credence, especially his inclusion of certain liturgical and theological elements that could be interpreted as heathen, elements that we shall engage with presently.[19] In this hostile climate, Rātana protected his mission by registering as a denominated church on Pentecost, 31 May 1925. By then he had caught in his net 18 per cent of the Māori population, who declared themselves members.[20] For the first time the Te Ua prophetic tradition – the pursuit of kingly *mana motuhake* for the redemption of suffering multitudes – was housed in a registered, nationwide institution.

Rātana took his mission to the world. One year prior to registration Rātana had embarked on an international tour with an entourage that included 24 musicians. The purpose was to present to George V in London the petition that Rātana had gathered (with 34,000 signatures) calling for the honouring of Te Tiriti o Waitangi (The Treaty).[21] Rātana subsequently made another tour to the USA in 1925 that was much more focused upon building funds for his movement.[22] In the spiritual hinterlands Te Ua had witnessed the solidarity of Ham and Shem as they faced colonial injustices in the manifest domain. Now Rātana would retrieve this anti-colonial relationship as he travelled the colonial world.

En route to Britain in 1924, the entourage passed through South Africa. In Durban, Rātana was distressed to find out that a Zulu chief had been reduced to driving a rickshaw. He took a photo of himself with the *rangatira* (chief) to convey to his followers their fate should Te Tiriti (The Treaty) remain dishonoured: they would become slaves (*mōkai*) with no standing, a fate intimately known to Te Ua and many of his contemporaries.[23] In Cape Town, Rātana noted the ill-treatment of African dock workers by whites and laid out a mat of *kai* (food) on the wharf for them.[24] He did the same for Black dock workers upon arrival in England.[25] During the South African stop-over, Rātana prophesied:

> I have seen and indeed witnessed these black-skinned people treated like dogs; I am hurt by this. Yet it shall come to pass, that in Jehovah's time and place, he shall lift these people up.

The Rātana faithful point out that 70 years later, almost to the month, Nelson Mandela became the first Black president of South Africa.[26]

Rātana's groundings with the children of Legba is notable. But his world tours can also be placed within the *whakapapa* of *mana motuhake* that, a couple of chapters prior, I demonstrated binds together Ethiopia and Aotearoa NZ. In fact, Rātana seems to have been aware of the fabled African land of Prester John. It is said, for instance, that Rātana wished to visit a number of polities on the African continent, including sovereign Ethiopia, but was blocked by authorities in South Africa.[27] Had Rātana read or been informed by his elders of that report on the Battle of Adwa and the Kingdom of Ethiopia published in 1900 by the Māori Parliament newspaper?

In any case, Rātana's extended sojourn in Britain coincided with the short visit by Crown Prince Ras Tafari of Ethiopia in the summer of 1924. Both attended the British Empire Exhibition at Wembley.[28] Whether or not their paths crossed, Rātana soon left for Geneva to present the case of the Māori people to the seat of world governance – the League of Nations in Geneva.[29] Although Rātana deposited the petition at the League, he won no formal hearing. Sitting in the chair of the president, while the League was out of session, Rātana remarked that all nations were represented there except for Māori.[30] Haile Selassie I would make the same journey from Britain for the same reasons 12 years later and stand in front of the chair of the president to make an appeal for international morality that fell on deaf ears. Yet nevertheless, Ruia Aperahama, historian and adherent of the Rātana faith, argues that Selassie I provides an important message for Māori: the need to pursue and preserve *mana motuhake*. For unlike the emperor, Rātana could not even speak at Geneva because Māori had lost their self-governance to the settler state of New Zealand.[31]

For every king there is a prophet. And the next year Rātana was to actually cross paths with the prophet of the Hamitic King RasTafari, Marcus Garvey. Aperahama has revealed that Rātana visited Garvey during his second world tour to the USA in August 1925, as he languished in an Atlanta prison on charges of mail fraud.[32] In their brief encounter, Garvey had even provided Rātana with a guest ticket for his Black Star shipping line.[33] The shipping line was – and remains – incredibly symbolic for the African Diaspora, manifesting, especially for members of the RasTafari faith, repatriation back across the Atlantic to the African continent. It is striking that Rātana, the Shemetic prophet, is offered passage on the vessel of Ham's redemption. In October 1925 Rātana was witness to the parades of Garvey's UNIA in New York. And the Māori prophet part modelled the uniform for the Katipa – the Rātana faith's wardens – along the lines of the UNIA's police force.[34]

Shem and Ham walk together in the uncolonized spiritual hinterlands. Sometimes they are visible. Sometimes they recede from manifest sight. But now, the Shemetic prophet and the Hamitic king walk parallel paths in the manifest domain, on the stage of international politics, and the paths of the Shemetic and Hamitic prophets actually cross. The ground has thus been prepared on which RasTafari can be enfolded into the Māori prophetic tradition. But because this ground is material-and-spiritual we will have to witness this enfolding through a theological register. And at this point I will call upon a Rātana theology that is elaborated by Te Whakaotinga Ron Smith, who was chair of Te Omeka Marae Trust, an important institution in the Rātana world.

It will be remembered that, under pressure through the Suppression of Tohunga Act, Rātana took a strategic decision to register as a Christian denomination. Smith argues that, in fact, the faith possesses its own distinct theology and philosophy.[35] For Smith, the Rātana creed is eschatological (concerned with the ultimate destiny of humanity) and also steeped in the *whakataukī* (proverbs, utterances, wordsound) of the Māori prophets.[36] Central to Rātana theology, therefore, is a focus on acculturation, i.e. that Māori come to know the Good News (Rongo Pai) through their extant customs and ways of life, which are also gifts of Jehovah.[37] Against the colonial gloss of John 5.23 the Rātana faith asserts that the word of God is not solely carried by European avatars; it can also be heard in the utterances of ancestors. RasTafari follow prophet Garvey's cognate commandment that Africans must worship God through the lens of Ethiopia,[38] or, in the language of liberation theology, they must become Black with God. Hence they must also stop worshipping the white Christ presented in the missionary reading of John 5.23.

There are significant theological differences within the RasTafari faith over the manifestation of the Black Christ. Nevertheless, most seek to reappropriate Jesus at the level of wordsoundpower: the subservient sound of 'me' is removed so that Jesus (pronounced J-ee-sus) becomes Iyesos (I-yes-os) Kristos.[39] The prophet Rātana also considered the name Jesus Christ to have been desecrated and made *noa* (profane) by Pākehā.[40] Hence, while Jesus Christ was the name of the physical manifestation that suffered and died on the cross, Rātana argued that the everlasting and living spiritual agency of that person was *tama* – the Son (of God).[41] *Tama* – the Son – is the name that is uttered at the beginning of creation.[42] By this reasoning Smith argues that the covenant of Iyesos (the word made flesh) cannot be the final dispensation of God's will, closing the drama with the death of Jesus on the cross; rather, there are subsequent dispensations because the spiritual agency of the Son (*Tama*) lives on.[43] As Black Israel takes back guardianship of the Black Christ, so does Indigenous Israel take back guardianship of the Māori *Tama*.

With guardianship retrieved, new covenants can be made with the Shemetic and Hamitic sufferers. For RasTafari, the dispensation of Haile Selassie I exceeds the end of the Bible, and his 'new name' opens the 'seven seals' of Revelation 5.5 to usher in African redemption through the covenant of the Organisation of African Unity (OAU). In Rātana's covenant of the 'New Heaven and New Earth'[44] the prophet takes the name of Te Māngai. *Mā* can be glossed as 'by means of', and *Ngai* is an ancient word for breath.[45] This name therefore references the prophetic tradition of channelling energies between the spiritual and manifest domains through means of wordsoundpower as, for example, undertaken by the followers of Te Ua as they rapidly uttered '*hau*' (wind, breath). In this sense, although Rātana was flesh and blood as was Jesus, Te Māngai manifests the ever-living spiritual agency of *tama*.[46]

The new covenants of Rātana and RasTafari radically upset the narratives of missionary Christianity, which place the beginning and the end firmly within colonial history. Alluding to Revelation 1.8 both Aperahama and Ron Smith make a cognate distinction between Jesus as the 'beginning and the end' of the book, and 'Alpha and Omega' (first and last) that precedes and succeeds the book.[47] Likewise, for RasTafari, Selassie I, with Empress Menen, represent not the beginning and the end of the book, but the Alpha and Omega. Smith puts it this way: the beginning and the end – i.e. the story of the Bible – belongs to all humanity, but Alpha/Omega is the spiritual seedbed of creation and belongs to 'us' who in this time are the *mōrehu*.[48] This word can be glossed as 'remnants', those who have been disregarded and dispossessed,[49] not victims nor dying but living survivors,[50] or, as RasTafari would say, the Black Survivors or 'sufferers'.

Both Rātana and RasTafari extend the dispensations of the Bible before and after colonial rule so as to place *kaitiakitanga* (guardianship) of the Bible with the (post)colonized suffering multitudes. These are the indigenous liberation theologies sought by Spivey, Borrie, Gnanasundaram and Reeves. In this decolonial temporality, no (post)colonized people would consider themselves to be subaltern but they would apprehend themselves rather as sanctified sufferers who relate to each other through the spiritual hinterlands and across the manifest domain by means of wordsoundpower: 'Shem, Ham, Father Glory, verily, Hau!' Take, for instance, Miriama Rauhihi-Ness, the first Sister Dinah of the Twelve Tribes of Israel in Aotearoa NZ. Rauhihi-Ness grew up in a Rātana household and so the image of a white Jesus was absent. For this reason, her 'sighting up' of Haile Selassie I as Kristos did not have to traverse any colonially induced racial segregation between the saviours and the damned, the avatars and the unsanctified.[51]

Rauhihi-Ness's experience signals the intimate theological connections between RasTafari and Rātana. And one of the Rātana faithful has creatively reconstituted this connection through a 'Shemetic *whakapapa*'.

It is no surprise that roots reggae received an early prominence among Rātana musicians who were already attuned to the relationship between songs, music and spirit.[52] One such musician is Carl Perkins, one-time member of the famous reggae band Herbs, and current member of the House of Shem.[53] Perkins' family is steeped in the Rātana faith. His father and aunt were baptized and named by Rātana himself as Pa-o-te-omeka (Peter Perkins) and Te Wai-o-turi (Turi Kui). Even Perkins' English grandfather, who had settled from England, was baptized into the Rātana faith. Perkins is a RastaFari follower of the prophet Gad of the Twelve Tribes of Israel, but he has also been rebaptized in the Rātana faith; Rātana and RasTafari iconography both adorn his workplace. In Perkins' estimation, Rātana opened a space for RasTafari. The purpose of Rātana's mission, argues Perkins, is to seek justice and redemption, and Selassie I 'reminds us of that', as does Gadman (the prophet of the Twelve Tribes of Israel), as did Jesus, as did Noah.

Perkins catalogues this relationship of Rātana to RasTafari through what he calls a 'shemetic *whakapapa*'. He starts by situating Ham within the African Garden of Eden from whence Adam and Eve came. The vocation of Shem – the peoples of Oceania – is consonant with the archetypal journeyman Māui: to undertake significant migrations. Leaving the garden and the corrupted old world far behind him, Shem travels far into the sea of islands. In this Oceanic environment, morally unpolluted by the ancient world, Shem safeguards 'zeal' and 'faith' in order to one day return it to the rest of humanity. Perkins likens this purpose to the lot of Shem that in *John Gill's Expositions of the Entire Bible* (1746–8) is documented as the duty to return Adam's body to Eden in order to ensure proper burial.[54]

Perkins' *whakapapa* creatively re-constitutes a deep, global infra-structure of anti-colonial connectivity. If we consider, as RasTafari do, that the first human (Adam/Eve) is African, then in this story of creation, indigenous Shem has a special part to play in the repatriation of Ham. As the archetypal sojourner, Shem is tasked with bringing Ham home. In this respect, the birthright from which Shem has been recently dispossessed – *mana whenua* (authority of the land) – is once again intimately related to the liberation of Ham from unjust bondage, as had been the case in Te Ua's gospel. This is a Shemetic *whakapapa* wherein Alpha and Omega precedes and succeeds the beginning and the end of the white man's Bible. RasTafari has been enfolded into the Māori prophetic tradition.

Hemi, Ngā Mōkai and an African tribesman

In Aotearoa NZ, Catholicism was a minor denomination of European Christianity compared to the Protestant-led Church Missionary

Society (CMS) and was ambiguously and tenuously related to colonial rule. Catholicism was influential in the Māramatanga movement that Rātana's aunt, Rikiriki, was a member of.[55] In fact, not too far from Rātana Pa, up the Whanganui River, the Catholic Society of Mary (Marists) had, in the later nineteenth century, set up mission stations. Marists such as Mother Suzanne Aubert took a vow of poverty and so did not, as was often the case with the CMS, engage in land buying and speculation. Mother Aubert even argued that Māori should not be made 'second-rate Europeans' and that the job of the missionary should be to help to preserve and encourage the good qualities of Māori culture.[56] Like Ngā Tamatoa, Mother Aubert disliked the concept of 'brown skinned Pākehā'.

By the 1970s a number of Pākehā who had received Catholic instruction of various kinds (including training in the Marist order) became involved in experiments to rekindle and refashion an *agape* (beloved community) specific to Aotearoa NZ. Many were influenced by Vatican II, some by Paolo Friere,[57] but the closest figure that they responded to was James K. Baxter. Baxter's life is marked by a rebaptizing from 'Jim the Catholic family man' to 'Hemi the prophet' (Hemi being the Māori transliteration of Jim). His internationally renowned poetic work is marked by a concomitant shift from classical Greek to Māori myth structures and the *tēina/tuākana* (younger and elder sibling) relationship.[58] In Baxter we might identify a poet of Arcadian Hermes.

Hemi's visit to India in the late 1950s on a UNESCO fellowship seems to have prompted his efforts to ground with Te Ao Māori (the Māori world) as he became exposed to not just extreme poverty but also the dignity of the poor.[59] Consequently Hemi set about re-examining the morality of the apparently more advanced society that Pākehā settlers had built in Aotearoa NZ. He found it absent of an 'ethical code'.[60] In fact, the depersonalization and de-sacralization of social relations encouraged by modern urban culture had produced instrumental creatures who related to others as things rather than as beings.[61] Meanwhile, schooling operated along the lines of authoritarian rule, treating students as if they were 'Israelites in Egypt'.[62] Love, proposed Hemi, 'has to share, directly or indirectly, the pain of the beloved'.[63] But settler society had destroyed the social bases of *agape* except for in the stifled air of the nuclear patriarchal family.[64]

Hemi's proposed resolution to this crisis was in many ways unprecedented: the younger siblings (*tēina*), the Pākehā, could only redeem themselves by appealing to their elder siblings (*tuākana*), the Māori, for guidance. Instead of a colonial science of segregation, Hemi opted for a decolonial science on the terms of those who already inhabited the ground for relating. He approached this science through the language of liberation theology.[65] And to this end Hemi decided to take on the prophetic role of Jeremiah, redirecting the people away from the disenchanted Pākehā church towards the streets and their inhabitant poor, where God dwelled.[66] There, outside of Pākehā institutions, they would find Jesus walking – a Māori Jesus.

Hemi's 1966 poem, *Māori Jesus*, can be read as a Pākehā articulation of the RasTafari and Rātana practice of refiguring the key avatar of God on earth as the (post)colonized sufferer.[67] The Māori Jesus, in Hemi's poem, is poor, even uncouth, and the light of the world. He is lobotomized for uttering 'I am who I am' – a wordsound that is offensive to settler colonialism in so far as it manifests a personal relation to the seedbed of creation. This was a relation that, as Hone Kaa had demonstrated in the Programme to Combat Racism workshops, not even the European avatars of Christ could claim. That is why the wordsound of 'Māori Jesus' must be violently blocked.

But through this violent act, darkness descends upon settler society. Hemi is at pains to point out that Pākehā youth are especially affected by these ramifications. Caught between the promise of counter-cultural values and the lack of directive resources in their settler heritage, some would become urban outcasts, homeless, junkies, at least partially sharing the fate of young Māori who, of course, received the truly hard end of the law. Bill Maung, a political refugee from Burma, an acquaintance of Baxter and subsequent advisor to the Black Power gang, summarizes Hemi's suspicion that no one colonizes without cost:

'Perhaps the range of the colonized now extends beyond the *tāngata whenua*.'[68]

It is interesting to note that, just as the Kīngitanga (King Movement) had done, Hemi also mused on the fate of the settler state by reference to Haiti:

> Baron Saturday ... whose altar is always a grave at the crossroads
>   You have shifted, man, out of thin Haiti. Now you grow fat on
> the fears of five thousand junkies in Auckland ... The servants of the
> Zombie king.[69]

Certainly, Hemi's use of Haitian spirituality evinces a fair degree of missionary sensationalism with little cultivated appreciation of Papa Legba. And Hemi's negative indictment of Haiti is far removed from the Kīngitanga's positive identification with the first postcolonial post-slaveholding state in the Americas. Nonetheless, it is striking that Hemi expressed the colonial fates of both Pākehā and Māori through the trope of the Zombie, which in Haitian Vodou embodies the condition of living death that was suffered under enslavement, a condition that one must never ever return to.[70] To avoid the zombie fate visited upon Ham, Hemi hoped for resurrection through an honouring of Te Tiriti (The Treaty): 'Brother, when will your Māori church be built? When will you hoist us all out of the graveyard?'[71]

Against the colonial gloss of John 5.23, Hemi, as his poem would suggest, was adamant that 'the European face of Christ should not be allowed to obscure or annihilate his Polynesian face'.[72] Indeed, he argued that the Māori prophets had come to do the work that Pākehā Christians were incapable of performing. For instance, speaking of the Rātana faith, Hemi asserted that 'they drew from *te atua* [god] and from the hearts of *te mōrehu* [the remnants] a Māori Christianity, hidden, abused, fragmented, but still viable'.[73] Moreover, Hemi argued that in the face of the colonized Christ could be gleaned 'a spectrum of all races and all cultures',[74] and that 'the deepest traditions of the church do not contradict the communal life of Māori people. It is only our Western cultural emphasis that makes it seem so.' To this end, Hemi sought to *whakapapa* the saints and prophets of Pākehā Christianity to the Māori prophets: 'Bernard and Francis can live at peace with Te Kooti and Te Whiti and Rātana.'[75] As part of Pākehā redemption, settler society had to give way to a 'Māori Zion' on earth.[76]

In 1968 God came to Hemi in a vision and directed him towards the old Marist settlement, Hiruhārama (Jerusalem), on the Whanganui River. He left his family behind (Hemi seems not to have learnt the cardinal Māori value of *whanaungatanga*, i.e. family relations), and took with him just a few possessions including a Te Reo (Māori language) Bible. The area surrounding Hiruhārama had been heavily depopulated by the urban migrations that followed the Second World War.[77] Hemi nonetheless recognized the *mana whenua* (authority over the land) of Ngāti Hau, the local people of the land,[78] and even hoped that there he would find his spiritual *tuākana* (elder brother) as he proceeded to draw in predominantly Pākehā outcasts from the urban areas. Hemi's commune relied upon the goodwill of the Marist Sisters of Compassion convent and, especially, that afforded by the local *pā* (Māori settlement).[79] Contrasting the 'pā's love' to the 'church's law', Hemi hoped that Te Wairua Tapu (the Holy Spirit) would facilitate, for Pākehā, a decolonial communion.[80]

Hemi labelled the outcasts that arrived from Auckland and other urban areas as *ngā mōkai*. Mōkai, in the particular sense that Hemi gave the word, denotes the fatherless, the undirected or unprepared, those convinced of their own uselessness, a 'tribe ... who can do nothing well'.[81] But Hemi did not believe them to be powerless. In one poem he goes so far as to call his tribe 'the *tama toa*' (young warriors), thereby invoking the inter-generational rebirth of *mana motuhake* that coincided with his commune project.[82] Hemi supported the young Pākehā non-conformists who in the late 1960s protested against a number of social and political issues, especially the Vietnam War. He believed these confrontations to be a way in which Pākehā youth might exorcise the 'guilt of history' buried by their own 'elders' that now manifested in the drab contemporary notion of New Zealand exceptionalism.[83]

Hemi personally supported Ngā Tamatoa's protest at Waitangi in 1971 while spending the weekend catching the 'new mood' among Māori.[84] And Hemi himself was well respected by many of the new generation of Māori radicals. On the night of Hemi's passing in October 1972 members of Ngā Tamatoa undertook a vigil at the morgue and provided the van and driver that delivered the prophet back to Hiruhārama for burial.[85] Hemi's influence survived his passing and even reached Māori gangs. The Mongrel Mob, for example, presented Prime Minister Robert Muldoon with Hemi's *Collected Works* on the occasion of his retirement from parliament.[86] Additionally, Eugene Ryder, a Black Power spokesperson, counts Hemi and the Hiruhārama (Jerusalem) project as one of the key influences upon the politicization of his group alongside key Māori advocates of *mana motuhake* such as Matiu Rata and Eva Rickard.[87]

Certainly, Hemi's prophetic message was contentiously and critically interrogated by Pākehā.[88] Nevertheless his decolonial mission became a strong undercurrent that moved many Pākehā in the 1970s to cultivate principled and committed relationships to *tāngata whenua* (peoples of the land) as partners in the long-maligned Treaty. This under-current affected many of the Pākehā members of Keskidee Aroha, or at least pushed them into collaborations with each other through community-development initiatives (e.g. Community Volunteers), work cooperatives (e.g. Ponsonby Labour Cooperative) and detached youth worker schemes (e.g. Te Kaha Trust).[89] Most of these projects engaged with Hemi's imperatives to make work meaningful again as *mahi* (collective, purposeful activity)[90] and to redress the colonial wounds suffered by *ngā mōkai* which, as urbanization proceeded, increasingly encompassed a multi-racial constituency.

We know, however, that the nineteenth-century meaning of *mōkai* denoted not simply the fatherless but more acutely the enslaved. And by mobilizing this term, Hemi, intentionally or otherwise, bound his Pākehā mission to that of Te Ua's: a kingly *mana motuhake* that sought the redemption of the enslaved and dispossessed – Ham and Shem. Hemi argued that his *mōkai* (young outcast Pākehā) could not be redeemed by 'Pākehā books' but only by some of the cardinal values of Te Ao Māori (the Māori world). We might say, then, that Hemi sought to redeem the relationship between Japheth and Shem so that the former would dwell not with dominion but with peace, love and justice in the latter's tent (Gen. 9.27). However, unlike Te Ua and Rātana, Hemi did not intentionally include Ham in his decolonial mission. In fact, in Hemi's wordsound, the land of Black liberation, Haiti, represented only the zombie, an enslaved condition that was to be avoided at all cost.

Nonetheless, the most audacious attempt to put into action Hemi's mission, Keskidee Aroha, sought to redress the relationship between Japheth and Shem precisely through the intervention of Ham, wherein Keskidee and the Ras Messengers would provide the catalyst for sufferers to walk out of Egypt, the settler wasteland. Denis O'Reilly's vision of the Keskidee Aroha project proposed the cultivation of a decolonial Pākehā/Māori relationship that was directly influenced and explicitly modelled on Hemi's mission – 'a loving and respectful relationship between *tēina* (younger sibling) and *tuākana* (older sibling)'.[91] O'Reilly sought out a *kaumātua* (respected elder) who could sanction and guide the project. And he found this person in Hiruhārama.[92] There, Hemi had considered Wehe Wallace to be the 'Māori mother of the community'.[93] She was also a relative of Taape O'Reilly, a member of the Keskidee Aroha national collective. Wallace agreed and led the troupe onto their first *marae* at Te Hāpua where the ancestors of Ham and Shem met, once more.[94]

Therefore, Keskidee Aroha can also be apprehended as a project that sought to enfold RasTafari into a Pākehā prophetic tradition endogenous (but not indigenous) to Aotearoa NZ. And I would like to finish this section by recalling parts of a recent workshop presentation wherein, 30 years later, O'Reilly enunciates this process of enfolding.[95]

O'Reilly begins by noting that, when the state apparatus takes on the modern-day form of Pharaoh, and the overseers are the police, the sufferers must use asymmetric warfare, especially the weapons of love – arts and music. These weapons are rooted in the long-standing tradition of the Māori prophets and their younger Pākehā relative, Hemi. Ngā Mōkai, O'Reilly reminds the audience, is nowadays composed disproportionately of Māori and Pasifika youth, especially those bound together through gang culture. The term *mōkai*, he notes, can also be translated as slave, a word that is 'memorable' to RasTafari. In this respect O'Reilly recalls recent comments by Shane Jones, a Māori MP, concerning gang members: 'They're not our people. In fact they are not people ... They are the slaves that would have been dispatched before Christianity without a sliver of doubt.'[96] With these words the Māori MP places himself in opposition to Te Ua's prophetic mission of redeeming the suffering multitudes through the pursuit of a kingly *mana motuhake*.

But who or what force might help to redeem Aotearoa's *mōkai* (slaves)/sufferers? O'Reilly reminisces that by the mid-1970s he had seen the Jamaican film, *The Harder They Come*, read a popular book exposing RasTafari to the world, *Babylon on Tin Wire*, and listened to the Wailers' *Burning*. Marley – *te māngai Ropata* (Robert the 'mouth-piece') as O'Reilly names him with Rātana terminology – revealed that the way to defeat Pharaoh was to burn down Babylon with wordsoundpower. Hemi, O'Reilly suggests, had prophesied just such an intervention by the children of Legba in his poem, *Complaint to a Friend*:

> But an African tribesman
> Smelling of mud and ochre took charge of my mind
> And hoisted me like a sack on his shoulder
> To teach me what I never knew.
> Well brother, today I walk the town as a new stranger
> and my heart is beating like an old buffalo drum.[97]

Presently, argues O'Reilly, Ngā Mōkai – specifically, Māori gang members – are excluded from the full rights of citizenship by virtue of new rules that block their access to state housing, give differential penalties, reverse the burden of proof and provide no presumption of innocence. At the same time, labour is degraded by current employment law and the benefit system so that it provides no dignity, promoting instead a contemporary slavery among the sufferers. What has been lost, claims O'Reilly, invoking Hemi's *Ballard of the Third Boobhead*, is precisely the quest for *mahi* – collective work for a communal purpose:

> It will take more than talk to make this a country
> Where the men who were treated like slaves will be able to work
> For other things than money

By this arrangement, O'Reilly bemoans, the essence of humanity is compromised, that is, the presence of god in each human or (and he uses the RasTafari pronoun) 'I and I'.

Nevertheless, O'Reilly holds on to the power of asymmetric warfare – wordsoundpower – and the prophecy of redemption signalled and shared by Te Ua, Rātana and the RasTafari ancients, and sounded by Hemi in *Pigeon Park Song*:

> Babylon, you
> Who sit on the waters
> In your market a man
> Costs less than a dollar
> I will play my guitar
> The day they burn you down

RasTafari has been enfolded into a Pākehā prophetic tradition, there to feed a decolonial relationship between *tāngata whenua* – the indigenous elder siblings – and *tāngata tiriti* – the younger endogenous siblings.

Conclusion

Through the channelling skills of the prophets, the anti-colonial relationship that Ham and Shem convey in the spiritual hinterlands has become manifest once more as RasTafari is enfolded into the indigenous and endogenous prophetic traditions of Aotearoa NZ. To arrive here we have travelled a path of many crossroads: from the public battles over Black Power to theological reasonings over Black liberation, to artistic projects and faith systems of Blackness; from comparison to identification to inhabitation to enfolding; from the present to the past; from the manifest to the spiritual. In wielding a decolonial science of deep relation we have sought to heal the wounds inflicted by colonial science upon the sanctified integrity of peoples, spirits and places – upon the very fabric of creation. And we have used the ethos of deep relation as a compass and energy store for the pursuit of restitutive justice in the present.

It remains for us to now exorcise the colonial history of Cook and Columbus through a collection of *whakapapa* that express the key contours of our journey. Long ago, we dispatched the figure of the subaltern: mute, passive, frozen, animated only by another's light and reason. So come now. Take your appropriate place around the campfire of liberation; perhaps it is at the front, at the side, or at the back. *Tātou tātou.* I and I. Let us tell some stories of Africa in Oceania.

Africa in Oceania

Māui and Legba

Hone Taare Tikao, an Ngāi Tahu scholar involved in Te Kotahitanga, the Māori Parliament movement of the late nineteenth century, puts the pieces together: Māui must have visited Africa in one of his epic journeys.[1] For once upon a time Māui had turned a thief called Irawaru into a dog, and since then some Māori have considered the dog to be their *tuākana* (elder sibling). In the 1830s a trading ship from South Africa arrives at Otago harbour. On board is a strange animal that the sailors call a monkey but that the local *rangatira* (chiefs) recognize to be, in fact, Irawaru. They make speeches of welcome to their elder brother.

It is 1924 and the prophet Rātana visits the land that Māui had trodden on so long ago. He finds a Zulu chief driving a rickshaw. He brings the evidence of this debasement back to the children of Tāne/Māui as a timely warning as to their own standing in the settler state of New Zealand. It is 1969 and Henderson Tapela, president of the African Student's Association in Aotearoa NZ, reminds the children of Tāne/Māui about their deep-seated relationship with the children of Legba. On a country-wide tour opposing sporting relations with an apartheid state, Tapela addresses the people of Mataatua marae thus: 'your [funeral] customs are very similar to ours. So you will understand what I mean when I say, don't go to South Africa to play the white team for if you do, you will be dancing on our bones!'[2] How could Māori refuse? After all, they have been reacquainted with their elder brother Irawaru by virtue of a trading ship that has arrived from South Africa. Are some of those bones their own relatives?

Ras Messengers ground with their hosts during the Keskidee Aroha tour. And occasionally some *kuia* (elder women) will *whakapapa* back to Africa to make the connection between host (*tangata whenua*) and guest (*manuhiri*). The basic principles of *whakapapa* impel acknowledgement of the seniority of African lineages within the human fabric.[3] And then there is Māui and Irawaru. So the *kuia* are not providing a convenient artifice but following an exacting science. A long-standing knowledge, skilfully retrieved and enunciated as living, deep relation.

Māui visits Africa on an epic journey. But Legba, that old African man, also visits Oceania in one of his epic journeys. Marcus Garvey recalls this visit as he speaks at Menelik Hall, Nova Scotia, on 1 October 1937. There, Garvey shakes the colonial world with his redemptive wordsound: 'We are going to emancipate ourselves from mental slavery because while others might free the body, none but ourselves can free the mind.'[4] But just prior to this, Garvey dispenses with the racist idea that African peoples are the 'missing link' between beasts and humanity. Rather than missing links, Africans, Garvey proposes, have woven the fundamental lattice of humanity:

> [N]ow they realize that the Negro is the oldest man [woman] in creation … The North American Indian, the Australian Aboriginal, the Aztecs of South America were all people who became what they were through the contact of Africans who had travelled across the continents … [B]efore modern history was written and produced in the different continents there were different shades of colour, each had their original civilization.[5]

It is the early 1990s. A grounation in Jamaica. And Ras Sam Brown, notable RasTafari elder, still claims this shared humanity and promotes an ethos for its restitution:

> Australia, New Zealand, the island of the East, all those lands, the lands of the long White Cloud [Aotearoa], all those lands are African

lands. When we shall free Africa from Cape to Cairo and from Timbuktu to the Nile, our job is not yet finished, for we shall free the sub-continent of Australia, and we shall free all the lands of the Pacific that bear the pigmentation of Black Humanity.[6]

In 1970 a future New Zealand Prime Minister writes an essay on Marcus Garvey and the Black Muslims. In 1989 Nation of Islam organizer Abdul Akbar Muhammad and his wife Maryam visit Aotearoa NZ to see for themselves. The Auckland branch of the Black Power gang hosts the couple. And Syd Jackson, that old *tamatoa*, invites them to stay with his family. Through these grounding sessions Muhammad notices that although many Māori have an appearance similar to whites they are nonetheless oppressed in similar ways to African Americans. Maryam reflects on their sojourn: 'I didn't feel any trends of racism … The Māori people have a habit of hugging and kissing. I got the feeling that we were finally meeting people the same as us.' Maryam shares with the Māori peoples a sense of being a 'distant relative'.[7] Less than ten years later Minister Louis Farakhan visits Aotearoa NZ to follow up on this relation. He is curious about the Rātana faith, its emblem of the moon and star, and the practice of women wearing headscarves. For there is a rumour that the Nation of Islam had been brought to Great Turtle Island by a Māori.[8]

Rātana adherent Ruia Aperahama stands in Bob Marley's mausoleum, St Anne's Bay, the Jamaican parish that birthed Marcus Garvey. He has given the Marley family a *taonga* (gift) from the children of Tāne/Māui that has inscribed on it the phrase 'it was Māui who changed our world forever, little by little'. Aperahama performs a *mihimihi* (greeting) to this great ancestor, a relative of Māui, and breathes in the air of the house in order to touch someone great in his life. Hauora, that great spiritual agent of reciprocity and balance, is at work. Marley intercedes with Aperahama and tells him that it is enough to be himself.[9]

Famous Jamaican author Erna Brodber writes a short story, a 'prince charming' for the Continent of Black Consciousness.[10] Two sojourners meet in the spiritual hinterlands, a woman and a man. They discuss how they have been travelling to significant sites across the continent, charting out a path for repatriation. Prince reveals to princess that he has been acting as a 'sort of ambassador for the return'. And that he was 'trying to make it to the Māori' when the two met. I ask Ms Brodber why she includes Māori in this Pan-African fairy tale? She replies to me, matter-of-factly, 'it came from considering the Māori part of us'.

Arcadian Hermes

Back in nineteenth-century England an amateur Egyptologist, Gerald Massey, makes a similar claim to that of Garvey, seeking to bind the origin of human civilization back to Africa through Egypt. Comparing Egyptian language and cosmology, Massey determines that Māori culture must have had African origins.[11] The roads no longer lead back to Britannica, the *faux* mother of civilization. Here, a child of Arcadian Hermes makes an early and hesitant foray into the decolonial science of deep relation. Waiting, perhaps, for an 'African tribesman', 'smelling of mud and ochre', to take charge of his mind and teach him what he never knew.

The coming of colonial science

Colonial science has never been concerned with deep relations. It is only concerned with cutting the ties that bind for the sake of endless accumulation. Dispossession of indigenous peoples to make way for the enslavement of other peoples; extraction of life force itself (*mauri ora*) from out of the soil, evaporating the blood. In the dispensation of European colonialism, the children of Legba arrive in Oceania once more, but this time bonded to – or fleeing from bondage to – European slavemasters, the children of Homeric Hermes.

In the late 1500s Spaniards meet the peoples of the Marquesas Islands who, when 'seeing a negro with the Spaniards, [make] signs toward the south, that there were such'.[12] At the turn of the seventeenth century Spanish sailors meet a Moor in New Guinea who bears the Spanish mark of enslavement – an S branded on the cheek. The Moor has been captured by Christians at the Battle of Lepanto, taken to Seville, sold and transported to Manila where he then steals a boat and heads south.[13]

The British enter the same region in the late 1500s. Francis Drake leaves on an island near Sulawesi 'two negro men and a woman whom he had carried off from the Spanish settlements on the west coast of America'.[14] The idea, according to Drake's nephew, is to form a colony of Africans that could feed English sojourners. The colonial science of extraction is implemented.

It is 1769 and Thomas Forrest, an English navigator employed by the East India Company, writes a pamphlet addressing the prospect of war against Spain in South America. Food, again, emerges as an issue of imperial administration. Concerned with providing a base for supplies in the broader region, Forrest suggests that a good location might be found at Dusky Bay in the extreme South West of the South Island of Aotearoa NZ. At Benkulen in Sumatra, notes Forrest, 'the Company has got a super abundance of Caffre [Africa] slaves, who speak the Malay tongue, may speak English, and are familiarized to our manners and customs'.[15] Forrest suggests that some slaves could be sent to far-off Dusky Bay, there to live free but on condition of supplying the English navy with agricultural products such as legumes, wildfowl and fish.

At Benkulen the East India Company operates a fort and, following its general policy for the Indian Ocean region, has established a pepper plantation. As early as 1704 a Caribbean planter by the name of Nathaniel Cox travels to Benkulen there to introduce sugar canes.[16] Enslaved Africans from or routed through Madagascar, as well as Africans forcibly routed through St Helena in the Atlantic Ocean and Madras in India, build the fort, guard the outpost and work the plantation. In this endeavour, members of the Company learn colonial sciences from fellow Portuguese and Dutch colonizers.[17] Forrest suggests the expansion of the enterprise into Oceania.

William Bligh enters Oceania in 1787 to transport and trans-
plant breadfruit from Tahiti into Britain's Caribbean plantations.
Bligh's mutinous missions are in large part funded by the Caribbean
plantocracy: able to grow on marginal land, and yielding a high
calorific crop, breadfruit is the planters' answer to the growing aboli-
tionist calls for 'humane' treatment of the enslaved.[18]

The extractive and segregational principles of colonial science
have been sharpened in the Atlantic and Indian Oceans. Forrest's
pamphlet announces their application to Oceania. An inequitable
current. Coming full circle with the mutiny on the *Bounty*.

Bondage

In the nineteenth century more Africans from the United States and
the Caribbean are travelling the islands of Oceania. Around 1809,
Captain Brown sails out of Boston with an intention to annex one of
the Mariana Islands from Spain and there to build a colony. Among the
men Brown deposits on Saipan (the island that he has landed upon due
to poor navigation) are 'a couple of negroes'. Brown's motley crew are
eventually taken by the Spanish to Guam and subsequently deported
to Hawai'i.[19] There, in Honolulu, a Black community has congealed as
early as 1833, and almost half of the whalers in the docks are Africans
from the Americas.[20] Most likely they are a combination of freed,
indentured and enslaved. Regardless, they ultimately attract a Ku Klux
Klan branch.

But it is not always the case that the children of Legba are powerless
in their Oceanic sojourns. In 1849 at Nukulau, New Caledonia, a US
consular agent and an English sea slug trader named Fitzgerald leave
20 Fijian workers under the command of an 'American man of colour'
while they sojourn in Fiji and Sydney.[21]

On another occasion an African American operates as recruitment
agent for a schooner, built in Auckland, and used for 'blackbirding', the

colloquial phrase for the Pacific slave-trade.[22] The civil war waging in the United States has created openings for 'entrepreneurs' in the cotton and sugar markets, and they proceed to open up plantations in Fiji and Queensland.[23] Former planters from Jamaica, Guiana and St Kitts swoop like vultures to settle around Brisbane.[24] This time, though, the captive plantation labour force are not 'negroes' but 'kanaka', that is, indigenous peoples of Oceania and especially those who Europeans define through their race science as Melanesian – more 'negroid' in character as opposed to the more 'Asiatic' Polynesian.[25] Kanaka bondage is further complemented by indentured servants from South Asia. 'I and I come to the Pacific in the ships of Babylon', laments a natty dread in 1980s Auckland. 'I and I suffer at the hands of Babylon. I and I moving out. To New Zealand. To Ethiopia.'[26]

It is not only the British that create imperial world maps. Dumont d'Urville, naval officer, botanist and cartographer, produces the French map of 'the [subaltern] islands of the great ocean'.[27] He divides Oceania into racial zones that exhibit more or less savagery: Polynesia might be saved; Melanesia is damned; Micronesia is between. Other colonial scientists replicate these hierarchies and segregations. Some suggest that as Māori migrate from Asia into Oceania they 'degenerate into barbarism, from a high state of civilization, the consequence most probably of their seclusion from the continent'.[28] Others comment at length on the miscegenation of Negroid, Malayan and other races,[29] suggesting that most Māori are 'Asiatic' yet 'betray evident marks of a Negro extraction'.[30] Segregated into new races by colonial science, some of these children are made to work the plantations on account of their melanin. Bondage segregates the children of Tāne/Māui among themselves.

In the Oceanic world, the epithet 'nigger' is used more for Kanaka than for Africans.[31] Later, in the inner cities of Auckland, groups of Nigs will attempt to redeem the segregated family of Tāne/Māui. They will rebaptize themselves as Polynesian Panthers. As Panthers they will defend their own, and refuse to let the category of Polynesian segregate themselves from their 'Melanesian' siblings. In order to cultivate the

ground for this reunion they will use Black matter. A Blackness other-
wise to colonial science. Some will then realize that RasTafari is an
'inborn concept', one that sutures the hacking of the sanctified root of
Kanaka by colonial machetes. At some point in his life Tigilau Ness,
Niuean Panther and RasTafari, realizes that the Christ of the Bible is
not white after all. The 23 July (the birthday of Haile Selassie I) is the
'birth of Christ', and Christ, proclaims Ness as he points to himself, 'is
like me'.[32]

Plantations

The plantation system consolidates itself in Oceania, uprooting the
soil, evaporating the blood. All for the sake of sugar in the Islands and
pine in the land of the long white cloud. There, swathes of expropriated
and/or disputed land are turned over to commercial forestry concerns,
many of which are foreign run. But pines tend to make soil acidic and,
once cleared of indigenous bush, little else will grow back upon the
land, even after the pine has been harvested. The Caribbean poets of
Legba wax lyrical of plantation landscapes turned over to extraction
and death.[33] So, too, do Māori. Veteran activist Titewhai Harawira
demands 'people on our land, not pines!'[34] Hone Heeney, Ruatoria
Dread, provides his cosmology of Babylon:

> The Baldheads decided to plant all our *whenua* [land] in pine trees,
> plantation work. Cutting down all our native trees, making our lands
> desolate ... They, the Baldheads, set it up so we are the 'niggers'
> working their 'cotton picking pine plantation' ... We laid our hands
> down on the table for the War-God-Jah-Tumatauenga, colonization,
> western imperialism, them all be Baldhead words of slavery, standover
> tactics.[35]

Hemi Baxter, the poet of Arcadian Hermes, also writes in cognate
cosmological terms: 'below the pines nothing can grow. One finds only
pine needles and dog manure ... The pines are an image of deism. The

broad-leafs are an image of humanism. Was the lord Jesus a pine or a broad leaf?'[36]

Tāne/Māui and Legba. Cook and Columbus. Pine and sugar. Shem and Ham. But fear not. Te Ua has found his way into the spiritual hinterlands.

Legba bears witness

The children of Legba bear witness to key moments that bring forth the pan-Māori struggle for *mana motuhake*. That old emissary of colonial science, Captain Cook, brings two African 'servants' on board his first voyage to Oceania. They do not survive past Cape Horn.[37] But for his second voyage Cook is accompanied by Tobias Furneaux, captain of the ship, *Adventure*. James Swilley, the 'Captn's Man' of this vessel, is a child of Legba. When anchored in Charlotte Sound, Swilley apparently catches a Māori in the act of theft and beats him. Later the crew find Swilley's cooked body on an adjacent beach.[38] Grounding can be bittersweet. There is something to redeem here, too.

In 1839 agents of the New Zealand Company sail from London on board the *Tory*, intent on undertaking the first systematic colonization of the islands. En route to Port Nicholson (present-day Wellington) the *Tory* stops at Queen Charlotte Sound, there picking up an English whaler, Dicky Barrett, along with his charge, 'a powerful negro who had escaped from an American ship, and went by the name of Sippy or Scipio'.[39] Barrett, presumably with Scipio in tow, immediately makes his way to Te Whanganui-a-Tara, the natural harbour of Port Nicholson, and there helps to negotiate the occupation of land that would ultimately become the colony capital, Wellington.

It is 25 May 1978 and over 500 police have been sent to arrest 200 people who protest against the expropriation of Ngāti Whatua tribal land at Bastion Point. In the temporary *marae* set up to cater for the people, Marley's redemption songs are regularly played. The songs of Legba's children bear witness too.

Race science versus decolonial science

What does any of this matter for European sojourners? The children of Legba cannot bear witness, they are mute. And they must be defined. Categorically. Segregationally. What is more, with the aid of race science Māori will be placed on a comparative spectrum of complexion between white (European) and black (African).

It is 1833 and, enslaved at Kawhai, Te Ua studies the Bible, seeking agents of intercession. He will find them in the uncolonized spiritual hinterlands where Tāne/Māui and Legba, as Ham and Shem, await his arrival. But meanwhile, Richard Hodgskin pursues a colonial science experiment. He notes the variance of Māori colour, pointing out that 'none approach the Negro hue'. In fact, 'owing to their being so dirty ... they appear much darker than they really are'. Hodgskin's racial comparison is made in the physical presence of both Māori and Africans: 'we [have] a black seaman on board, and many jests they [indulge] in at darkey's expense'.[40] Meanwhile, William Swainson judges Māori in the negative as having 'nothing of the gentle, loving nature, the affectionate disposition, and the child-like docility of the negro race'.[41]

Māori do not consider their *tuākana* (elder siblings) to be child-like and docile but rather exemplars of revolution. Wait a little, suggests Wiremu Pātara Te Tuhi of the Kīngitanga, and this island shall be like Haiti; perhaps God will protect his black-skinned children who are living in Aotearoa. Objects sanctified in Blackness are worn upon the rebellious children of Legba and protect them against the bullets of the Caribbean Pākehā.[42] Thirty years after the proclamation of the free empire of Haiti, the Māori prophet Papahurihia assures Hone Heke that in battle he can divert all bullets away from him by holding up printed texts of the Bible.[43] Thirty years later still, Te Ua's flock will shout 'E riki kawea' as they ambush colonial troops, requesting a divine diversion of bullets.[44]

And 30 years after Te Ua's capture, the Paremata Māori o te Kotahitanga (the Māori Parliament) will acknowledge the manifest power of Blackness in the pursuit of kingly *mana motuhake* in a newspaper article entitled 'Te Kīngi o Etiopia'. As a gift of the gods, *mana* is stronger than bullets. 'An uprising, that's how it began', recalls Hone Heeney, Ruatoria Dread: 'the spirit from Ethiopia, Bob sent it to us through the ray of sunlight.'[45] Sanctified Blackness is given the name of Ethiopianism; and dreadlocked *kowhaiwhai* adorn the cherub who guards the gates of Eden.

Black Power in the hinterlands

It is 1772 and in between Cook's two voyages Marion du Fresne embarks on a trading and exploration voyage of Oceania. Anchoring in Aotearoa at the Bay of Islands a 'negro belonging to Marion' deserts the ship.[46] Across Oceania, Africans working in commercial ventures, often whaling, occasionally jump ship upon landfall and take their chances inland with indigenous inhabitants. Sometimes they are forced to.

It is 1831 and at the estuary of the Whanganui river estuary, Joe Rowe, a Kapiti-based trader in dried human heads, arrives in a whaling boat and promptly comes into conflict with local Māori.[47] The contention is most probably due to the fact that some of the heads that Rowe carries are *rangatira* (chiefs) from Taupo whom the Māori at Whanganui are related to. Rowe and his crew are killed except for a white man, Andrew Powers, and 'a negro ... who, being a man of colour, [is] spared'.[48] Powers is subsequently taken to Taupo.[49] At Taupo, Powers is bartered for by a Danish trader called Hans Homman Felk, popularly known as Philip Tapsell, a resident of Maketu (a small village in the Bay of Plenty).[50]

The Black sailor is also taken to chief Te Heuheu Tukino in Taupo. Identified as 'an American negro' he is also called, probably after his white downpressor, 'Powers'.[51] Tapsell barters for the white and Black Powers, as well as for a captive Lascar. While resident in Maketu, Tapsell utilizes the Black Powers as a 'special messenger'.[52] He is, after all, a child of Legba. After some time, both of the Powers depart Maketu in a ship arriving from Sydney.

It is the 1980s. A few individuals have travelled to the countryside surrounding Whakatane, not far from Maketu. They have also run into the interior, to escape from Babylon. There they survive for a time by raiding orchards, cultivating their own Black powers as 'Nyahbinghis in the Ureweras'.[53]

Black redemption

Ethiopians arrive in Aotearoa NZ at the *fin de siècle*, followed later by African-American soldiers, billeted in Paekakariki as part of the world war in Oceania, themselves followed by African university students taking part in the Colombo Plan. A certain casual racism meets these African arrivants, as it always has.

Account books of the 1870s held by Messrs Jones and Morrison of Greymouth contain random, untitled racial caricatures of a Chinese and African man.[54] A sketch of 'George', a crew member of the *Duke of Portland* arriving in Lyttelton, Christchurch in 1851 from London, is accompanied by the aliases of 'jumbo, sambo, snowball darkie, blackie, cootes'.[55] That is down south. Up north, a couple of years later, Edward Crewe is told a story on Queen Street, Auckland, of a canoe accident in the nearby area. The only sober passenger, 'a black fellow – a nigger', drowns, and in suffering this fate the 'African' is 'washed white'.[56]

Further down river, though, at precisely this time, the Kīngitanga resistance is gathering pace. And Hōri Ngātai-rākaunui refuses to be whitewashed: 'my skin is black skin, my canoe is a Māori canoe'. Over

100 years later, Black Women chant the same; only 'the blanket of black skin' can act as 'a *whāriki* – a cloak of dignity'. The Stormtroopers: front-liners in the colonial fatal impact. They might not hold university degrees but they know enough of their ancestry to raise clenched fists in the Black Power salute.

Shem, Ham, Father Glory, verily, Hau!

After the departure of Black Powers, another schooner arrives from Sydney carrying merchandise for Tapsell. It is beached in a storm at Maketu. On board is a 'black cook, a big Jamaican man'.[57] Between 1821 and 1837 approximately 150 mostly Black convicts are deported to New South Wales from the British Caribbean colonies.[58] The crime of some is to have taken part in rebellions against colonial rule. Those deported from Jamaica might even have been fighting in the Baptist War of 1830/31 led by the preacher Sam Sharpe. This Jamaican cook: perhaps he is one of those riotous subjects?

Now it is 1860, and Māori are being told in Pākehā-written propaganda newspapers that the formerly licentious Jamaicans have, thankfully, given up their '*mahi māori*' – native work, uncivilized pursuits – for a new devoutness to Christian revivalism.[59] The Pākehā have fooled themselves. Five years later Edward Eyre, an ex-Lieutenant Governor of New Munster Province in New Zealand, will preside as Governor of Jamaica over the massacres that punish the participants of the Morant Bay uprising led by Paul Bogle, another Baptist deacon and revivalist.[60]

I am discussing two very different tours with Merata Mita: Keskidee Aroha and the Springboks.[61] A seminal figure in indigenous film making, Merata has taken part in directing the documentaries of both tours. I ask Merata where her politics comes from. And she starts by talking about her father. Merata explains that, during his day, Black men – especially African Americans – were heroes to many Māori men. Her father and his friends adored Joe Lewis; they would sing the lines of Black vocalists rather than their white dualists; and her father once drove through the night so that they could see Louis Armstrong perform in Hamilton in 1963. By the early 1970s, in the new era of Black Powers, Merata is a member of Ngā Tamatoa. In retrospect Merata realizes that while her father was not explicitly political he was, nonetheless, attempting to demonstrate to her that it was not just white people who could possess world-class skills and perform notable feats.

I ask Merata where she thinks her father got his compass and energy store of social justice from. She replies, 'no idea'. But Merata also speaks of her treasured ancestor. His name is Tame Haika, which literally translates as Tommy Anchor. This child of Legba had been caught in a storm and forced to jump ship. He was found by Merata's people, who took him in. Merata tells me that, when she was growing up, elderly Māori called her people 'the niggers of Maketu'. Yet this name 'was whispered in awe more than [as an] insult'.

****

The *whakapapa* of the children of Tāne/Māui and Legba begins not in the laboratories of colonial race science but in the invisible institutions and *whare wānanga* that teach the sciences of deep relation. Therein, the manifest and spiritual domains are bound together with the present and past and with peoples and peoples – *tātou tātou*, I and I. The material is material-and-spiritual. It is luminous. Potent. Shem and Ham stand together in the spiritual hinterlands. Before they were *tāngata whenua/manuhiri* (peoples of the land and guests) they knew each other as *tēina/tuākana* (younger and elder siblings). As the sky is separated from the earth, Tāne/Māui and Legba walk together across Africa and Oceania to inaugurate the manifest domain of human being. All the relations between their children cultivate from this ground. No human hand could uproot.

Conclusion

If we think differently about the past then different possibilities open up for our present. Instead of an imperial world map, we might begin to glean a global infrastructure of anti-colonial connectivity; and rather than reproducing categories of segregation we might start to live an ethos of humanity, deeply relating. I hope that this book has contributed to such revisionings. But I cannot conclude its stories. They are living and will continue to be retrieved and remade. I have opened a space on my blog where you can, if you wish, carry them on, deepen them, revise them, contest them (http://robbieshilliam. wordpress.com/blackpacific/). And there are no subalterns reading this book. So instead, I will finish briefly with some further reflections on the purposes which I set out with on this journey.

First, and most importantly, I wanted to retrieve a science of relationality that could support the Māori struggle for *mana motuhake* in an era marked by polite civil violence and the slow strangling of the spirit of Te Tiriti o Waitangi (The Treaty) by neo-liberal government. It is also an era marked by significant increases in migrant peoples, many of whom do not now arrive through old colonial circuits but via new ones carved out by global capital. Will their arrival merely extend the palette of identity politics? What investment can/do they make in the Treaty? Are they meaningfully encouraged to do so, and supported when they do? Pākehā are now partially being displaced as the usurpers; and at least Pākehā would have to admit that the document is written to them as much as to Māori.

I follow Manuka Henare when he argues that Te Tiriti (the Treaty) – so too the Declaration of Independence – are manifestations of the cardinal values arising out of Māori cosmology and *mātauranga* Māori (knowledge systems). There is more to these *taonga* (treasures) than the text. This being the case, the spirit of the Treaty provides ample resources through which to refigure the multicultural present of global capital and pursue restitution for capital's original colonial sins. The spirit of Te Tiriti provides rich resources through which to cultivate deep relations with diverse peoples – *tātou tātou*. I have demonstrated these capacities in the groundings of the children of Tāne/Māui and Legba. Many more multicultural relations might be cultivated along these lines, even in the era of global capital. In some ways, then, this book is a precocious essay on multiculturalism before Multiculturalism: of multiplicity as deep relation rather than as categorical segregation.

I hesitate somewhat to say this, but I do believe that what Māori should demand from Pākehā systems is not cultural 'recognition' but strictly legal restitution. At the very least, little investment should be made in a rarefied 'settler studies' that seeks, in melancholy fashion, to preserve a pristine encounter between the native and the settler. This was never the case, and it never will be the case. The material-and-spiritual domain is more potent than that.

Second, I intended to provide some strength to the children of Legba, especially those of the Diaspora, in our struggle for confidence in a global colonial system that has treated whole peoples only as beasts, beasts of burden, poor devils, and devils. But now Africans are abroad again, ejected or launching themselves into global capital circuits. They meet their long-sojourning Diaspora relatives. And other sufferers too. (How) will they ground? All roads lead to Rome, says massa. Crop, mineral, goods, bodies, value, narrative, concept, Jesus. Rome guards all the old gates and pathways. South–South trade, presently, is a veneer of postcoloniality, neo-Roman. Can self-determination be kingly without the redemption of the suffering multitudes?

In this context a Pan-Africanism must be renewed that has as its compass the ethos of humanity. And if Africans possess an energy store so great that it can help charge the self-determination and redemption of peoples half a world away, what can they not do? The *tuākana* (elder siblings) of humanity have great responsibility to step away from Rome and find other pathways through uncolonized spiritual hinterlands so that African redemption will proceed for the sake of humanity. Let the hungry be fed, the naked clothed, the sick nourished, the ancients protected and the infants cared for.

Third, I wanted to mark the importance of the fact that European colonization has depended upon an interlocking super-exploitation of labour and super-dispossession of land organized along lines of race: a world of natives and negroes. Certainly, the exploiters and dispossessors are nowadays multi-coloured (as in truth they always were, although less visibly so). Yet the racial interlocking of enslavement, exploitation and dispossession remains fundamental to global capital. The *whakapapa* of global capital starts with colonialism – a plantation on expropriated land next to a provision ground – and not in a factory next to an enclosure. Te Ua's gospel has lost none of its prescience. Ham and Shem still walk together in the spiritual hinterlands. And there are many other such agents, waiting with motile energies, compass in hand. Who will channel these forces on your behalf?

My fourth and final intention was to encourage a political commitment among critical intellectuals (especially those occupying the Western academy) to displace current academic endorsements of privileged narcissism and, instead, to help make more intelligible the deep, global infrastructure of anti-colonial connectivity. To this provocation, I can only add: colonial science is a science that you can use or discard; decolonial science is another science.

Appendix

Archives

Alexander Turnball Archives	(AT)	Wellington
Auckland University Archives	(AU)	Auckland
Bob Chapman Archives, University of Auckland	(BCA)	Auckland
British National Archives	(BA)	London
Hocken Archives	(HA)	Dunedin
London Metropolitan Archives	(LMA)	London
Māori Niupepa Collection, New Zealand Digital Archive	(MNC)	Online
New Zealand Archives	(NZA)	Wellington
New Zealand Film Archives	(FA)	Wellington
New Zealand Sound Archives /Ngā Taonga Kōrero	(SA)	Christchurch
Personal Archive of Author	(PAA)	
World Council of Churches	(WCC)	Geneva

Interviews

Paul Buchanan	Upper Hutt	10/3/09
Don Borrie	Porirua	1/5/09
Carl Perkins	Whanganui	3/5/09
Denis O'Reilly	Wellington	5/5/09
Matiu Te Huki	Raumati	10/5/09
Wanjiku Kiare and Martyn Sanderson	Otaki	23/5/09
Brian Ruawai	Raglan	16/6/09
Nandor Tanczos	Ngaruawahia	16/6/09
Alma Rei	Porirua	27/6/09
Darcy Nicholls	Porirua	1/7/09
Denis O'Reilly and Taape Tareha-O'Reilly	Wellington	8/7/09
Ngahiwi Apanui	Wellington	9/7/09
Hone Harawira	Wellington	25/7/09
Dale Hunter	By Phone	4/8/09
David Grace	Porirua	9/8/09
Merata Mita	Coromandel	13/9/09
Warren Lindberg	Wellington	17/9/09
James Moss	By Phone	19/8/09
Roimata Kirikiri	Wellington	1/10/09
Brian Potiki	Wellington	3/10/09
Tim Dyce	By Phone	9/10/09
Duncan Campbell	By Phone	9/10/09
Eruera Ted Nia	Rarotonga	1/11/09
Paul Chalmers	By Phone	11/11/09
Kirk Service	By Phone	14/11/09
Reihana Ngatoro	Porirua	27/11/09
Tigilau Ness	Auckland	30/11/09
Bob Scott	Auckland	1/12/09

Keskidee and Ras Messengers	London	10/12/09
Zena Tamanui	Auckland	20/1/10
Ron Smith	Matamata	21/1/10
Hone Heeney	Ruatoria	29/1/10
Atareta Pounanga	Gisborne	4/2/10
Wally Te Ua	Gisborne	5/2/10
Jules Issa	Auckland	9/2/10
Will 'Ilolahia	Auckland	10/2/10
Ruia Aperahama	Auckland	11/2/10
Tim Dyce	Wellington	1/3/10
Ben Dalton	Wellington	7/3/10
Gary Foley	Melbourne	21/3/10
George McLeod	By Phone	6/5/10
Ross France	Auckland	26/6/10
Miriama Rauhihi-Ness	Auckland	2/7/10
Oblex Brown	By Email	25/10/10
Ron Smith	Matamata	18/2/11
Chris McBride	Auckland	21/2/11
Roger Fowler	Auckland	22/2/11
Miriama Rauhihi-Ness	Auckland	22/2/11
Denis O'Reilly	Wellington	3/3/11
Nopera Pikari	Rawene	21/5/11
David Cuthbert	Wellington	11/2/11
Mitzi Nairn	Auckland	22/2/11
Eugene Ryder	Wellington	3/3/11
Eugene Ryder	Wellington	10/3/11
Tony Tafari	Bath, UK	23/7/13
Right Hon. Binghi Congo-Nyah	Bath, UK	23/7/13
Ras Shango Baku	London	16/12/13
Ras Bongo Spear	By Email	6/1/14
Dr Desta Meghoo	By Email	4/6/14
Carl Perkins	By phone	20/7/14

Notes

Introduction

1 Mita and Sanderson, *Keskidee Aroha*.
2 O'Reilly, Denis, 'Report on Keskidee Tour', 1980. AANV W4445 4/11/1. NZA.
3 Colomb, 'Imperial Federation'.
4 Driver, 'In Search of The Imperial Map'.
5 Ibid., 149–50. Colomb, 'Imperial Federation', 91.
6 See Biltcliffe, 'Walter Crane and the Imperial Federation Map'.
7 Sartre, 'Preface to the Wretched of the Earth', 141.
8 In general see Young, *Postcolonialism*; Ahluwalia, 'Out of Africa'; Sajed, *Postcolonial Encounters in International Relations*; Arthur, *Unfinished Projects*; Robinson, 'The Appropriation of Frantz Fanon'.
9 Sarkar, 'The Decline of the Subaltern in Subaltern Studies', 83–5; Chakrabarty, *Habitations of Modernity*, 7; Ludden, 'A Brief History of Subalternity', 11.
10 Prakash, 'Subaltern Studies as Postcolonial Criticism', 1475–6.
11 Guha, 'The Prose of Counterinsurgency'; Guha, *History at the Limit of World-History*, 6.
12 See Chakrabarty, 'Invitation to a Dialogue', 370.
13 Guha, 'The Small Voice of History', 11.
14 See Chakrabarty, *Habitations of Modernity*, 19.
15 Spivak, 'Can the Subaltern Speak?'
16 Spivak, 'Subaltern Studies: Deconstructing Historiography'.
17 Ibid., 339–40.
18 See Prakash, 'Subaltern Studies as Postcolonial Criticism', 1481.
19 On these issues in general see Sarkar, 'The Decline of the Subaltern in Subaltern Studies', 93; Chakrabarty, *Habitations of Modernity*, 16.
20 Chakrabarty, *Habitations of Modernity*, 33.
21 Chakrabarty, 'The Politics and Possibility of Historical Knowledge', 245–7.
22 Spivak, 'Subaltern Studies: Deconstructing Historiography', 342.

23 Spivak, 'The New Subaltern: A Silent Interview', 333; see also Spivak, 'Scattered Speculations on Geography', 10.

24 See Moorehead, *The Fatal Impact*.

25 Gramsci, *Selections from the Prison Notebooks of Antonio Gramsci*, 5–7; on the issues see also Beverley, 'The Dilemma of Subaltern Studies'; Green, 'Rethinking the Subaltern'.

26 See Icaza and Vázquez, 'Social Struggles as Epistemic Struggles'; and Mignolo and Vasquez, *The Decolonial Option*.

27 Shilliam, 'Living Knowledge Traditions'.

28 Bob Marley and the Wailers, *Babylon System*.

29 The term 'sufferer' is an Anglo-Caribbean term that describes the socio-economically dispossessed and downtrodden. For more context, see Bogues, 'Black Power, Decolonization, and Caribbean Politics'.

30 Harris, Reitu, 'Letter to the Evening Post', 12 August 1991. PAA.

31 See, for example, Smith, Hoskins and Jones, 'Interview: Kaupapa Māori'; Smith, *Decolonizing Methodologies;* and Bishop, 'Freeing Ourselves from Neo-Colonial Domination in Research'. For cognate projects in Oceania and the wider world of indigenous peoples, see, for example, Kabina Sanga, 'Making Sense of Indigenous Pacific Research' and Hokowhitu et al., *Indigenous Identity and Resistance;* and for the African Diaspora, see for example, Brodber, 'Re-Engineering Blackspace'.

32 For an extended argument on this issue see Shilliam, 'Caribbean Slavery, Constructivism and Hermeneutic Tensions'.

33 See, for example, Green, *Black Yanks in the Pacific;* Taketani, 'The Cartography of the Black Pacific'; Luciou, 'In the Black Pacific'; and from a somewhat different position see Horne, *The White Pacific*.

34 See, for example, Feldman, 'The Black Pacific'.

35 Gilroy, *The Black Atlantic*.

36 Piot, 'Atlantic Aporias'. See also Sweet, 'Reimagining the African-Atlantic Archive'.

37 Hau`ofa, 'Our Sea of Islands'.

38 Hau`ofa, 'The Ocean in Us'.

39 Teaiwa, 'On Analogies'.

40 See Jones and Singh, 'Guest Editor's Introduction'; Amadahy and Lawrence, 'Settlers or Allies?'; Kidane and Martineau, 'Building

Connections Across Decolonization Struggles'; Tuck and Yang, 'Decolonization Is Not a Metaphor'; DeLoughrey, *Routes and Roots*. See also the Islands of Globalization Project at the University of Hawai'i.

41 See especially Wolfe, 'Land, Labor, and Difference'.

Chapter One

1 On the wound as a metaphor see Ramazani, 'The Wound of History'. However, my use of the term is ontological: see Mignolo and Vázquez, 'Decolonial AestheSis'.

2 Smith et al., *Negotiated Space*; Airini, Anae and Mila-Schaaf, *Teu Le Va*; Thaman, 'Nurturing Relationships and Honouring Responsibilities'.

3 Smith, *Decolonizing Methodologies*, 120; Pere, *Ako*, 81; Vaioleti, 'Talanoa Research Methodology: A Developing Position on Pacific Research'.

4 As well as in footnotes these people are listed in the Appendix to this book.

5 Brodber, *The Continent of Black Consciousness*.

6 In general see Moules, 'Hermeneutic Inquiry'.

7 Nilsson, *Greek Popular Religion*, 9; Brown, *Hermes the Thief*, 43, 48. Fletcher, 'A Trickster's Oaths'.

8 Baer, *Conversations with Derek Walcott*, 216–17.

9 See Buxton, 'Introduction'; Schrempp, *Magical Arrows*.

10 Farnell, *The Cults of the Greek States*, 11–15.

11 Nilsson, *Greek Popular Religion*, 9.

12 Farnell, *The Cults of the Greek States*, 17, 25; Nilsson, *Greek Popular Religion*, 8–9.

13 Brown, *Hermes the Thief*, 7–10; Farnell, *The Cults of the Greek States*, 23.

14 Brown, *Hermes the Thief*, 21.

15 Ibid., 12, 19.

16 Ibid., 21.

17 Mead and Grove, *Ngā Pēpeha a Ngā Tīpuna*, 315.

18 Te Haupapa-o-Tane, 'Io, the Supreme God', 142; Marsden, *Kaitiakitanga*, 56–7.

19 See in general Luomala, *Maui-of-a-thousand-tricks*.

20 Orbell, *Māori Myth and Legend*, 114.

21 Pomare and Cowan, *Legends of the Māori*, 14–15. Wohlers, *Mythology and Traditions of the Māori*, 9; Orbell, *The Illustrated Encyclopedia of Māori Myth and Legend*, 114.

22 In some South Island Māori cosmologies, Māui is cast into a thorn bush and retrieved by wingless birds; Wohlers, *Mythology and Traditions of the Māori*, 9.

23 Orbell, *Māori Myth and Legend*, 114.

24 Pomare and Cowan, *Legends of the Māori*, 17.

25 Keelan and Woods, 'Māuipreneur'; Orbell, *Māori Myth and Legend*, 115.

26 Desmangles, 'The Christian Cross in Vodun', 16; Herskovits, *Dahomey*, 229.

27 Cosentino, 'Who Is That Fellow in the Many-Colored Cap?', 266.

28 Hurbon, *Voodoo*, 16; Herskovits, *Dahomey*, 201; for a critical exegesis of Herskovits' influential text see Gai, 'The Herskovits Legacy'.

29 Herskovits, *Dahomey*, 203.

30 Ibid., 222; Hurbon, *Voodoo*, 16.

31 Herskovits, *Dahomey*, 223, 229.

32 Herskovits, *Dahomey*, 203, 207.

33 Dayan, *Haiti, History, and the Gods*, 112; Brathwaite, *The Arrivants: A New World Trilogy*, 224.

34 Ibid., 263–4; Cosentino, 'Who Is That Fellow in the Many-Colored Cap?', 265; Hutton, 'Creative Ethos of the African Diaspora', 128.

35 Desmangles, 'The Christian Cross in Vodun', 16.

36 See Ikenga-Metuh, 'Religious Concepts in West African Cosmogenies'.

37 Buxton, 'Monsters in Greek Ethnography'; Clifford, 'On Ethnographic Allegory'.

38 See, for example, Asad, *Anthropology and the Colonial Encounter*; Clifford, *Writing Culture*.

39 See, for example, Price, *First-Time*.

40 See in general Atal, 'The Call for Indigenisation'.

41 This, of course, returns us to the founding problematique of subaltern studies discussed in the last chapter. See, additionally, Seth, '" Once Was Blind but Now Can See"'.

42 Marsden, *Kaitiakitanga*, 63.

43 Ibid., 62.

44 Marsden, *Kaitiakitanga*, 61.

45 See also Walcott, 'The Muse of History'.

46 Binney, 'The Ringatū Traditions of Predictive History', 169. For the wider Oceania context see also Hauʻofa, 'Pasts to Remember'.

47 See Salmond, 'Te Ao Tawhito'.

48 Temple, 'The Emergence of Sankofa Practice in the United States'. My thanks to Dr Lez Henry for pointing out this connection to me.

49 Desmangles, 'The Christian Cross in Vodun', 20.

50 Afari, *Overstanding RasTafari*.

51 Zahan, *The Religion, Spirituality and Thought of Traditional Africa*, 26.

52 Desmangles, 'The Christian Cross in Vodun', 20; Young III, *A Pan-African Theology*, 102.

53 Young III, *A Pan-African Theology*, 102.

54 Schuler, *Alas, Alas, Kongo*, 95.

55 Zane, *Journeys to the Spiritual Lands*, 85, 137; Stewart, *Three Eyes for the Journey*, 147.

56 Figiel, 'Song of the Banyan Tree'.

57 On these issues see also Seth, '"Once Was Blind but Now Can See"'.

58 Chatterjee, 'Talking About Modernity in Two Languages'.

59 Marsden, 'The Natural World and Natural Resources', 44.

60 Henare, 'Changing Images of Nineteenth Century Māori Society', 145.

61 Roberts et al., 'Whakapapa as a Māori Mental Construct', 4.

62 Hudson et al., 'Whakapapa – A Foundation for Genetic Research?', 44.

63 Pere, *Ako*, 80–1; see also Royal, 'Te Ao Mārama'.

64 See Piripi and Body, 'Tihei-Wa Mauri Ora'.

65 Henare, 'Changing Images of Nineteenth Century Māori Society', 125.

66 See in general Penetito, 'A Sociology of Māori Education: Beyond Mediating Structures', 103. Royal, 'Exploring Indigenous Knowledge', 2.

67 Pere, *Ako*, 68.

68 See, for example, Harris, 'Sharing Our Differences Together'. In building relationships with some of my interlocutors I have had to communicate my own expansive *whakapapa*.

69 Ryder, Interview.

70 Hudson et al., 'Whakapapa – A Foundation for Genetic Research?'

71 Royal, 'Te Ao Mārama', 80; Roberts et al., 'Whakapapa as a Māori Mental Construct', 13.

72 Nicholls, Interview.

73 Tamanui, Interview.

74 Drake, *The Redemption of Africa and Black Religion*, 25–6.

75 Bongo Spear, 'Groundation'.

76 Ibid.

77 Afari, *Overstanding RasTafari*, 88.

78 Homiak, 'The "Ancients of Days" Seated Black', 235.

79 Iah C, 'Nyahbinghi Order'; Ras Shango Baku, 'Groundation'.

80 Centenary Committee for RasTafari, 'Ancient Nyabinghi Guidelines', Centenary News, 1996. PAA.

81 Ras Shango Baku, 'Groundation'.

82 For some detailed thoughts on this issue see Stewart, *Three Eyes for the Journey*.

83 Sawyerr, *God, Ancestor or Creator?*, 6; Ikenga-Metuh, 'Religious Concepts in West African Cosmogonies', 22.

84 Cited in Homiak, 'The "Ancients of Days" Seated Black', 233.

85 Mack, *From Babylon to RasTafari*, 81; Homiak, 'The "Ancients of Days" Seated Black', 32.

86 Rodney, *The Groundings with My Brothers*, 83.

87 Césaire, *Discourse on Colonialism*, 42.

88 Ras Shango Baku, 'Groundation'; see also Lewis, 'The Groundings of Walter Rodney'.

89 Yasus Afari, 'Footprints and Visions of RasTafari'.

90 Dr Desta Meghoo, 'Question'.

91 Henare, 'Changing Images of Nineteenth Century Māori Society', 24–5.

Chapter Two

1 Hunn, *Report on Department of Maori Affairs*, 16.

2 See Fleras and Spoonley, *Recalling Aotearoa*, 194–201.

3 See Ngā Tamatoa, 'The Fly'.

4 The literature is too voluminous to comprehensively cite. For examples, see Joseph, *The Black Power Movement*, and Slate and Trotter, *Black Power Beyond Borders*.

5 Ausubel, *The Fern and the Tiki*.

6 Henderson, J. M., 'Letter to Race Relations Council', 3 August 1972. MS Papers 1617/656. AT.

7 See, for example, 'Black Power, White Peril'; 'Black Panthers: The New Revolt'.

8 New Zealand Post-Primary Teachers' Association, *Maori Education*, 1.

9 Maung, Bill, 'Untitled Letter', n.d. PAA. See also New Zealand Race Relations Council, 'Minutes', 20 June 1970. MS Papers 1617/665. AT.

10 Walker, 'Manifesto of the New Zealand Maori Council on the Race Relations Bill', 6.

11 Te Roopu o te Matakite 'Manifesto', 1975. 85-080-07/01. AT.

12 Smithyman, 'N.Z. has Nothing to Learn from Americans Says Amos'.

13 Rudman, 'Auckland's Racial Problems'.

14 'Common Problems for New Zealanders'.

15 See Sutherland et al., 'Justice and Race: A Monocultural System in a Multicultural Society'.

16 Andi, 'United Brown Brothers'.

17 'Ilolahia, Interview.

18 Dalton, Interview.

19 Kirikiri, Interview; Dalton, Interview; Lindberg, Interview.

20 'N.Z.F.M.S. Conference at Wellington'.

21 Chapman, Bob, 'Notes on Student Essays', 1970. MSS Archives 2006/2 Item 420–1. BCA.

22 Pounanga, Interview.

23 Reid, 'Interview with Syd Jackson', 22.

24 Te Rangihiroa, 'He Poroporoaki', 22; Royal, 'Te Ao Mārama'.

25 Cited in Ihimaera, *Growing up Māori*, 38.

26 Te Rangihiroa, 'He Poroporoaki', 22; Henare, 'Changing Images of Nineteenth Century Māori Society', 20.

27 Te Rangihiroa, 'He Poroporoaki', 25.

28 Douglas, 'Young Maori Leaders' Conference in a Developmental Context'.

29 'Young Maori Leaders Conference', 1959, 10–11. MS Papers 3776 7/13. AT.

30 Ibid., 33.

31 *Young Maori Leaders Conference*, 1970, 1–2.

32 Ibid., 9–10.

33 Ibid., 14.

34 'Tamatoa Council', 1971. MS Papers 1617/667. AT.

35 However, one of the organization's most famous members, Tame Iti, was not university educated and grew up in his *tūrangawaewae* (place of belonging).

36 'Young Māori Opinion', 1971. 44525. SA.

37 Mita, Interview; McAvinue, 'Tamatoa'.

38 Jackson, 'We Want a Truly Non-Racial Society'; McAvinue, 'Tamatoa'. The three key aims of Ngā Tamatoa in Christchurch and Wellington were the return of land, making Te Reo compulsory in schools, and the protection of land and sea resources; (Nia, Interview).

39 Pounanga, Interview.

40 'Tamatoa Council'.

41 Jackson, 'We Want a Truly Non-Racial Society'.

42 Ngā Tamatoa, 'The Resurrection of Maori Identity', 1.

43 Ngā Tamatoa, 'Submissions on the Treaty of Waitangi Bill', 3. n.d. PAA.

44 Awatere et al., 'Wahine Ma Kōrerotia', 24.

45 Ngā Tamatoa, 'Race Relations Bill 1972', 15.

46 'Kei Te Ora Te Wairua O Te Iwi Maori'.

47 Elder, 'Hone Kaa's Good Fight', 85.

48 Awatere et al., 'Wahine Ma Kōrerotia', 27.

49 Cooper, Whina, 'Telegram to Matt Rata', 15 October 1975. MSS Archives 2006/2 Item 173. BCA.

50 See, for example, Murch, *Living for the City*.

51 'Pat Hohepa in U.S.A.'; Taepa, 'The Ford Foundation Exchange'.

52 Reeder, C. et al., 'Stereotypes and People'.

53 Ibid.

54 'Brown Power and the Pākehā Problem', 4 May 1968. 41101. SA.

55 Clements, 'Brown Power: Otaki'.

56 *Young Maori Leaders Conference*, 1970, 16.

57 '"Brown Power" Emergent'.

58 *Young Maori Leaders Conference*, 1970, 16.

59 '"Brown Power" Emergent'.

60 Ibid.

61 *Young Maori Leaders Conference*, 1970, 16.

62 Harawira, Interview.

63 'Warning of Racial Conflicts'.

64 *1977 Young Maori Leaders Conference*.

65 Walker, 'Early Storm-Warnings'.

66 Moore, M. K., 'Press Statements', 11 February 1980. MSS Archives 2006/2
    Item 174. BCA.

67 Reid, 'Interview with Syd Jackson', 22; 'Interview with Nga Tamatoa
    Tuatoru'.

68 *Nga Tamatoa: 40 Years On.*

69 Reid, 'Interview with Syd Jackson'.

70 Leigh, 'Let's Head Off Racial Strife'.

71 Kennedy, 'Gang's Sights on Parliament'; Gee, 'Rei Harris Interview'.

72 O'Reilly, Interview.

73 Gee, 'Rei Harris Interview', 13.

Chapter Three

1 'Ilolahia, Interview.

2 Pālagi is the Samoan equivalent to Pākehā (European settlers and their
   descendents).

3 Miriama Rauhihi-Ness made these comments at 'Ilolahia, Rauhihi-Ness
   and Ness, 'Polynesian Panthers Lecture'.

4 *Our People / Our Century.*

5 Anae, *Polynesian Panthers*, 31.

6 'Ilolahia, Interview; 'Interview with Polynesian Panthers', The Press, June
   1973. 99-278-08/09. AT.

7 Ness, Interview.

8 'Ilolahia, Interview.

9 Anae, *Polynesian Panthers*, 62.

10 Baysting, Arthur, 'The Pakeha Problem', n.d. 94-106-19/07. AT.

11 Polynesian Panther Party, 'Panther Action', 1973. 94-106-19/07. AT.

12 Polynesian Panther Movement, 'Platform of Movement Positions and
    Structure of Organisation', 1971. 94-106-19/07. AT.

13 Polynesian Panther Movement, 'Investigation Period', 1972. PAA.

14 Reeves, Paul, 'Letter to Baldwin Sjollema, World Council of Churches',
    1973. 4223.13.32. WCC.; Polynesian Panther Movement, 'Where We
    The Panther Movement Have Aided Our People', 1972. PAA; Fowler,
    Interview.

15 Photographs in author's possession.

16 Polynesian Panther Party, 'P.P.P.' 1973. 99-278-08/10. AT; Polynesian Panther Party, 'Platform and Programme, January '74', 94-106-19/07. AT. It is interesting to note that Black Power groups in urban Australia were involved in an almost exactly the same problem-solving activity; Foley, Interview.

17 'Ilolahia, Interview; Foley, Interview.

18 Fepulea'l, *Dawn Raids*. The Panthers were not alone in this regard; Māori women activists also organized against the campaign; Awatere et al., 'Wahine Ma Kōrerotia', 30.

19 Polynesian Panther Movement, 'Investigation Period'.

20 Ibid.

21 Anae, *Polynesian Panthers*, 98.

22 Satele, 'The Polynesian Panthers', 93.

23 Ness, Interview.

24 Anae, *Polynesian Panthers*, 52–4.

25 'Midnight Rider', 1973. 99-278-08/09. AT.

26 Reeves, 'Letter to Baldwin Sjollema, World Council of Churches'.

27 Baysting, 'The Pakeha Problem'.

28 Wishart et al., 'Talking to Polynesian Women Part 2', 9.

29 Rauhihi-Ness, Interview.

30 Wishart et al., 'Talking to Polynesian Women Part 2', 9.

31 Anae, *Polynesian Panthers*, 98; Papali'i, 'Interview with Peta Siulepa', n.d. PAA.

32 Harawira, Interview.

33 Will 'Ilolahia, the Chairman of the PPP, was especially attracted to this notion; Anae et al., 'The Polynesian Panthers'.

34 Newton, 'Speech Delivered at Boston College', 169–71. See also Hayes III and Kiene III, 'All Power to the People', 157–76.

35 'Ilolahia, 'We Are All Polynesians', Rongo, 1973. 4223.13.32. WCC.

36 McDonald, Brian and Tuiasau, Norman, 'Conference Advertisement', 1974. Ms Papers 1617/670. AT.

37 'Ilolahia, 'We Are All Polynesians'.

38 'Ilolahia, Interview; Ness, Interview. Although Rauhihi-Ness, as a Māori, took an active part in organizing the Land March; Interview.

39 'Ilolahia, 'We Are All Polynesians'.

40 'Ilolahia, 'Maori Organisation on Human Rights Newsletter: Letter from Will Ilolahia', October 1972. 2004-024-3/02. AT.

41 Polynesian Panther Party, 'Newsletter Nov 1974', 1974. MS Papers 8958-24.

42 Gump, 'The Imperialism of Cultural Assimilation'.

43 Limb, 'The Anti-Apartheid Movements', 915.

44 Sorensen, 'Vern Turns Down South Africa Tour'.

45 Limb, 'The Anti-Apartheid Movements', 911.

46 Potter, 'Veteran Scorns Muldoon Analogy'.

47 Maori Organization on Human Rights, 'Newsletter', September 1972, 2.

48 'Days of Rage', 20.

49 Limb, 'The Anti-Apartheid Movements', 915.

50 Ngā Tamatoa Tuarua, 'Statement of Aims'.

51 Limb, 'The Anti-Apartheid Movements', 909.

52 Kia Ngawari Youth Club, 'Press Statement'.

53 'Nga Tamatoa Conference'; see also Te Matakite, 'Newsletter', 5.

54 See, for example, 'Kei Te Ora Te Wairua O Te Iwi Maori'.

55 Awatere, 'Rugby, Racism and Riot Gear'; see also Alba, 'Who Is Steve Biko?' As I noted in the preceding chapter, Houpapa had been shot dead during a police shootout with the Mongrel Mob in 1976.

56 Tirikatene-Sullivan, 'Press Statement'. 15 September 1980. MSS Archives 2006/2 Item 129. BCA.

57 Harawira, Hone, 'Māori and Polynesian Groups Against the Tour', n.d. 93-043-Hart-Box 9. AT.

58 Mita, Interview.

59 Nia, Interview.

60 'Ilolahia, Interview.

61 Nia, Interview.

62 For example, after the experience of touring the very conservative South Island; Polynesian Panther Party, 'Newsletter'. See also Polynesian Panther Party, 'Panther Action'.

63 'Ilolahia, Interview.

64 Awatere, 'Rugby, Racism and Riot Gear', 11; Ryder, Interview.

65 Chalmers, Interview.

66 Mita, Interview.

67 *From Street to Sky*.

68 Awatere, 'Rugby, Racism and Riot Gear', 11.

69 Halkyard, 'Otara Black Woman Batonned'.

70 Rei, Interview.

71 Waitangi Action Committee, 'Newsletter'.

72 Mobilisation to Stop the Tour, 'Defence & Aid Fund'.

73 'Violence in Court Disrupts Hearing'.

74 'Ilolahia, Interview; Harawira, Interview.

75 'Ilolahia, Interview.

76 Nia, Interview; 'Ilolahia, Interview.

77 Nairn, Interview.

78 Minto, 'Kaupapa Māori'.

79 'Deep Split Indicated by Conflicting Answers'.

80 Nairn, Interview.

81 Greig, 'The Police and the Tour', 16.

82 Te Ua, Interview.

83 Mita, Interview.

84 Ibid.

85 'Pan-Māori Hui'.

86 Waitangi Action Committee, 'Leaflet'.

87 For a ground-breaking analysis of the movement see Okeroa, 'The Black Women's Movement 1978–1982'.

88 Biko, 'Black Consciousness and the Quest for a True Humanity'.

89 Awatere, 'Kōrero-Tia Wahine Ma!', 14.

90 Grey Lynn/Ponsonby Black Womens Collective, 'First National Hui of Black Women'. See, in general, Okeroa, 'The Black Women's Movement 1978–1982', 72–8.

91 Grey Lynn/Ponsonby Black Womens Collective, 'First National Hui of Black Women', 12.

92 Evans, 'The Politics of Blackness and Black–White Relationships', 18.

93 Evans, 'Black Unite', 11; Awatere et al., 'Wahine Ma Kōrerotia', 30.

94 'Policies MPLM'.

95 For example, 'Black Dykes'; 'Black Women's Hui'.

96 Taylor, 'Hui Wahine Maori Kei Otaua'.

97 Evans, 'Hui Wahine Maori'. On mana wahine (glossed as 'women's power/authority') see, for example, Smith, 'Māori Women'; and Te Awekotuku, 'Mana wahine Māori'.

98 Tamanui, Interview; Dalton, Interview.

99 MacGregor, 'Black Is Beautiful'.

100 Tamanui, Interview.

101 On these broad issues see, for example, Durie, *Te Mana, Te Kawanatanga;* Rata, 'Theory of Neotribal Capitalism'.

102 See Charters and Erueti, *Māori Property Rights;* Bargh, *Resistance.*

103 On identity politics see Mignolo, 'The De-colonial Option'.

104 On rethinking the chronology of civil rights movements see Hall, 'The Long Civil Rights Movement'.

105 Eruera, 'Letter to Don Borrie'.

106 Ibid.

Chapter Four

1 Cone, *A Black Theology of Liberation,* 45.

2 Ibid., 63, see also 66.

3 See West, *Prophesy Deliverance!,* 109.

4 Jackson, 'Research and The Colonisation of Māori Knowledge', 71.

5 See Wynter, 'Unsettling the Coloniality of Being/Power/Truth/Freedom'.

6 Sjollema, Boudewijn, 'Combating Racism: A Chapter in Ecumenical History'.

7 Cited in CARE, 'Newsletter', 3, April 1971. 4223.13.31. WCC.

8 These biographical notes are from an interview with Borrie.

9 Sjollema, Boudewijn, 'Letter to D. Taylor', 16 April 1970. MS Papers 1617/658. AT.

10 Borrie, Don, 'Letter to B. Sjollema', 20 April 1970. MS Papers 1617/658. AT.

11 Borrie, Don, 'Letter to B. Sjollema', 3 December 1970. 4223.13.31. WCC.

12 Findlay, *Church People in the Struggle,* 188; 'Charles S. Spivey Jr.'s Obituary'.

13 'Charles S. Spivey Jr.'s Obituary'.

14 See Newman, *Freedom's Prophet.*

15 Spivey, Charles, 'Summary of Visit to Australia, New Zealand, Fiji and Hong Kong', 11 January 1972. 4223.13.31. WCC.

16 Ness, 'Charles Spivey'.

17 Spivey, 'Summary of Visit to Australia, New Zealand, Fiji and Hong Kong'.

18 'Churchmen It's Time to Speak Out'.

19 'Panthers Justified, Says Churchman', 3 December 1970. 4223.13.31. WCC.

20 Cull, S. G., 'Letter to H. W. Baines', 15 February 1972. 4223.13.31. WCC.

21 Roberts, T. A., 'Letter to Allan Brash', 16 February 1971. 223.13.31. WCC.

22 Cited in Taylor, David, 'Grants to Liberation Movements: A View From the Congo', 20 May 1971. 223.13.31. WCC.

23 Poata, Tom, 'Letter to Charles Spivey', 5 March 1972. 4223.13.31. WCC.

24 Leigh, 'Let's Head Off Racial Strife'.

25 Spivey, Charles, 'Letter to Wil Ilolahia', 16 February 1972. 4223.13.31. WCC; Spivey, Charles, 'Letter to Syd and Hana Jackson', 28 February 1972. 4223.13.31. WCC.

26 Borrie, 'Letter to B. Sjollema', 10 December 1971. 4223.13.31. WCC.

27 Gnanasunderam, A., 'Letter to B. Sjollema', 2 June 1971. 4223.13.31. WCC.

28 Gnanasunderam, A., 'Letter to C. Spivey', 15 February 1972. 4223.13.31. WCC.

29 Spivey, Charles, 'Letter to A. Gnanasunderam', 23 February 1972. 4223.13.31. WCC.

30 Spivey, 'Letter to A. Gnanasunderam', 8 May 1972. 4223.13.31. WCC.

31 Spivey, Charles, 'Letter to Syd Jackson', 13 June 1972. 4223.13.31. WCC.

32 Spivey, 'Letter to A. Gnanasunderam'.

33 See also McIntosh, 'White Privilege and Male Privilege'.

34 Terry, Robert, 'New Whites: Justice and Racism', 4. 1971. MS Papers 1617/665. AT.

35 Ibid.

36 Gnanasunderam, A., 'Letter to C. Spivey', 5 June 1972. 4223.13.31. WCC.

37 Reeves, Paul, 'Letter to C. Spivey', 30 March 1972. 4223.13.31. WCC.

38 Ibid.

39 Spivey, Charles, 'Letter to P. Reeves', 30 June 1972. 4223.13.31. WCC.

40 Spivey, Charles, 'Letter to P. Reeves', 30 April 1972. 4223.13.31. WCC.

41 Reeves, Paul, 'Letter to C. Spivey', 3 July 1972. 4223.13.31. WCC.; Reeves, Paul, 'Letter to C. Spivey', 30 June 1972. 4223.13.31. WCC.

42 Borrie, Don 'Letter to C. Spivey', 19 July 1972. MS Papers 1617/650. AT.

43 Reeves, Paul, 'Letter to D. Taylor', 2 May 1972. 4223.13.31. WCC.

44 See, for example, Reeves, Paul, 'Letter to C. Spivey', 30 March 1972.

45 Nairn, Interview.

46 Borrie, Don, 'Reactions to America', 21 November 1972. MS Papers 1617/650. AT.

47 Grundy, John, 'Report on the Visit of a New Zealand Team to the USA'. 1972. MS Papers 1617/650. AT.

48 As part of the selection of participants for the trip, Syd Jackson of Ngā Tamatoa was asked to nominate names of Pākehā that he trusted. Borrie, Don 'Letter to C. Spivey', 10 August 1972. MS Papers 1617/650. AT.

49 Grundy, 'Report on the Visit of a New Zealand Team to the USA'.

50 'PCR Programme Project List No.9'. 1973. 4223.13.32. WCC.

51 Nairn, Interview.

52 Programme to Combat Racism, 'Anti-Racism Training Programme in New Zealand', 1973. 4223.13.32. WCC.

53 Reeves, Paul, 'Letter to Baldwin Sjollema', 16 November 1973. 4223.13.32. WCC.

54 Scott, Bob, 'A Letter From Bob', MS Papers 1617 / 679. AT.

55 Scott, Interview.

56 These comments resonate with Biko, 'Black Souls in White Skins?'

57 Scott, Interview.

58 Nairn, Interview.

59 Elder, 'Hone Kaa's Good Fight', 88.

60 Scott, Interview.

61 Nairn, Interview.

62 Scott, Bob, 'Letter to Whom It May Concern', 4 May 1984. MS 92 085 2/3. AT.

63 Scott, Interview.

64 Ibid.

65 Gnanasunderam, A., 'The Birthday Celebrations at the Rātana Pa', 1 February 1972. MS Papers 1617/656. AT.

66 Gnanasunderam, A., 'Maori Theology and Black Theology, or a Theology of Liberation', 6 February 1974. 4223.13.32. WCC.

67 Tahere, T. R., 'Letter to Rev E.G. Buckle', 6 July 1971. 4223.13.31. WCC.

68 Buckle, E. G., 'Letter to B. Sjollema', 5 July 1971. 4223.13.31. WCC.

69 Gnanasunderam, A., 'Letter to B. Sjollema', 7 March 1973. 4223.13.32. WCC.

70 Ibid.

71   Elder, 'Hone Kaa's Good Fight', 86.

72   Tamanui, Interview.

73   Anae et al., 'The Polynesian Panthers'.

74   Spivey, Charles, 'Letter to N. Perry', 13 October 1972. 4223.13.31. WCC.;
     Spivey, Charles, 'Letter to W.S. Andrews', 13 October 1972. 4223.13.31.
     WCC.

75   Scott, Interview.

76   Gnanasunderam, A., 'Letter to P. Reeves', 5 September 1972. MS Papers
     1617/650. AT.

77   Spivey, Charles, 'Letter to R. Tekaha', 20 November 1972. 4223.13.31. WCC.

78   Schulze, Paul, 'Letter to Borrie, Gnanasunderam and Jackson', 22
     November 1972. MS Papers 1617/650. AT.; Gnanasunderam, A., 'Letter
     to B. Sjollema', 12 January 1973. 4223.13.31. WCC.

79   'Profile: Al Ragland'.

80   Nia, Interview. In making these connections I am also indebted to
     participating in some workshops by Ruakere Hond at Parihaka in
     November 2011. Acknowledgements to Tahu Wilson and Erina Okeroa
     for taking me to this weekend *hui*.

Chapter Five

1   *Te Raukura*, 25.

2   Dansey, *Te Raukura*, xv.

3   See Peterson, 'Reclaiming the Past, Building a Future', 16–17.

4   Potiki, 'It Is Political If It Can Be Passed On', 173.

5   Keskidee Aroha National Collective, 'Minutes', January 1979. PAA.

6   O'Reilly, Denis, 'Letter to Michael Volkerling', 7 December 1978. PAA.

7   O'Reilly, Denis, 'Report on Keskidee Tour', 1980. AANV W4445 4/11/1.
     NZA.

8   O'Reilly and Tareha-O'Reilly, Interview.

9   The Keskidee Trust, 'A Community Discovering Itself Creates Its Own
     Future', n.d. LMA/446VC/09/01/001. LMA.

10   Dein, 'The Keskidee'.

11   The Keskidee Trust, 'A Community Discovering Itself Creates Its Own
     Future', 4–5.

12 Keskidee and Ras Messengers, Interview; Ness, Tigilau, 'Letter to Ross France', 28 March 1979. PAA.

13 Keskidee Aroha National Collective, 'Minutes'.

14 Keskidee Aroha, 'Co-Opting Committee Agenda', 1979. PAA.

15 O'Reilly, 'Letter to Michael Volkerling'; Lindberg, Interview.

16 Keskidee Aroha, 'Mission', 1979. PAA.

17 Keskidee Aroha, 'Mission'.

18 O'Reilly, 'Letter to Michael Volkerling'.

19 Ibid.

20 Edgar White, *Lament for Ras Tafari*, 78.

21 'The Symbol of Keskidee Aroha', 4. Keskidee Aroha, 20 February 1979. PAA.

22 O'Reilly, 'Letter to Oscar Abrams'.

23 Steven, *Te Matakite O Aotearoa*.

24 Māori Organization on Human Rights, 'Report on Te Hapua'. 1972. 4223.13.32.043. WCC.

25 Keskidee Aroha, 'Te Hāpua Report', 7 May 1979. PAA.

26 Murray, Saana, 'Letter to Tom Poata', 17 January 1972. 4223.13.31. WCC.

27 Keskidee Aroha National Collective, 'Minutes'.

28 Kiarie and Sanderson, Interview.

29 O'Reilly, 'Report on Keskidee Tour'.

30 Kiarie and Sanderson, Interview; O'Reilly, Interview. See also Desmond, *Trust*.

31 Mita, Interview; O'Reilly and Tareha-O'Reilly, Interview.

32 Mita, Interview.

33 Anon, 'Letter to the Minister of Internal Affairs', 1 June 1979. AANV W4445 4/11/1.NZA.

34 O'Reilly, 'Report on Keskidee Tour'.

35 Wairarapa Times-Age, 'Audience Involved in Performance', 6 June 1979. LMA/4463/C/09/08/001.LMA.

36 Kiarie and Sanderson, Interview.

37 Mita and Sanderson, *Keskidee Aroha*.

38 Service, Interview.

39 Hunter, Interview, 13 December 2009.

40 'Keskidee Aroha Promotional Material', 1979. PAA.

41 O'Reilly and Tareha-O'Reilly, Interview.

42 Kiarie and Sanderson, Interview.

43 Hunter, Interview, 4 August 2009.

44 Kiarie and Sanderson, Interview.

45 For cognate thoughts in the field of literature see James, 'Black Literatures in the Pacific'. Interestingly, Wanjiku Kiarie, the only continental African member of Keskidee, was so affected by the intimate relationship between Māori and the land that she subsequently started to write poetry about her relationship to her own mother-land – Kenya; Kiarie and Sanderson, 'Interview'.

46 Rosso, *Babylon*.

47 Mita and Sanderson, *Keskidee Aroha*.

48 Kiarie and Sanderson, Interview; Mita, Interview.

49 O'Reilly, 'Report on Keskidee Tour'.

50 McCormick, Gary, 'Letter to Jim Booth, QE2 Arts Council', 10 June 1979. AANV W4445 4/11/1. NZA.

51 Lindberg, Interview.

52 Mitchell and Kirikiri, *Polynesian Youth in Otara*.

53 Lindberg, Interview.

54 Bray, *Proposals for Te Puke O Tara*, 4.

55 Tamanui, Interview.

56 'New Streets: South Auckland, Two Cities'.

57 Kirikiri, Interview.

58 Tamanui, Interview; Bray, *Proposals for Te Puke O Tara*, 7.

59 Tamanui, Interview.

60 *Eye Witness News: Māori Activists*.

61 Dalton, Interview.

62 Lindberg, Interview.

63 'Keskidee Aroha Hui: 30 Years On'.

64 'Toko Turns Troops to Work'.

65 Manukau Arts Collective, 'Evaluation of Keskidee Tour', 1979. AANV W4445 4/11/1. NZA; Mcleod, Interview.

66 Cited in Homiak, 'The "Ancients of Days" Seated Black', 233.

67 Tamanui, Interview.

68 Manukau Arts Collective, 'Evaluation of Keskidee Tour'.

69 Ibid.

70 Manukau Arts Collective, 'Evaluation of Keskidee Tour'.

71 Ibid.

72 Ibid.

73 Lindberg, Interview.

74 'Keskidee Aroha Hui: 30 Years On'.

75 Ibid.

76 Ibid.

77 Ibid.

78 Ibid.

79 Mcbride, Interview.

80 Keskidee Aroha, 'Keskidee Aroha Community Development Course', n.d. PAA.

Chapter Six

1 Savishinsky, 'Transnational Popular Culture and the Global Spread of the Jamaican RasTafarian Movement'; Alvarez, 'Reggae Rhythms in Dignity's Diaspora'; Boxill, 'Atlantic Meets Pacific'. Maaka Mcgregor of the group *Wai 100%* remembers that 'we were being told by Bob Marley to get up, stand up … and we related to it instantly'. See 'Native Affairs'.

2 Pikari, Interview; Rei, Interview.

3 Hawkeswood, 'I'n'I Ras Tafari', 74; Ness, Interview; O'Reilly, 'Ngā Mōkai'.

4 Brown, 'Twelve Tribes'; Grace, Interview; Aperahama, 'Māori Prophets'.

5 Moss, Interview; Rei, Interview; Ness, 'Reggae and RasTafari'; Hawkeswood, 'I'n'I Ras Tafari', 76; Solomon, 'Tēnā Koe – Greetings'.

6 Ness, Interview; O'Reilly and Tareha-O'Reilly, Interview.

7 Ness, 'Reggae and RasTafari'.

8 Aperahama, 'Māori Prophets'.

9 Aperahama, Interview.

10 Apanui, 'Kaupapa Māori'; Apanui, Interview.

11 Heeney, Interview.

12 Davidson and Lineham, *Transplanted Christianity*, 167.

13 Kaiwai and Zemke-White, 'Kapa Haka', 143.

14 Orbell, *Māori Myth and Legend*, 115.

15 Apanui, Interview. For more on rhythms see Cattermole, *The Routes of Roots Reggae in Aotearoa/New Zealand*, 21–4.

16 Aperahama, Interview; Apanui, Interview.
17 Mita, *Dread*.
18 Grace, Interview; Ruawai, Interview.
19 Buchanan, Interview.
20 O'Reilly and Tareha-O'Reilly, Interview.
21 Campbell, 'Dread Inna Western Springs'; Ness, Interview.
22 Interview.
23 Rauhihi-Ness, 'Twelve Tribes of Israel Aotearoa New Zealand'; Campbell, Interview.
24 Rauhihi-Ness, 'Twelve Tribes of Israel Aotearoa New Zealand'.
25 Mita, Narbey and Pohlmann, *Bastion Point Day 507*.
26 Dalton, Interview.
27 France, Interview.
28 Ibid.; Kiarie and Sanderson, Interview.
29 'Multicultural Herbs Ready to Go Back to Their Roots', 10.
30 France, Interview.
31 Solomon, 'Tēnā Koe – Greetings'.
32 Grace, Interview.
33 The difference, of course, is that most of the youth in Ōtara were migrants to that place.
34 Ngatoro, Interview.
35 Ibid.
36 Moss, Interview; Apanui, Interview; Apanui, 'Kaupapa Māori'; 'Native Affairs'.
37 Aperahama, Interview.
38 Katchafire, Te Ahi Kaa.
39 Aperahama, Interview.
40 *He Koha Ma Bob Marley*.
41 Nandor Tanczos (2009) made this observation to me.
42 Biographic detail is sourced from 'Death of Captain Speedy'; 'Speedy of Abyssinia'; 'Emir Ali'.
43 My thanks to Ras Mark Solomon for alerting me to the story of Emir Ali.
44 'Lecture by Captain Speedy'; 'Lecture on Abyssinia'.
45 'Te Kīngi O Etiopia', *Te Puke Ki Hikurangi* 2, no. 22 (1900), 6-7. MNC.
46 'Abyssinia: List of Telegrams from 1923', 1923. EA1 134 10/111927. NZA.

47 McIntosh, A. D., 'Memorandum to Parliamentary Library of New Zealand: Attitude to Abyssinia', 20 May 1946. EA1 134 260/4/2. NZA.

48 Selassie I, Haile. 'Telegram to Mr Jordan', 7 May 1941. EA1 134 260/4/3. NZA.

49 McIntosh, 'Memorandum to Parliamentary Library of New Zealand: Attitude to Abyssinia'.

50 'Fighting Lead from New Zealand Workers'.

51 'Emir Ali'.

52 For example, 'End of Slavery in Ethiopia'.

53 'Lecture on Abyssinia'.

54 Rauhihi-Ness, Interview, 22 February 2011.

55 'Tribute to New Zealand'.

56 O'Reilly and Tareha-O'Reilly, Interview.

57 Buchanan, Interview.

58 Campbell, 95bFM Historical Society.

59 'Fete's Letter', 1982. PAA.

60 Ness, Interview.

61 Mita, *Dread*.

62 Ness, Interview.

63 On the Dread see Douglass and Boxill, 'Lantern and the Light'; Mita, *Dread;* Patel, *Children of Zion;* and the work forthcoming from David Robinson's ground-breaking PhD thesis.

64 Heeney, Interview.

65 Gillies, *Ngati Dread*, 13.

66 Turner, Harold, 'Letter to Hensley Dyer', 29 December 1989. MS 1321 002/130. HA.

67 Heeney, Hone, 'Letter to Harold Turner', 12 November 1990. MS 1431 002/127. HA; Turner, Harold, 'Note Fragment', 1993. MS 1431 001/066. HA.

68 O'Reilly and Tareha-O'Reilly, Interview.

69 Ashton, 'Tame Te Maro'.

70 Mita, *Dread*.

71 Rauhihi-Ness, Interview, July 2010.

72 Campbell, 'Rasta in Aotearoa', 18.

73 Ibid., 19.

74 Ibid.; Hawkeswood, 'I'n'I Ras Tafari', 84.

75   Ness, Interview; Buchanan, Interview; Rauhihi-Ness, Interview, July 2010; Reid, 'The Twelve Tribes of Israel'.

76   Rauhihi-Ness, 'Twelve Tribes of Israel Aotearoa New Zealand'.

77   Rauhihi-Ness, Interview, July 2010.

78   Issa, Interview.

79   Brown, 'Twelve Tribes'.

80   Campbell, Interview.

81   Rauhihi-Ness, 'Twelve Tribes of Israel Aotearoa New Zealand'.

82   Turner, Harold, 'Notes on Interview with Hensley Dyer', 1990. MS 1431 002/130. HA.

83   Hawkeswood, 'I'n'I Ras Tafari', 106; Rauhihi-Ness, Interview, 22 February 2011.

84   Turner, Harold, 'Notes on RasTafarians for Prison Superintendents, Wellington', 1989. MS 1431 002/127. HA; Legat, 'Rastaman Vibration'.

85   On the concomitant disarming and commodification of Marley's message by the music industry see Stephens, 'Babylon's "natural mystic"'.

86   I have had insightful reasonings with Zena Tamanui and Ruia Aperahama regarding this issue.

87   Apanui, Interview; see also Miriama Rauhihi-Ness's comments in Babington, *Nga Reo: Jah.*

88   A number of correspondents have conveyed this point to me in different ways.

89   Cited in Hogg, 'Real Rastaman Fights Back'.

90   Woods, *Highway 35*, 37; Heeney, Interview.

91   Ness, Interview.

92   Babington, *Nga Reo: Jah.*

93   Ness, Interview; Rauhihi-Ness, Interview, July 2010; Perkins, Interview.

94   Sutherland and Parsons, 'Background to WAI 262'.

95   Grace, Interview.

96   Mita, *Dread.*

97   Heeney, Interview.

Chapter Seven

1 Huie-Jolly, 'Maori "Jews" and a Resistant Reading of John 5.10-47'.
2 See, for example, Comaroff and Comaroff, *Of Revelation and Revolution*; and Sugirtharajah, *The Bible and the Third World*.
3 Henare, 'Changing Images of Nineteenth Century Māori Society', 95; Young III, *A Pan-African Theology*, 18.
4 Henare, 'Changing Images of Nineteenth Century Māori Society', 62.
5 See variously, Hegel, *Lectures on the Philosophy of World History*; Freud, *Moses and Monotheism*; Pettazzoni, 'The Formation of Monotheism'.
6 Sawyerr, *God, Ancestor or Creator?*, 96.
7 Gell, 'Closure and Multiplication', 23-5.
8 Aperahama, 'Atua'.
9 Tony Tafari, Interview.
10 Te Haupapa-o-Tane, 'Io, the Supreme God', 141.
11 For an overview of the debates see Simpson, 'Io as Supreme Being'.
12 Henare, 'Changing Images of Nineteenth Century Māori Society', 74. See also Best, *Māori Religion and Mythology*, 22; Witchel, 'A Forceful Lever', 29.
13 Zahan, *The Religion, Spirituality and Thought of Traditional Africa*, 20-1; Van Stipriaan, 'Watramama/Mami Wata'. Schuler, *Alas, Alas, Kongo*, 72.
14 Pere, *Ako*, 14.
15 Nicholas, *Narrative Of A Voyage To New Zealand*, 286-7.
16 Best, *The Whare Kohanga and Its Lore*, 28-34.
17 Marsden, 'God, Man and Universe', 4.
18 Metge, 'Returning the Gift', 317.
19 Sawyerr, *God, Ancestor or Creator?*, 105.
20 Young III, *A Pan-African Theology*, 108; Elsmore, *Like Them That Dream*, 80-1.
21 See Sugirtharajah, *The Bible and the Third World*, 182.
22 Heschel, *The Prophets Vol. 1*, 21.
23 Ibid., 4, 31; Shulman, *American Prophecy*, 4.
24 Zahan, *The Religion, Spirituality and Thought of Traditional Africa*, 85-6.
25 Aperahama, 'The Campaign Against Tohunga by Te Māngai and Hamuera'.
26 Smith, 'Tohu and Māori Knowing', 266; see also Pere, *Ako*, 64-5.

27 Heschel, *The Prophets Vol. 1*, 25; and in general see Heschel, *The Prophets Vol. 2*, Ch. 11.

28 Ong, *Orality and Literacy*, 32.

29 Horton, 'African Traditional Thought and Western Science', 157.

30 Pollard, 'Dread Talk'.

31 Right Hon. Binghi Congo Nyah, Interview.

32 Hutton and Murrell, 'Rastas' Psychology of Blackness', 50; Owens, *Dread*, 179.

33 Ong, *The Presence of the Word*, 113; Tambiah, 'The Magical Power of Words', 184.

34 Smith, 'Tohu and Māori Knowing', 267.

35 Witchel, 'A Forceful Lever', 28–9.

36 See, for example, Stewart, *Three Eyes for the Journey*.

37 Clark, *Hauhau*, 82.

38 See Heschel, *The Prophets Vol. 1*, 12, 21; Young III, *A Pan-African Theology*, 3, 18.

39 See also Shulman, *American Prophecy*, 10.

40 Bi-cultural Commission of the Anglican Church, *Te Ripoata a Te Komihana*, 3; Te Ua, Interview.

41 Bi-cultural Commission of the Anglican Church, *Te Ripoata a Te Komihana*, 3; Sinclair, *Prophetic Histories*, 18.

42 Newman, *Bible and Treaty*, 121.

43 Binney, 'Papahurihia', 322.

44 Ibid., 325.

45 Ibid.

46 See Binney, 'Papahurihia, Pukerenga, Te Atua Wera and Te Nākahi'.

47 Wilson, 'Papahurihia, First Maori Prophet', 476.

48 Binney, 'Papahurihia', 327.

49 Wilson, 'Papahurihia, First Maori Prophet', 476.

50 See, for example, Drake, *The Redemption of Africa and Black Religion*, 23.

51 Gibson, *Comfa Religion and Creole Language*, 56–7.

52 Wilson, 'Papahurihia, First Maori Prophet', 477.

53 Davidson and Lineham, *Transplanted Christianity*, 224.

54 Elsmore, *Like Them That Dream*, 72.

55 Wilson, 'Papahurihia, First Maori Prophet', 475.

56 Binney, 'Papahurihia', 323.

57 Buick, *New Zealand's First War, Or, The Rebellion of Hone Heke*, 29.

58 Apanui, Interview.

59 Henare, 'Changing Images of Nineteenth Century Māori Society', 96.

60 Ibid., 221–2.

61 Davidson and Lineham, *Transplanted Christianity*, 130.

62 Henare, 'Changing Images of Nineteenth Century Māori Society', 194.

63 Royal, 'A Modern View of Mana', 6.

64 Swainson, *New Zealand and Its Colonization*, 4–5.

65 Stokes, *Wiremu Tamihana*, 171.

66 Royal, 'A Modern View of Mana', 6.

67 Newman, *Bible and Treaty*, 127.

68 Elsmore, *Like Them That Dream*, 27.

69 Sinclair, *Prophetic Histories*, 18.

70 Henare, 'Changing Images of Nineteenth Century Māori Society', 74.

71 Davidson and Lineham, *Transplanted Christianity*, 138.

72 Ibid., 130; Stokes, *Wiremu Tamihana*, 301.

73 Ibid., 40 fn. 115; Clark, *Hauhau*, 81–2.

74 Clark, *Hauhau*, 79, 85; Davidson and Lineham, *Transplanted Christianity*, 142.

75 See, in general, Stokes, *Wiremu Tamihana*, 405–35.

76 Head, 'The Gospel of Te Ua Haumene', 12.

77 Henare, 'Changing Images of Nineteenth Century Māori Society', 151.

78 Clark, *Hauhau*, 85.

79 Ibid., 97–8; Head, 'The Gospel of Te Ua Haumene', 31 fn. 32.

80 Clark, *Hauhau*, 93.

81 Stokes, *Wiremu Tamihana*, 433.

82 Head, 'The Gospel of Te Ua Haumene', 11.

83 Ibid., 17.

84 Ibid., 17–18.

85 See especially Paterson, 'Kiri Mā, Kiri Mangu'; see also Belich, 'Myth, Race and Identity in New Zealand'.

86 Head, 'The Gospel of Te Ua Haumene', 35 fn. 77.

87 Elsmore, *Lke Them That Dream*, 63.

88 Paterson, 'Kiri Mā, Kiri Mangu', 89.

89 Ibid.

90 Ibid.

91 Clark, *Hauhau*, 74.

92 Paterson, 'Ngā Reo O Ngā Niupepa', 131, 134. My thanks to Lachlan Paterson for informing me of this episode at the first academic conference that I attended in Aotearoa NZ.

93 Cited in ibid., 132.

94 Clark, *Hauhau*, 97.

95 Head, 'The Gospel of Te Ua Haumene', 29.

96 By the prophet Te Kooti. See Binney, *Redemption Songs*, 66–71.

97 Gudgeon, 'Maori Religion', 118.

98 Shilliam, 'Intervention and Colonial-Modernity'.

99 It was Richard Hill who first suggested to me that RasTafari could be considered in the context of the Māori prophetic tradition.

Chapter Eight

1 Aperahama, Interview.

2 Smith and Smith, *Te Omeka Pa*, 6–7.

3 Sinclair, *Prophetic Histories*, 38; Newman, *Rātana Revisited*, 45.

4 Newman, *Rātana Revisited*, 45.

5 Sinclair, *Prophetic Histories*, 37.

6 Newman, *Rātana Revisited*, 54.

7 Ibid.

8 Henderson, *Rātana*, 87.

9 Raureti, 'The Rātana Movement', 16–17; Henderson, *Rātana*, 82; Aperahama, Interview.

10 Henderson, *Rātana*, 55.

11 Ibid., 283.

12 Rātana, T. W., 'Greetings to British Prime Minister', 1924. MSY 4976. AT.

13 See Dow, 'The Tohunga Suppression Act 1907'.

14 Davidson and Lineham, *Transplanted Christianity*, 166.

15 Binney, *Redemption Songs*.

16 Smith, Interview, 21 January 2010.

17 Newman, *Rātana Revisited*, 105.

18 Clark, *Hauhau*, 124.

19 Bi-cultural Commission of the Anglican Church, *Te Ripoata a Te Komihana*, 5; Henderson, *Rātana*, 42.

20 Newman, *Rātana Revisited*, 162, 197.

21 Ibid., 119.

22 Ibid., 172.

23 Aperahama, 'Māori Prophets'.

24 Ibid.

25 Newman, *Rātana Revisited*, 127.

26 Ibid., 119; Aperahama, 'Māori Prophets'.

27 Aperahama, 'Rātana and Garvey'; Perkins, Interview.

28 'Programme of the Visit of His Imperial Highness Taffari Makonnen'. 1924. PRO 30/69/27. BA.

29 Newman, *Rātana Revisited*, 138.

30 Henderson, *Rātana*, 58–9.

31 Aperahama, 'Māori Prophets'.

32 Aperahama, 'Garvey'.

33 Aperahama, 'Rātana's American Tour and Garvey'.

34 Aperahama, 'Rātana's American Tour and Garvey'; Aperahama, 'Māori Prophets'.

35 Smith, Interview, 21 January 2010; Smith and Smith, *Te Omeka Pa*, 34.

36 Smith and Smith, *Te Omeka Pa*, 37.

37 Ibid., 34–5.

38 Garvey, *Philosophy and Opinions of Marcus Garvey*, 34.

39 Tony Tafari, Interview.

40 Gnanasunderam, 'Birthday Celebrations at the Rātana Pā'.

41 Smith and Smith, *Te Omeka Pa*, 37; Aperahama, Interview.

42 Newman, *Rātana Revisited*, 213.

43 Smith, Interview, 18 February 2011.

44 Aperahama, 'Where Did the Name Māngai or Mouth of God Come From?'

45 Ibid.

46 Ibid.

47 Aperahama, Interview; Smith, Interview, 18 February 2011.

48 Smith and Smith, *Te Omeka Pa*, 37; Smith, Interview, 18 February 2011.

49 'Rātana's Book Closes'; Newman, *Rātana Revisited*, 368.

50 Aperahama, Interview.

51 Rauhihi-Ness, Interview.

52 Ibid., 32; Perkins, Interview.

53 The following information is sourced from Perkins, Interview.

54 *Gill's Expositions of the Bible.*

55 Sinclair, *Prophetic Histories*, 31.

56 Ibid., 33; Newman, *Bible and Treaty*, 136–7.

57 Chalmers, Interview.

58 Brown, 'James K. Baxter', 134; Dennison, 'Ko Te Pakeha Te Tēina'; Dyce, 'Stories of Development', 17–19.

59 Newton, *The Double Rainbow*, 31.

60 Baxter, James K., 'Talk to Training College Students', n.d. MS Papers 8856. AT, 31.

61 Ibid., 14; see also Phillips, 'James K. Baxter', 269.

62 Baxter, 'Talk to Training College Students', 10.

63 Ibid., 32.

64 Baxter, 'Pig Island Letters', 115.

65 Baxter, 'Talk to Training College Students', 31.

66 Phillips, 'James K. Baxter', 270; Baxter, *Jerusalem Daybook*, 16.

67 Baxter, 'The Māori Jesus'.

68 Maung, 'Letter from Te Waka E Manaaki Trust'.

69 Baxter, 'Ballard of the Junkies and the Fuzz', 192.

70 See Hurbon, *Voodoo*.

71 Baxter, 'Jerusalem Sonnets: Poems for Colin Durning', 204.

72 Phillips, 'James K. Baxter', 272.

73 Ibid.

74 Ibid.

75 Baxter, *Jerusalem Daybook*, 41.

76 Brown, 'James K. Baxter', 134.

77 Newton, *The Double Rainbow*, 29.

78 Baxter, *Jerusalem Daybook*, 50.

79 Ibid., 22.

80 Ibid., 7.

81 Baxter, 'He Waiata Mo Taku Tangi', 227; Newton, *The Double Rainbow*, 86; Baxter, *Jerusalem Daybook*, 21.

82 Baxter, *Jerusalem Daybook*, 48.

83 Ibid., 9, 40–1.

84 McKay, *The Life of James K. Baxter*, 268; 'The Pot is on the Boil'; De Nave, 'Ko Te Whenua Te Whaea Kore E Mate'.

85 McKay, *The Life of James K. Baxter*, 289.

86 O'Reilly, 'Muldoon of the Five Stones', 21.

87 Ryder, Interview.

88 Dyce, Interview.

89 France, Interview; Dyce, Interview; O'Reilly and Tareha-O'Reilly, Interview.

90 See Baxter, *Jerusalem Daybook*, 44, 54–5; see also Pere, *Ako*, 57–9.

91 O'Reilly, 'Vision of Keskidee Aroha'.

92 'Minutes of Keskidee Aroha Meeting'.

93 McKay, *The Life of James K. Baxter*, 39.

94 O'Reilly, Interview.

95 The following is sourced from O'Reilly, 'Ngā Mōkai'.

96 'Gang Bills Spark Debate'.

97 In reading this poem Tiopira McDowell has pointed out to me that ochre – or *kura* – is a sacred colour for Māori. Hence, this tribesman must be a *rangatira* (chief).

Chapter Nine

1 Beattie, 'Traditions and Legends'.

2 Newnham, *Apartheid is Not a Game*, 40.

3 Aperahama, Interview.

4 Garvey, 'Speech by Marcus Garvey, 1937', 791.

5 Ibid., 790–1.

6 Cited in McPherson, *RasTafari and Politics: Sixty Years of a Developing Cultural Ideology*, 15.

7 Thompson, 'New Zealand Liberation Struggle Seeks Base of Black Struggles'.

8 Mita, Interview.

9 Aperahama, Interview.

10 Brodber, 'Sleeping's Beauty'.

11 Massey, *The Natural Genesis*, 535–98.

12 Dalrymple, *An Account of Discoveries*, 18.

13 Dunbabin, *Slavers of the South Seas*, 44.

14 Ibid., 59.

15 Forrest, 'Extract', 1779. MS-0793. AT.

16 Ibid., 206.

17 On this history see ibid., 198–219; Logan, 'East India Company'; Silva Jayasuriya, 'East India Company in Sumatra'.

18 DeLoughrey, 'Routes of Breadfruit'.

19 Dunbabin, *Slavers of the South Seas*, 117–19.

20 Horne, *The White Pacific*, 7.

21 Dunbabin, *Slavers of the South Seas*, 141.

22 Horne, *The White Pacific*, 137.

23 See especially Horne, *The White Pacific*.

24 Ibid., 5.

25 Graham, *Sugar Slaves*; Tate and Foy, 'Slavery and Racism in South Pacific Annexations'.

26 Hawkeswood, 'I'n'I Ras Tafari', 128.

27 Clark, 'Dumont d'Urville's Oceania'.

28 Nicholas, *Narrative Of A Voyage To New Zealand*, 266–7.

29 Dieffenbach, *Travels in New Zealand*, 1–12.

30 Power, *Sketches*, 143.

31 See Horne, *The White Pacific*, 134–5.

32 Ness, 'Reggae and RasTafari'.

33 For example Glissant, *Caribbean Discourse*.

34 Harawira, 'Proposal – Funding for Rural Development'. 'Pining for Native Bush'.

35 John Heeney, cited in Iti et al., *Moko – Maori Tattoo*, 131, 133.

36 Cited in Phillips, 'James K. Baxter: A Dialogue with His Later Theological and Philosophical Thought in the Context of Aotearoa/New Zealand', 273.

37 Snell, 'Captain Cook's Surgeons', 43–4.

38 See Davies, 'Cook'.

39 Wells, *The History of Taranaki*, 19.

40 Hodgskin, *Eight Month's Sojourn*, 14.

41 Swainson, *New Zealand and Its Colonization*, 9.

42 See Hutton, *The Logic and Historic Significance of the Haitian Revolution*.

43 Newman, *Bible and Treaty*, 119; Binney, 'Papahurihia', 327.

44 Clark, *Hauhau*, 81.

45 Gillies, *Ngati Dread*, 45.

46 Crozet, *Crozet's Voyage to Tasmania*, 3.

47 For this story see Thomson, *The Story of New Zealand*, 253; Buller, *Forty Years in New Zealand*, 251; and Downes, *Old Whanagui*, 167–70.

48 Downes, *Old Whanagui*, 168.

49 Ibid.

50 Cowan, *Trader in Cannibal Land*; and Tapsell, *Historic Maketu*, who seems to derive most of her information from Cowan.

51 Cowan, *Trader in Cannibal Land*, 74, 137.

52 Ibid., 105.

53 Buchanan, Interview.

54 'Account Books'.

55 'George Alias Jumbo'.

56 Baines, *The Narrative of Edward Crewe*, 214–15.

57 Ibid., 148.

58 Paton, 'An Injurious Population'.

59 Paterson, 'Kiri Mā, Kiri Mangu', 82.

60 See Evans, *Edward Eyre*.

61 Mita, Interview.

Bibliography

1977 Young Maori Leaders Conference. University of Auckland Library.

Afari, Yasus. *Overstanding RasTafari: Jamaica's Gift to the World*. Kingston: Senya-Cum, 2007.

—'Footprints and Visions of RasTafari'. Presented at the RasTafari Studies Conference, University of West Indies, 2010.

Ahluwalia, P. 'Out of Africa: Post-Structuralism's Colonial Roots'. *Postcolonial Studies* 8, no. 2 (2005): 137–54.

Airini, Melani Anae and Karlo Mila-Schaaf. *TEU LE VA — Relationships Across Research and Policy in Pasifika Education*. Wellington: Ministry of Education, 2010.

Alba, Pilar. 'Who Is Steve Biko and Does He Live in Ponsonby?' *Bitches, Witches & Dykes*, November 1981.

Alvarez, Luis. 'Reggae Rhythms in Dignity's Diaspora: Globalization, Indigenous Identity, and the Circulation of Cultural Struggle'. *Popular Music and Society* 31, no. 5 (2008): 575–97.

Amadahy, Zainab and Bonita Lawrence. 'Indigenous Peoples and Black People in Canada: Settlers or Allies?' In *Breaching the Colonial Contract: Anti-Colonialism in the US and Canada*, ed. A. Kempf, 105–36. New York: Springer Publishing, 2009.

Anae, Melani, ed. *Polynesian Panthers: The Crucible Years*. Auckland: Reed Publishing, 2006.

Anae, Melani, Tigilau Ness, Alec Toleafoa and Will 'Ilolahia. 'The Polynesian Panthers – Political Activism in Aotearoa New Zealand'. Presented at the OCIS IV Conference, University of Auckland, July 2010.

Andi. 'United Brown Brothers'. *P.D. Barb.*, 1970.

Apanui, Ngahiwi. 'Kaupapa Māori and Reggae Music'. Presented at the Caribbean Connections Workshop, Victoria University of Wellington, 12 August 2011.

Aperahama, Ruia. 'Atua'. *Te Māngai Pono*, 3 October 2011.

—'The Campaign Against Tohunga by Te Māngai and Hamuera'. *Te Māngai Pono*, 2011.

—'Garvey', 10 February 2012. Email.

—'RasTafari and the Māori Prophets'. Presented at the Caribbean Connections Workshop, Victoria University of Wellington, 12 August 2011.

—'Rātana and Garvey', 8 September 2011. Email.

—'Rātana's American Tour and Garvey', 14 August 2011, Email.

—'Where Did the Name Māngai or Mouth of God Come From?' *Te Māngai Pono*, 3 October 2011.

Arthur, Paige. *Unfinished Projects: Decolonization and the Philosophy of Jean-Paul Sartre*. London: Verso, 2010.

Asad, Talal. *Anthropology and the Colonial Encounter*. New York: Humanities Press, 1973.

Ashton, Lloyd. 'Tame Te Maro'. *Mana* 26, no. 2 (2005): 6–8.

Atal, Yogesh. 'The Call for Indigenisation'. In *Indigeneity and Universality in Social Science: A South Asian Response*, eds P. N. Mukherji and C. Sengupta. New Delhi: Sage, 2004, 99–113.

Ausubel, David. *The Fern and the Tiki: An American View of New Zealand National Character, Social Attitudes and Race Relations*. New York: Holt, Rinehart and Winston, 1965.

Awatere, Donna. 'Kōrero-Tia Wahine Ma!' *Broadsheet*, November 1980.

—'Rugby, Racism and Riot Gear'. *Broadsheet*, November 1981.

Awatere, Donna, Hana Jackson, Eva Rickard, Titewhai Harawira and Hilda Halkyard. 'Wahine Ma Kōrerotia'. *Broadsheet*, 1982.

Babington, Kirsty. *Nga Reo: Jah*. Front of the Box Productions, 2002.

Baer, William, ed. *Conversations with Derek Walcott*. University Press of Mississippi, 1996.

Baines, William Mortimer. *The Narrative of Edward Crewe, Or, Life in New Zealand*. London: Sampson Low, Marston, Low & Searle, 1874.

Bargh, Maria. *Resistance: An Indigenous Response to Neoliberalism*. Wellington: Huia, 2007.

Barrowman, Rachel. 'A Report on the Molesworth Street Incident'. In *The Police and the 1981 Tour*, 23–50. Occasional Papers 2. Victoria University History Department, 1985.

Baxter, James K. 'Ballad of the Junkies and the Fuzz'. In *Selected Poems*, ed. Paul Millar, 192–194. Manchester: Carcanet Press Limited, 2010.

—'He Waiata Mo Taku Tangi'. In *Selected Poems*, ed. Paul Millar, 226–30. Manchester: Carcanet Press Limited, 2010.

—*Jerusalem Daybook*. Wellington: Price Milburn, 1971.

—'Jerusalem Sonnets: Poems for Colin Durning'. In *Selected Poems*, ed. Paul Millar, 194–219. Manchester: Carcanet Press Limited, 2010.

—'The Māori Jesus'. In *Selected Poems*, ed. Paul Millar, 145–7. Manchester: Carcanet Press Limited, 2010.

—'Pig Island Letters'. In *Selected Poems*, ed. Paul Millar, 114–24. Manchester: Carcanet Press Limited, 2010.

Beattie, H. 'Traditions and Legends Collected from the Natives of Murihiku'. *The Journal of the Polynesian Society* 24, no. 95 (1915): 98–112.

Belich, James. 'Myth, Race and Identity in New Zealand'. *The Journal of the Polynesian Society* 31, no. 1 (1997): 9–22.

Best, Elsdon. *Māori Religion and Mythology Part 1*. Wellington: Government Printer, 1976.

—*The Whare Kohanga and Its Lore*. Wellington: Government Printer, 1975.

Beverley, John. 'The Dilemma of Subaltern Studies at Duke'. *Nepantla: Views from the South* 1, no. 1 (2000): 33–44.

Bi-cultural Commission of the Anglican Church. *Te Ripoata a Te Komihana Mo Te Kaupapa Tikanga Rua Mo Te Tiriti O Waitangi*. Auckland: Church of the Province of New Zealand, 1986.

Biko, Steve. 'Black Consciousness and the Quest for a True Humanity'. In *I Write What I Like*, 87–99. London: Heinemann, 1979.

—'Black Souls in White Skins?' In *I Write What I Like*, 19–26. London: Heinemann, 1979.

Biltcliffe, Pippa. 'Walter Crane and the Imperial Federation Map Showing the Extent of the British Empire (1886)'. *Imago Mundi* 57, no. 1 (2005): 63–9.

Binney, Judith. 'Papahurihia, Pukerenga, Te Atua Wera and Te Nākahi: How Many Prophets?' *The Journal of the Polynesian Society* 116, no. 3 (2007): 309–20.

—'Papahurihia: Some Thoughts on Interpretation'. *The Journal of the Polynesian Society* 75, no. 3 (1966): 321–31.

—*Redemption Songs: A Life of the Nineteenth Century Maori Leader Te Kooti Arikirangi Te Turuki*. Auckland: Auckland University Press, 1995.

—'The Ringatū Traditions of Predictive History'. *The Journal of Pacific History* 23, no. 2 (1988): 167–74.

Bishop, Russell. 'Freeing Ourselves From Neo-Colonial Domination in Research: A Māori Approach to Creating Knowledge'. *International Journal of Qualitative Studies in Education* 11, no. 2 (1998): 199–219.

'Black Dykes'. *Bitches, Witches & Dykes*, November 1981.

'Black Panthers: The New Revolt'. *Listener*, 12 January 1969.

'Black Power, White Peril'. *Listener*, 29 April 1968.

'Black Women's Hui'. *Broadsheet*, September 1982.

Bob Marley and the Wailers. 'Babylon System'. Vol. *Survival*. Tuff Gong, 1979.

Bogues, Anthony. *Black Heretics, Black Prophets: Radical Political Intellectuals.* New York: Routledge, 2003.

—'Black Power, Decolonization, and Caribbean Politics: Walter Rodney and the Politics of The Groundings with My Brothers'. *Boundary 2* 36, no. 1 (20 March 2009): 127–47.

Boxill, Ian. 'Atlantic Meets Pacific: Music as an Element of Struggle in Aotearoa/New Zealand'. *Critical Criminology* 7, no. 2 (1996): 108–22.

Brathwaite, Edward. *The Arrivants: A New World Trilogy.* Oxford: Oxford University Press, 1973.

Bray, D. H. *Proposals for Te Puke O Tara.* Ministry of Recreation and Sport, 1981.

Brodber, Erna. *The Continent of Black Consciousness.* London: New Beacon Books, 2003.

—'Re-Engineering Blackspace'. *Caribbean Quarterly* 43, no. 1/2 (1997): 70–81.

—'Sleeping's Beauty and the Prince Charming'. In *Stories from Blue Latitudes: Caribbean Women Writers at Home and Abroad*, ed. Elizabeth Nunez and Jennifer Sparrow, 27–31. Emeryville: Seal Press, 2006.

Brown, Danielle. 'James K. Baxter: The Identification of the "Poet" and the Authority of the "Prophet"'. *Journal of New Zealand Literature*, no. 13 (1995): 133–42.

Brown, Norman Oliver. *Hermes the Thief: The Evolution of a Myth.* Madison: University of Wisconsin Press, 1947.

Brown, Oblex. 'Twelve Tribes', 25 October 2010. Email.

'"Brown Power" Emergent'. *The Dominion Weekend Magazine*, 12 September 1970.

Buick, Thomas Lindsay. *New Zealand's First War, Or, The Rebellion of Hone Heke.* Cambridge: Cambridge University Press, 2011.

Buller, James. *Forty Years in New Zealand.* London: Hodder & Stoughton, 1878.

Buxton, R. G. A. 'Introduction'. In *From Myth to Reason? Studies in the Development of Greek Thought*, ed. R. G. A. Buxton, 1–24. Oxford: Oxford University Press, 1999.

—'Monsters in Greek Ethnography and Society in the Fifth and Fourth Centuries BCE'. In *From Myth to Reason? Studies in the Development of Greek Thought*, ed. R. G. A. Buxton, 197–214. Oxford: Oxford University Press, 1999.

Campbell, Duncan. 95bFM Historical Society, 6 April 2009. http://www.95bfm.co.nz/assets/sm/190920/3/duncanwebversion.mp3

Campbell, Gordon. 'Dread Inna Western Springs'. *Listener*, 12 May 1979.

—'Rasta in Aotearoa'. *Listener*, 17 January 1981.

Cattermole, Jennifer A. 'The Routes of Roots Reggae in Aotearoa/New Zealand: The Musical Construction of Place and Identity'. MA Thesis. University of Otago, 2004.

Césaire, Aimé. *Discourse on Colonialism*. Princeton, NJ: Princeton University Press, 2007.

Chakrabarty, Dipesh. *Habitations of Modernity: Essays in the Wake of Subaltern Studies*. Chicago: University of Chicago Press, 2002.

—'Invitation to a Dialogue'. *Subaltern Studies* IV (1985): 364–76.

—'The Politics and Possibility of Historical Knowledge: Continuing the Conversation'. *Postcolonial Studies* 14, no. 2 (2011): 243–50.

'Charles S. Spivey Jr's Obituary'. *Florida Times-Union*. http://www.legacy.com/obituaries/timesunion/obituary.aspx?n=charles-s-spivey&pid=147197058&fhid=3409 (accessed 20 July 2013).

Charters, Claire and Andrew Erueti (eds). *Māori Property Rights and the Foreshore and Seabed: The Last Frontier*. Wellington: Victoria University Press, 2007.

Chatterjee, Partha. 'Talking About Modernity in Two Languages'. In *A Possible India: Essays in Political Criticism*, 263–85. New Delhi: Oxford, 1998.

—'Whose Imagined Community?' *Millennium* 20, no. 3 (1991): 521–5.

Clark, Geoffrey. 'Dumont d'Urville's Oceania'. *The Journal of Pacific History* 38, no. 2 (2003): 155–61.

Clark, Paul. '*Hauhau*': *The Pai Mārire Search for Māori Identity*. Auckland: Auckland University Press, 1975.

Clements, D. 'Brown Power: Otaki'. *Salient*, 1971.

Clifford, James. 'On Ethnographic Allegory'. In *Writing Culture: The Poetics and Politics of Ethnography*, eds J. Clifford and G. E. Marcus, 98–121. Berkeley: University of California Press, 1986.

—*Writing Culture: The Poetics and Politics of Ethnography*. Berkeley: University of California Press, 1986.

Colomb, John C. R. 'Imperial Federation'. *The Graphic*, 24 July 1886.

Comaroff, Jean and John L. Comaroff. *Of Revelation and Revolution: Christianity, Colonialism and Consciousness in South Africa*, Vol. 1. Chicago: University of Chicago Press, 1991.

Cone, James H. *A Black Theology of Liberation*. Philadelphia: J. B. Lippincott, 1970.

Cosentino, Donald. 'Who Is That Fellow in the Many-Colored Cap? Transformations of Eshu in Old and New World Mythologies'. *The Journal of American Folklore* 100, no. 397 (1987): 261–75.

Cowan, James. *A Trader in Cannibal Land: The Life and Adventures of Captain Tapsell*. Wellington: A. H. and A. W. Reed, 1935.

Crozet, Julien Marie. *Crozet's Voyage to Tasmania, New Zealand, The Ladrone Islands, and the Philippines in the Years 1771–1772*. Trans. H. Ling Roth. London: Truslove & Shirley, 1891.

Dalrymple, Alexander. *An Account of the Discoveries Made in the South Pacifick Ocean*. Potts Point, NSW: Hordern House Rare Books, 1996.

Dansey, Harry. *Te Raukura: The Feathers of the Albatross – A Narrative Play in Two Acts*. Auckland: Longman Paul, 1974.

Davidson, Allan K. and Peter J. Lineham. *Transplanted Christianity: Documents Illustrating Aspects of New Zealand Church History*. Palmerston North: Dunmore Press, 1989.

Davies, John. 'Cook: The "Adventure" and Misadventure in Queen Charlotte Sound'. *Journal of the Nelson and Marlborough Historical Societies* 2, no. 1 (1987).

Dayan, J. *Haiti, History, and the Gods*. Berkeley: University of California Press, 1995.

'Days of Rage'. *Listener*, 22 August 1981.

De Nave, Kathryn. 'Ko Te Whenua Te Whaea Kore E Mate'. *Craccum*, 4 March 1971.

'Death of Captain Speedy'. *New Zealand Herald*, 22 August 1910.

'Deep Split Indicated by Conflicting Answers'. *The Evening Post*, 13 August 1981.

Dein, Alan. 'The Keskidee'. BBC Radio 4, 7 May 2009.

DeLoughrey, Elizabeth M. 'Globalizing the Routes of Breadfruit and Other Bounties'. *Journal of Colonialism and Colonial History* 8, no. 3 (2007).

—*Routes and Roots: Navigating Caribbean and Pacific Island Literatures*. Honolulu: University of Hawai'i Press, 2007.

Dennison, John. 'Ko Te Pakeha Te Tēina: Baxter's Cross-Cultural Poetry'. *Journal of New Zealand Literature*, no. 23 (2005): 36–46.

Desmangles, Leslie Gerald. 'African Interpretations of the Christian Cross in Vodun'. *Sociological Analysis* 38, no. 1 (1977): 13–24.

Desmond, Pip. *Trust: A True Story of Women and Gangs.* Auckland: Random House New Zealand, 2009.

Dieffenbach, Ernest. *Travels in New Zealand: Vol. 2.* London: Murray, 1843.

Douglas, Edward Te Kohu. 'Foreword – The 2001 Hui a Taiohi – Young Maori Leaders' Conference in a Developmental Context'. *First Found* 207 (n.d.). http://www.firstfound.org/Vol.%207New_Folder/foreword.htm

Douglass, Te Kohu and Ian Boxill. 'The Lantern and the Light: RasTafari in Aotearoa (New Zealand)'. In *The Globalization of RasTafari*, ed. Ian Boxill, 70–97. Kingston, Jamaica: Arawak Publications, 2008.

Dow, Derek A. '"Pruned of Its Dangers": The Tohunga Suppression Act 1907'. *Health and History* 3, no. 1 (2001): 41–64.

Downes, T. W. *Old Whanagui.* Hawera, NZ: W. A. Parkinson & Co., 1915.

Drake, St Clair. *The Redemption of Africa and Black Religion.* Chicago: Third World Press, 1970.

Driver, Felix. 'In Search of The Imperial Map: Walter Crane and the Image of Empire'. *History Workshop Journal* 69, no. 1 (2010): 146–57.

Dunbabin, Thomas. *Slavers of the South Seas.* Sydney: Angus & Robertson, 1935.

Durie, Mason. *Te Mana, Te Kawanatanga: The Politics of Māori Self-Determination.* Auckland: Oxford University Press, 1998.

Dyce, Tim. 'Stories of Development: New Zealand Community Developing in the 1970s'. Presented at the Conference of the New Zealand Council of Social Services, Ashburton, 17 October 2006.

Elder, Ann. 'Hone Kaa's Good Fight'. *Metro* 35 (1984): 82–8.

Elsmore, Bronwyn. *Like Them That Dream: The Maori and the Old Testament.* Auckland: Reed, 2000.

'Emir Ali'. *Auckland Star*, 27 February 1935.

'End of Slavery in Ethiopia'. *The Dominion Post*, 23 May 1942.

Eruera, Taura. 'Common Problems for New Zealanders'. MOOHR Newsletter, January 1971. University of Auckland Library.

Evans, Julie. *Edward Eyre: Race and Colonial Governance.* Dunedin, NZ: University of Otago Press, 2005.

Evans, Rebecca. 'The Politics of Blackness and Black–White Relationships'. *Bitches, Witches & Dykes*, November 1981.

Evans, Ripeka. 'Black Unite'. *Bitches, Witches & Dykes*, December 1980.

—'Hui Wahine Maori'. *Craccum*, 17 April 1984.

Eye Witness News: Māori Activists, 1979.

Farnell, Lewis. *The Cults of the Greek States*. Oxford: Clarendon Press, 1909.

Feldman, Heidi C. 'The Black Pacific: Cuban and Brazilian Echoes in the Afro-Peruvian Revival'. *Ethnomusicology* 49, no. 2 (2005): 206–31.

Fepulea'l, Damon. *Dawn Raids*. Isola Productions, 2005.

'Fighting Lead from New Zealand Workers'. *New Leader: Paper of the Independent Labour Party*, 15 November 1935.

Figiel, Sia. 'Song of the Banyan Tree'. *The Contemporary Pacific* 22, no. 2 (2010): 273–6.

Findlay, James F. *Church People in the Struggle: The National Council of Churches and the Black Freedom Movement, 1950-1970*. New York: Oxford University Press, 1997.

Fleras, Augie and Paul Spoonley. *Recalling Aotearoa: Indigenous Politics and Ethnic Relations in New Zealand*. Auckland: Oxford University Press, 1999.

Fletcher, Judith. 'A Trickster's Oaths in the Homeric Hymn to Hermes'. *American Journal of Philology* 128 (2008): 19–46.

Freud, S. *Moses and Monotheism*. London: Hogarth Press, 1939.

From Street to Sky, Blue Batch Productions, 2007.

Gai, Olabiyi Babalola J. 'The Herskovits Legacy in African Narrative Analysis and Beyond'. *Diálogos Revista Electrónica de Historia* 3, no. 1 (2002). http://www.redalyc.org/pdf/439/43930104.pdf

'Gang Bills Spark Debate'. *New Zealand Herald*, 29 October 2009. http://www.nzherald.co.nz/nz/news/article.cfm?c_id=1&objectid=10606034

Garvey, Marcus. *Philosophy and Opinions of Marcus Garvey or Africa for the Africans: Two Vols in One*, ed. Amy Jacques Garvey. London: Frank Cass, 1967.

—'Speech by Marcus Garvey, Menelik Hall, Sydney, Nova Scotia, 1 Oct 1937'. In *The Marcus Garvey and Universal Negro Improvement Association Papers. Volume VII, November 1927–August 1940*, ed. Robert A. Hill, 788–94. University of California Press, 1991.

Gee, Debby. 'Rei Harris Interview'. *Agenda*, 1988.

Geggus, David. 'The Bois Caïman Ceremony'. In *Haitian Revolutionary Studies*, 81–92. Bloomington: Indiana University Press, 2002.

Gell, Alfred. 'Closure and Multiplication: An Essay on Polynesian Cosmology and Ritual'. In *Cosmos and Society in Oceania*, 21–56. Oxford: Berg, 1995.

Gibson, Kean. *Comfa Religion and Creole Language in a Caribbean Community*. Albany: State University of New York Press, 2001.

Gill's Expositions of the Bible, n.d. http://biblehub.com/commentaries/gill/john/19.htm

Gillies, Angus. *Ngati Dread: Vol. 3*. Auckland: Rogue Monster Books, 2011.

Gilroy, Paul. *The Black Atlantic: Modernity and Double Consciousness*. Cambridge, MA: Harvard University Press, 1993.

Glissant, Édouard. *Caribbean Discourse: Selected Essays*. Charlottesville: University Press of Virginia, 1989.

Graham, Trevor. *Sugar Slaves*. Film Australia, 1995.

Gramsci, Antonio. *Selections from the Prison Notebooks of Antonio Gramsci*, ed. Quintin Hoare and Geoffrey Nowell-Smith. London: Lawrence & Wishart, 1971.

Green, Marcus E. 'Rethinking the Subaltern and the Question of Censorship in Gramsci's Prison Notebooks'. *Postcolonial Studies* 14, no. 4 (2011): 387–404.

Green, Michael C. *Black Yanks in the Pacific: Race in the Making of American Military Empire after World War II*. Ithaca, NY: Cornell University Press, 2010.

Greig, Louise. 'The Police and the Tour'. In *The Police and the 1981 Tour*, 4–22. Occasional Papers 2. Victoria University History Department, 1985.

Grey, Lynn/Ponsonby Black Womens Collective. 'First National Hui of Black Women'. *Bitches, Witches & Dykes*, December 1980.

Gudgeon, W. E. 'Maori Religion'. *The Journal of the Polynesian Society* 14, no. 3 (1905): 107–30.

Guha, Ranajit. *History at the Limit of World-History*. New York: Columbia University Press, 2002.

—'The Prose of Counterinsurgency'. *Subaltern Studies* II (1983).

—'The Small Voice of History'. *Subaltern Studies* IX (1996): 1–12.

Gump, James O. 'The Imperialism of Cultural Assimilation: Sir George Grey's Encounter with the Maori and the Xhosa, 1845–1868'. *Journal of World History* 9, no. 1 (1998).

Halkyard, Hilda. 'Otara Black Woman Batonned'. *Broadsheet*, August 1982.

Hall, Jacquelyn D. 'The Long Civil Rights Movement and the Political Uses of the Past'. *The Journal of American History* 91, no. 4 (2005): 1233–63.

Harris, Aroha. "'Sharing Our Differences Together": Whakapapa of Experience in Post-War Auckland'. Australian Institute of Aboriginal and Torres Strait Islander Studies Conference, Canberra, 2009.

Hau`ofa, Epeli. 'The Ocean in Us'. In *We Are the Ocean*, 41–59. Honolulu: University of Hawai'i Press, 2008.

—'Pasts to Remember', in *We Are the Ocean*. Honolulu: University of Hawai'i Press, 2008.

Hawkeswood, William G. 'I'n'I Ras Tafari: Identity and the Rasta Movement in Auckland'. MA in Anthropology, University of Auckland, 1983.

Hayes III, Floyd W. and Francis A. Kiene III. "'All Power to the People": The Political Thought of Huey P. Newton and the BPP'. In *In Search of the Black Panther Party: New Perspectives on a Revolutionary Movement*, eds Jama Lazerow and Yohuru R. Williams, 157–76. Durham: Duke University Press, 2006.

He Koha Ma Bob Marley. Toa TV, 2009.

Head, Lyndsay. 'The Gospel of Te Ua Haumene'. *The Journal of the Polynesian Society* 101, no. 1 (1992): 7–44.

Hegel, G. W. F. *Lectures on the Philosophy of World History – Introduction: Reason in History*. Cambridge, UK: Cambridge University Press, 1975.

Henare, Manuka Arnold. 'The Changing Images of Nineteenth Century Māori Society – From Tribes to Nation'. DPhil Thesis, Victoria University of Wellington, 2003.

Henderson, J. McLeod. *Rātana: The Origins and the Story of the Movement*. Wellington: The Polynesian Society, 1963.

Herskovits, Melville J. *Dahomey, An Ancient West African Kingdom*. Evanston: Northwestern University Press, 1967.

Heschel, Abraham Joshua. *The Prophets Vol. 1*. New York: Harper Torchbooks, 1969.

—*The Prophets Vol. 2*. New York: Harper & Row, 1972.

Hodgskin, Richard. *A Narrative of Eight Month's Sojourn in New Zealand*. Coleraine: S. Hart, 1841.

Hogg, Colin. 'Real Rastaman Fights Back'. *New Zealand Times*, 2 March 1986.

Hokowhitu, Brendan, Nathalie Kermoal, Chris Andersen, Anna Petersen, Michael Reilly, Isabel Altamirano-Jiménez and Poia Rewi. *Indigenous Identity and Resistance: Researching the Diversity of Knowledge*. Dunedin: Otago University Press, 2010.

Homiak, John P. 'The "Ancients of Days" Seated Black: Eldership, Oral Tradition and Ritual in RasTafari Culture'. PhD Thesis, Brandeis University, 1985.

Horne, Gerald. *The White Pacific: U.S. Imperialism and Black Slavery in the South Seas after the Civil War*. Honolulu: University of Hawai'i Press, 2007.

Horton, Robin. 'African Traditional Thought and Western Science'. *Africa* 37, no. 2 (1967): 155–87.

Hudson, Maui L., Annabel L. M. Ahuriri-Driscoll, Marino G. Lea and Rod A. Lea. 'Whakapapa – A Foundation for Genetic Research?' *Journal of Bioethical Inquiry* 4, no. 1 (1 March 2007): 43–9.

Huie-Jolly, Mary. 'Maori "Jews" and a Resistant Reading of John 5:23.10-47'. In *The Postcolonial Biblical Reader*, 224–37. London: Wiley-Blackwell, 2005.

Hunn, J. K. *Report on Department of Maori Affairs*. Wellington: R. E. Owen, 1961.

Hurbon, Laënnec. *Voodoo: Search for the Spirit*. New York: H. N. Abrams, 1995.

Hutton, Clinton. 'The Creative Ethos of the African Diaspora: Performance Aesthetics and the Fight for Freedom and Identity'. *Caribbean Quarterly* 53, no. 1 (2007): 127–49.

—*The Logic and Historic Significance of the Haitian Revolution and the Cosmological Roots of Haitian Freedom*. Kingston: Arawak, 2007.

Hutton, Clinton and Nathaniel Samuel Murrell. 'Rastas' Psychology of Blackness, Resistance, and Somebodiness'. In *Chanting Down Babylon: The RasTafari Reader*, ed. Nathaniel S. Murrell, William D. Spencer and Adrian A. McFarlane, 36–54. Philadelphia: Temple University Press, 1998.

Iah, C. 'Nyahbinghi Order'. *Jahug* 2, no. 2 (1992): 5.

Icaza, R. and R. Vázquez. 'Social Struggles as Epistemic Struggles'. *Development and Change* 44 (2013): 683–704.

Ihimaera, Witi, ed. *Growing Up Māori*. Auckland: Tandem Press, 1998.

Ikenga-Metuh, Emefie. 'Religious Concepts in West African Cosmogenies: A Problem of Interpretation'. *Journal of Religion in Africa* 13, no. 1 (1982): 11–24.

'Ilolahia, Will, Miriama Rauhihi-Ness and Tigilau Ness. 'Polynesian Panthers Lecture'. Victoria University of Wellington, 14 May 2010.

'Interview with Nga Tamatoa Tuatoru'. Maori Organization on Human Rights, September 1971. University of Auckland Library.

Iti, Tame Wairere, Nicole MacDonald, Hans Neleman and Pita Turei. *Moko – Maori Tattoo*. Zurich: Edition Stemmle, 1999.

Jackson, Moana. 'Research and The Colonisation of Māori Knowledge'. In *Proceedings of Te Oru Rangahau Māori Research and Development Conference*, 78–86. Palmerston North: Massey University, 1998.

Jackson, Syd. 'We Want a Truly Non-Racial Society'. *Te Maori* 5, no. 3 (1973): 32–3.

James, Trevor. 'Black Literatures in the Pacific: The Spider and the Bee'. In *Connections: Essays on Black Literatures*, ed. E. S. Nelson, 61–74. Canberra: Aboriginal Studies Press, 1988.

Jones, Andrew F. and Nikhil P. Singh. 'Guest Editor's Introduction'. *Positions* 11, no. 1 (2003): 1–9.

Joseph, Peniel E. *The Black Power Movement: Rethinking the Civil Rights– Black Power Era*. New York: Routledge, 2006.

Kaiwai, Hector and Kirsten Zemke-White. 'Kapa Haka as a Web of Cultural Meanings'. In *Cultural Studies in Aotearoa New Zealand*, ed. C. Bell and S. Matthewman, 139–49. Auckland: Oxford University Press, 2004.

Katchafire. *Te Ahi Kaa*. Radio, 19 December 2010. Radio New Zealand National.

Keelan, Teorongonui Josie and Christine Woods. 'Māuipreneur: Understanding Māori Entrepreneurship'. *International Indigenous Journal of Entrepeneurship, Advancement, Strategy & Education* 2, no. 2 (2006). http://www.indigenousjournal.com/

'Kei Te Ora Te Wairua O Te Iwi Maori'. *Craccum*, 4 March 1971.

'Keskidee Aroha Hui: 30 Years On'. Te Herenga Waka Marae, Victoria University of Wellington, 15 May 2010.

Kidane, Luam and Jarrett Martineau. 'Building Connections Across Decolonization Struggles'. *ROARMAG*, 2013. http://roarmag.org/2013/10/african-indigenous-struggle-decolonization/

'Lecture by Captain Speedy'. *Waikato Times*, 25 February 1886.

'Lecture on Abyssinia'. *Grey River Argus*, 7 January 1868.

Legat, Nicola. 'Rastaman Vibration'. *Metro*, May 1985.

Leigh, Jackie. 'Let's Head Off Racial Strife'. *Auckland Star*, 5 February 1972.

Lewis, Linden. 'The Groundings of Walter Rodney'. *Race & Class* 33, no. 1 (1991): 71–82.

Limb, Peter. 'The Anti-Apartheid Movements in Australia and Aoetearoa/ New Zealand'. In *The Road to Democracy in South Africa, Vol. 3, International Solidarity, Part II*, 907–82.

Logan, Frenise A. 'The British East India Company and African Slavery in Benkulen, Sumatra, 1687–1792'. *The Journal of Negro History* 41, no. 4 (1956): 339–48.

Luciou, Bernard S. 'In the Black Pacific: Testimonies of Vietnamese Afro-Amerasian Displacements'. In *Displacements and Diasporas: Asians in the Americas*, ed. W. W. Anderson and G. L. Lee, 122–58. New Brunswick: Rutgers University Press, 2005.

Ludden, David. 'Introduction: A Brief History of Subalternity'. In *Reading Subaltern Studies: Critical History, Contested Meaning and the Globalization of South Asia*, ed. David Ludden, 1–42. London: Anthem Press, 2002.

Luomala, Katharine, *Maui-of-a-thousand-tricks: His Oceanic and European Biographers*. Honolulu: Bernice P. Bishop Museum, 1949.

MacGregor, Anne. 'Black Is Beautiful'. In *He Whakaaro Ke*, ed. Verna Winitana. Porirua, 1985.

Mack, Douglas R. A. *From Babylon to RasTafari: Origin and History of the RasTafarian Movement*. Chicago: Research Associates School Times Publications and Frontline Distribution Int. Inc., 1999.

Marsden, Māori. 'God, Man and Universe: A Māori View'. In *The Woven Universe: Selected Writings of Rev. Māori Marsden*, ed. Te Ahukaramū Charles Royal, 2–23. Masterton: The Estate of Rev. Māori Marsden, 2003.

—'The Natural World and Natural Resources: Maori Value Systems and Perspectives'. In *The Woven Universe: Selected Writings of Rev. Māori Marsden*, ed. Te Ahukaramū Charles Royal, 24–53. Masterton: The Estate of Rev. Māori Marsden, 2003.

Massey, Gerald. *The Natural Genesis: Or, Second Part of A Book of the Beginnings*. London: Williams and Norgate, 1883.

McAvinue, Adrienne. 'Tamatoa'. *Craccum*, 1 July 1971.

McIntosh, Peggy. 'White Privilege and Male Privilege'. In *Privilege: A Reader*, eds Michael S. Kimmel and Abby L. Ferber, 147–60. Boulder: Westview Press, 2003.

McKay, F. M. *The Life of James K. Baxter*. Auckland: Oxford University Press, 1990.

McPherson, E. S. P. *RasTafari and Politics: Sixty Years of a Developing Cultural Ideology*. Clarendon: Black International Iyahbinghi Press, 1991.

Mead, Hirimi Moko and Neil Grove, eds. *Ngā Pēpeha a Ngā Tīpuna*. Wellington: Victoria University Press, 2003.

Meghoo, Desta. 'Question'. 4 June 2014. Email.

Metge, Joan. 'Returning the Gift – "Utu" in Intergroup Relations: In Memory of Sir Raymond Firth'. *The Journal of the Polynesian Society* 111, no. 4 (2002): 311–38.

Mignolo, Walter. 'The De-colonial Option and the Meaning of Identity in Politics'. *Anales N. E.* 9/10 (2007): 43–72.

Mignolo, W. and Rolando Vázquez. 'Decolonial AestheSis: Colonial Wounds/ Decolonial Healing'. *Social Text: Periscope*, 2013. http://socialtextjournal.org/ periscope_article/decolonial-aesthesis-colonial-woundsdecolonial-healings/.

Mignolo, Walter and Rolando Vasquez. *The Decolonial Option*. London: Bloomsbury Academic, forthcoming.

Minto, John. '30 Years Commemoration of the Springbok Protests'. Victoria University of Wellington, 29 June 2011.

Mita, Merata. *Dread*. Ora Digital / NZ on Air, 1998.

Mita, Merata, Leon Narbey and Gerd Pohlmann. *Bastion Point Day 507*, 1980.

Mita, Merata and Martyn Sanderson. *Keskidee Aroha*. Scratch Pictures, 1980.

Mitchell, Ian and Roimata Kirikiri. *Polynesian Youth in Otara*, 1970. Young Maori Leaders Conference. University of Auckland Library.

Moorehead, Alan. *The Fatal Impact: An Account of the Invasion of the South Pacific, 1767–1840*. New York: Harper & Row, 1966.

Moules, Nancy. 'Hermeneutic Inquiry: Paying Heed to History and Hermes – An Ancestral, Substantive, and Methodological Tale'. *International Journal of Qualitative Methods* 1, no. 3 (2002). http://www.ualberta. ca/~iiqm/

'Multicultural Herbs Ready to Go Back to Their Roots'. *Tu Tangata*, 1982.

Murch, Donna. *Living For the City: Migration, Education, and the Rise of the Black Panther Party in Oakland, California*. Chapel Hill: University of North Carolina Press, 2010.

'N.Z.F.M.S. Conference at Wellington'. *Te Ao Hou*, 1967.

'Native Affairs'. Māori Television, 28 July 2009.

Ness, Tigilau. 'Charles Spivey', 15 September 2010.

—'Connecting Reggae and RasTafari in Aotearoa NZ'. Presented at the Caribbean Connections Workshop, Victoria University of Wellington, 12 August 2011.

New Zealand Post-Primary Teachers' Association. *Maori Education: An Interim Report*. Wellington, 1970.

Newman, Keith. *Bible and Treaty: Missionaries Among the Māori – A New Perspective*. Auckland: Penguin Books, 2010.

—*Rātana Revisited: An Unfinished Legacy*. Auckland: Reed Publishing, 2006.

Newman, Richard S. *Freedom's Prophet: Bishop Richard Allen, the AME Church, and the Black Founding Fathers*. New York: New York University Press, 2009.

Newnham, Tom. *Apartheid is Not a Game: The Inside Story of New Zealand's Struggle Against Apartheid Sport*. Auckland: Graphic Publications, 1975.

Newton, Huey. 'Speech Delivered at Boston College: November 18, 1970'. In *The Huey P. Newton Reader*, ed. D. Hilliard and D. Weise, 160–75. New York: Seven Stories Press, 2002.

Newton, John. *The Double Rainbow: James K. Baxter, Ngāti Hau, and the Jerusalem Commune*. Wellington: Victoria University Press, 2009.

Ngā Tamatoa. 'The Fly'. In *Ngā Tamatoa*, ed. Ranginui Walker, 1–3. Auckland University Library, n.d.

—'Race Relations Bill 1972'. *Craccum*, 9 March 1972.

—'The Resurrection of Maori Identity'. In *Ngā Tamatoa*, ed. Ranginui Walker, 1–2. Auckland University Library, n.d.

'Nga Tamatoa Conference'. *Salient* (1976): 12.

Ngā Tamatoa Tuarua. 'Statement of Aims'. Maori Organization on Human Rights, August 1972. University of Auckland Library.

Nga Tamatoa: 40 Years On. Maori Television, 2013.

Nicholas, John Liddiard. *Narrative of A Voyage To New Zealand: Performed in the Years 1814 and 1815, In Company With The Rev. Samuel Marsden, Principal Chaplain of New South Wales Vol. I. [...]*. London: Hughes and Baynes, 1817.

Nilsson, Martin. *Greek Popular Religion*. New York: Columbia University Press, 1940.

O'Reilly, Denis. 'RasTafari and Ngā Mōkai'. Presented at the Caribbean Connections Workshop, Victoria University of Wellington, 12 August 2011.

Okeroa, Erina. 'Unfurling Routes of Self-Determination in Aotearoa New Zealand: The Black Women's Movement 1978–1982'. MA in Political Science, Victoria University of Wellington, 2012.

Ong, Walter J. *Orality and Literacy: The Technologizing of the Word*. London: Methuen, 1982.

—*The Presence of the Word: Some Prolegomena for Cultural and Religious History*. New Haven: Yale University Press, 1967.

Orbell, Margaret R. *The Illustrated Encyclopedia of Māori Myth and Legend.* Christchurch: Canterbury University Press, 1995.

Our People / Our Century, Ninox Productions, 2000.

Owens, Joseph. *Dread: The RasTafarians of Jamaica.* London: Heinemann, 1979.

'Pat Hohepa in U.S.A.' *Te Ao Hou,* no. 43 (1963): 45–6.

Patel, Hitendra. *Children of Zion.* Auckland: Auckland University, 2002.

Paterson, Lachlan. 'Kiri Mā, Kiri Mangu: The Terminology of Race and Civilization in the Mid-Nineteenth-Century Māori-Language Newspapers'. In *Rere Atu, Taku Manu! Discovering History, Language and Politics in the Māori-Language Newspapers,* ed. J. Curnow, N. Hopa and J. McRae, 78–97. Auckland: Auckland University Press, 2002.

—'Ngā Reo O Ngā Niupepa: Māori Language Newspapers 1855–1863'. University of Otago, 2004.

Paton, Diana. 'An Injurious Population'. *Cultural and Social History* 5, no. 4 (2008): 449–64.

Penetito, Walter Takaha. 'A Sociology of Māori Education: Beyond Mediating Structures'. PhD Thesis, Victoria University of Wellington, 2005.

Pere, Rose. *Ako: Concepts and Learning in the Māori Tradition.* Wellington: Te Kōhanga Reo National Trust, 1994.

Peterson, William. 'Reclaiming the Past, Building a Future: Maori Identity in the Plays of Hone Kouka'. *Theatre Research International* 26, no. 01 (2001): 15–24.

Pettazzoni, Raffaele. 'The Formation of Monotheism'. In *Essays on the History of Religions,* 1–10. Leiden: Brill, 1954.

Phillips, Russell. 'James K. Baxter: A Dialogue with His Later Theological and Philosophical Thought in the Context of Aotearoa/New Zealand'. *Journal of New Zealand Literature,* no. 13 (1995): 267–84.

'Pining for Native Bush'. *Salient,* 2 May 1983.

Piot, Charles. 'Atlantic Aporias: Africa and Gilroy's Black Atlantic'. *The South Atlantic Quarterly* 100, no. 1 (2001): 155–70.

Piripi, Tēina and Vivienne Body. 'Tihei-Wa Mauri Ora: Te Tipuranga'. In *Pacific Identities and Well-Being: Cross-Cultural Perspectives,* eds M. N. Agee, T. McIntosh, P. Culbertson and C. Makasiale, 91–102. New York: Routledge, 2013.

Pollard, Velma. 'Dread Talk: The Speech of the RasTafarian in Jamaica'. *Caribbean Quarterly* 26, no. 4 (1980): 32–41.

Pomare, Maui and James Cowan. *Legends of the Māori Vol. 1.* Christchurch: Cadsonbury Publications, 2012.

'The Pot is on the Boil'. *Dominion Weekend Magazine*, 20 February 1971.

Potiki, Roma. '"It Is Political If It Can Be Passed On": An Interview with Roma Potiki'. In *The Intercultural Performance Reader*, ed. Patrice Pavis, 172–8. London: Routledge, 1996.

Potter, Basil. 'Veteran Scorns Muldoon Analogy'. *The Dominion Post*, 16 July 1981.

Power, W. Tyrone. *Sketches in New Zealand, With Pen and Pencil.* London: Longman, Brown, Green, and Longmans, 1849.

Prakash, Gyan. 'Subaltern Studies as Postcolonial Criticism'. *The American Historical Review* 99, no. 5 (1994): 1475–90.

Price, Richard. *First-Time: The Historical Vision of an Afro-American People.* Baltimore: Johns Hopkins University Press, 1983.

'Profile: Al Ragland'. *Pathfinder: Newsletter of the Midwest Institute for Native American Studies* 3, no. 1 (2002): 4.

Ramazani, Jahan. 'The Wound of History: Walcott's Omeros and the Postcolonial Poetics of Affliction'. *PMLA* 112, no. 3 (May 1997): 405–17.

Rata, Elizabeth. 'The Theory of Neotribal Capitalism'. *Review* 22, no. 3 (1999): 231–88.

Rauhihi-Ness, Miriama. 'The Twelve Tribes of Israel Aotearoa New Zealand'. Presented at the Caribbean Connections Workshop, Victoria University of Wellington, 12 August 2011.

Raureti, M. 'The Rātana Movement'. Diploma of Social Science, Victoria University of Wellington, 1954.

Reeder, C. et al. 'Stereotypes and People'. *NZ Listener*, 1973.

Reid, Graham. 'The Twelve Tribes of Israel'. *New Zealand Herald*, 28 September 1990.

Reid, Tony. 'The Laughing Revolutionary: Interview with Syd Jackson'. *NZ Listener*, 1989.

Roberts, Mere, Brad Haami, Richard Benton, Terre Satterfield, Melissa L. Finucane, Mark Henare and Manuka Henare. 'Whakapapa as a Māori Mental Construct: Some Implications for the Debate over Genetic Modification of Organisms'. *The Contemporary Pacific* 16, no. 1 (2004): 1–28.

Robinson, Cedric. 'The Appropriation of Frantz Fanon'. *Race & Class* 35, no. 1 (1993): 79–91.

Rodney, Walter. *The Groundings with My Brothers*. London: Bogle-L'Ouverture, 1990.

Rosso, Franco. *Babylon*, 1980.

Royal, Te Ahukaramū Charles. 'Exploring Indigenous Knowledge'. Presented at the Indigenous Knowledges Conference, Victoria University of Wellington, 2005. http://charles-royal.com/assets/exploringindigenousknowledge.pdf

—'A Modern View of Mana'. Presented at the Conference of Australian and New Zealand Psychological Society, University of Auckland, 2006. http://www.charles-royal.com/assets/apspaper.pdf

—'Te Ao Mārama – A Research Paradigm'. In *Proceedings of Te Oru Rangahau Māori Research and Development Conference*, 7–9. Massey University, 1998.

Rudman, Richard. 'Auckland's Racial Problems'. *Focus*, September 1970.

Sage, Eugenie and Rufus Collins. 'Keskidee'. *Craccum*, 26 June 1979.

Sajed, Alina. *Postcolonial Encounters in International Relations: The Politics of Transgression in the Maghreb*. London: Routledge, 2012.

Salmond, Anne. 'Te Ao Tawhito: A Semantic Approach to the Traditional Māori Cosmos'. *The Journal of the Polynesian Society* 87, no. 1 (1978): 5–28.

Sando, Joe S. 'My Visit with the Maoris'. *Te Maori* 1, no. 5 (1970): 29–31, 46.

Sanga, Kabina. 'Making Sense of Indigenous Pacific Research', in Tupeni Baba, Okusitino Mahina, Nuhisifa Williams and Unaisi Nabobo-Baba, eds, *Researching the Pacific and Indigenous Peoples: Issues and Perspectives*. Auckland: Centre for Pacific Studies, University of Auckland, 2004.

Sarkar, Sumit. 'The Decline of the Subaltern in Subaltern Studies'. In *Writing Social History*, 82–108. Delhi: Oxford University Press, 1997.

Sartre, Jean-Paul. 'Preface to the Wretched of the Earth'. In *Colonialism and Neocolonialism*, ed. J. Sartre, 136–55. London: Routledge, 2001.

Satele, Michael Fonoti. 'The Polynesian Panthers: An Assertion of Ethnic and Cultural Identities Through Activism in Auckland During the 1970s'. MA in Education Thesis, 1998.

Savishinsky, N. J. 'Transnational Popular Culture and the Global Spread of the Jamaican RasTafarian Movement'. *New West Indian Guide* 68, no. 3 (1994): 259–81.

Sawyerr, Harry. *God, Ancestor or Creator? Aspects of Traditional Belief in Ghana, Nigeria & Sierra Leone*. Harlow: Longmans, 1970.

Schrempp, Gregory. *Magical Arrows: The Māori, the Greeks, and the Folklore of the Universe*. Madison: University of Wisconsin Press, 1992.

Schuler, Monica. *'Alas, Alas, Kongo': A Social History of Indentured African Immigration into Jamaica, 1841–1865*. Baltimore: Johns Hopkins University Press, 1980.

Seth, Sanjay. "'Once Was Blind but Now Can See": Modernity and the Social Sciences'. *International Political Sociology* 7, no. 2 (2013).

Shepperson, George. 'Ethiopianism and African Nationalism'. *Phylon* 14, no. 1 (1953): 9–18.

Shilliam, Robbie. 'Intervention and Colonial-Modernity: Decolonising the Italy/Ethiopia Conflict Through Psalms 68:31'. *Review of International Studies* 39, no. 5 (2013): 1131–47.

—'Living Knowledge Traditions and the Priestly Caste of the Western Academy'. *The Disorder of Things*, 2013. http://thedisorderofthings. com/2013/12/01/living-knowledge-traditions-and-the-priestly-caste-of-the-western-academy/

—"'Open the Gates Mek We Repatriate": Caribbean Slavery, Constructivism and Hermeneutic Tensions'. *International Theory* 6, no. 2 (2014): 349–72.

—'Redemption from Development: Amartya Sen, RasTafari and Promises of Freedom'. *Postcolonial Studies* 15, no. 3 (2012): 331–50.

Shulman, George. *American Prophecy: Race and Redemption in American Political Culture*. Minneapolis: University of Minnesota Press, 2008.

Silva Jayasuriya, Shihan de. 'East India Company in Sumatra: Cross-Cultural Interactions'. *African and Asian Studies* 8 (2009): 204–21.

Simpson, Jane. 'Io as Supreme Being: Intellectual Colonization of the Māori?' *History of Religions* 37, no. 1 (1997): 50–85.

Sinclair, Karen. *Prophetic Histories: The People of the Māramatanga*. Auckland: Bridget William Books, 2002.

Sjollema, Baldwin. 'Combating Racism: A Chapter in Ecumenical History'. *Ecumenical Review* 56, no. 4 (2004): 470–9.

Slate, Nico and Joe Trotter, eds. *Black Power Beyond Borders*. New York: Palgrave, 2012.

Smith, Hingangaroa Graham, Te Kawehau Hoskins and Alison Jones. 'Interview: Kaupapa Māori: The Dangers of Domestication'. *New Zealand Journal of Educational Studies* 47, no. 2 (2012): 10–20.

Smith, Linda Tuhiwai. *Decolonizing Methodologies: Research and Indigenous Peoples*. London: Zed Books, 1999.

—'Māori Women: Discourses, Projects and Mana Wahine', in S. Middleton and A. Jones, eds, *Women and Education in Aotearoa*. Wellington: Bridget Williams Press, 1990.

Smith, Linda, Sarah-Jane Tiakiwai, Murray Hemi, Mau Hudson, Robert Joseph, Anthony Barrett and Merepaea Dunn. *Negotiated Space*. https://www.waikato.ac.nz/provcmaori/research/tehaumihiata/pdf/negotiated_space.01.pdf

Smith, T. W. R. and J. N. Smith. *Te Omeka Pa: The Passing Years 1937–1987*. Matamata: Te Omeka Marae Trustees, 1987.

Smith, Takirirangi. 'Tohu and Māori Knowing'. In *Proceedings of the Traditional Knowledge Conference 2008*, 266–70. Auckland: Ngā Pae o te Māramatanga, 2010.

Smithyman, Chris. 'N.Z. Has Nothing to Learn from Americans Says Amos'. *Craccum*, 9 July 1968.

Snell, W. E. 'Captain Cook's Surgeons'. *Medical History* 7, no. 1 (1963): 43–55.

Solomon, Mark. 'Tēnā Koe – Greetings', 11 February 2013. Email.

Sorensen, Klaus. 'Vern Turns Down South Africa Tour'. *Te Maori*, 1974.

'Speedy of Abyssinia'. *Auckland Star*, 17 July 1935.

Spivak, Gayatri. 'Can the Subaltern Speak?' In *Marxism and the Interpretation of Culture*, ed. C. Nelson and L. Grossberg, 271–313. Houndsmills: Macmillan, 1988.

—'The New Subaltern: A Silent Interview'. In *Mapping Subaltern Studies and the Postcolonial*, ed. Vinayak Chaturvedi, 324–40. London: Verso, 2000.

—'Scattered Speculations on Geography'. *Antipode* 46, no. 1 (2014): 1–12.

—'Subaltern Studies: Deconstructing Historiography'. *Subaltern Studies IV*, 1985.

Stephens, M. 'Babylon's "Natural Mystic": The North American Music Industry, the Legend of Bob Marley, and the Incorporation of Transnationalism'. *Cultural Studies* 12, no. 2 (1998).

Steven, Geoff. *Te Matakite O Aotearoa*, 1975.

Stewart, Dianne. *Three Eyes for the Journey: African Dimensions of the Jamaican Religious Experience*. Oxford: Oxford University Press, 2004.

Stokes, Evelyn. *Wiremu Tamihana: Rangatira*. Wellington: Huia Publishers, 2002.

Sugirtharajah, R. S. *The Bible and the Third World: Precolonial, Colonial and Postcolonial Encounters*. Cambridge: Cambridge University Press, 2001.

Sutherland, O. R. W., J. T. Hippolite, A. M. Smith and R. A. Galbreath. 'Justice and Race: A Monocultural System in a Multicultural Society', 1973.

Sutherland, Oliver and Murray Parsons. 'Background to WAI 262', 2011. http://wai262.weebly.com/uploads/7/4/6/3/7463762/the_background_to_wai_262.pdf

Swainson, William. *New Zealand and Its Colonization*. London: Smith, Elder, 1859.

Sweet, James H. 'Reimagining the African-Atlantic Archive: Method, Concept, Epistemology, Ontology'. *The Journal of African History* 55, no. 2 (2014): 147–59.

Taepa, Hohepa. 'The Ford Foundation Exchange'. *Te Ao Hou*, no. 67 (1969): 10–20.

Taketani, Etsuko. 'The Cartography of the Black Pacific: James Weldon Johnson's Along This Way'. *American Quarterly* 59, no. 1 (2007): 79–106.

Tambiah, S. J. 'The Magical Power of Words'. *Man* 3, no. 2 (1968): 175–208.

Tapsell, Enid. *Historic Maketu: Hui Hui Mai!* Rotorua: Rotorua Morning Post Printing House, 1940.

Tate, Merze and Fidele Foy. 'Slavery and Racism in South Pacific Annexations'. *The Journal of Negro History* 50, no. 1 (1965): 1–21.

Te Awekotuku, N. *Mana wahine Māori: Selected Writings on Māori Women's Art, Culture and Politics*. Auckland: New Zealand Women's Press, 1991.

Te Haupapa-o-Tane. 'Io, the Supreme God, and Other Gods of the Maori'. *The Journal of the Polynesian Society* 29, no. 115 (1920): 139–43.

Te Matakite. 'Newsletter', August 1976. NZYC Te Matakite. Auckland University Library.

Te Rangihiroa. 'He Poroporoaki – A Farewell Message'. *The Journal of the Polynesian Society* 60, no. 1 (1951): 22–31.

Teaiwa, Teresia. 'On Analogies: Rethinking the Pacific in a Global Context'. *The Contemporary Pacific* 18, no. 1 (2006): 71–87.

Temple, Christel N. 'The Emergence of Sankofa Practice in the United States'. *Journal of Black Studies* 45, no. 1 (2010): 127–50.

Thaman, Konai Helu. 'Nurturing Relationships and Honouring Responsibilities: A Pacific Perspective'. *International Review of Education* 54, no. 3/4 (2008): 459–73.

Thompson, Donald. 'New Zealand Liberation Struggle Seeks Base of Black Struggles'. *Te Iwi O Aotearoa*, February 1989.

Thomson, Arthur S. *The Story of New Zealand: Past and Present, Savage and Civilized.* London: J. Murray, 1859.

'Toko Turns Troops to Work'. *Auckland Star,* 17 October 1979.

'Tribute to New Zealand'. *New Times and Ethiopia News,* 24 October 1942.

Tuck, E. and K. Wayne Yang. 'Decolonization Is Not a Metaphor'. *Decolonization: Indigeneity, Education & Society* 1, no. 1 (2012). decolonization.org/index.php/des/article/download/18630/15554

Vaioleti, Timote M. 'Talanoa Research Methodology: A Developing Position on Pacific Research'. *Waikato Journal of Education* 12 (2006): 21–34.

Van Stipriaan, Alex. 'Watramama/Mami Wata: Three Centuries of Creolization of a Water Spirit in West Africa, Suriname and Europe'. *Matatu: Journal of African Culture and Society* 27 (n.d.): 323–37.

'Violence in Court Disrupts Hearing'. *Auckland Star,* 3 March 1982.

Walcott, Derek. 'The Muse of History'. In *Is Massa Day Dead? Black Moods in the Caribbean,* ed. O. Coombs, 1–27. New York: Anchor Books, 1974.

Walker, Ranginui. 'Early Storm-Warnings'. *NZ Listener,* 1979.

—'Innocence Lost, Amnesia Cured?' *Listener,* 10 October 1981.

—'Manifesto of the New Zealand Maori Council on the Race Relations Bill'. University of Auckland, 1971.

'Warning of Racial Conflicts'. *New Zealand Herald,* 12 February 1972.

Wells, B. *The History of Taranaki.* New Plymouth: Edmundson & Avery, 1878.

West, Cornel. *Prophesy Deliverance! An Afro-American Revolutionary Christianity.* Louisville: Westminster John Knox Press, 2002.

White, Edgar. *Lament for RasTafari and Other Plays.* London: M. Boyars, 1983.

Wilson, Ormond. 'Papahurihia, First Maori Prophet'. *The Journal of the Polynesian Society* 74, no. 4 (1965): 473–83.

Wishart, Kitty, Janet Bogle, Kate Jason-Smith and Sharon Alston. 'Talking to Polynesian Women Part 2'. *Broadsheet,* 1973.

Witchel, Diana. 'A Forceful Lever'. *Listener,* 8 November 1986.

Wohlers, J. F. H. *Mythology and Traditions of the Māori in New Zealand.* Christchurch: Kiwi Publishers, 1995.

Wolfe, Patrick. 'Land, Labor, and Difference: Elementary Structures of Race'. *The American Historical Review* 106, no. 3 (June 2001): 866–905.

Woods, John. *Highway 35: Travels Around East Cape.* Auckland: Reed, 1998.

Wynter, Sylvia. 'Unsettling the Coloniality of Being/Power/Truth/Freedom: Towards the Human, After Man, Its Overrepresentation – An Argument'. *CR: The New Centennial Review* 3, no. 3 (2003): 257–337.

Young III, Josiah Ulysses. *A Pan-African Theology: Providence and the Legacies of the Ancestors.* New York: Africa World Press, Inc., 1992.

Young Maori Leaders Conference, 1970. University of Auckland Library.

Young, Robert. *Postcolonialism: An Historical Introduction.* Oxford: Blackwell, 2002.

Zahan, Dominique. *The Religion, Spirituality and Thought of Traditional Africa.* Chicago: University of Chicago Press, 1983.

Zane, Wallace W. *Journeys to the Spiritual Lands: The Natural History of a West Indian Religion.* New York: Oxford University Press, 1999.

Index

Made in the USA
Columbia, SC
26 January 2019